The Good Gap
and Sixth Form Guide

The Good Schools Advisory Service

This is a consultancy run by the authors of this book and the *Good Schools Guide* to advise parents on choosing the best school and the next step for their son or daughter.

The authors are in a unique position to advise because they have visited hundreds of schools, colleges and courses, and gathered an enormous reservoir of information and experience. No money is taken at any stage from the schools: all advice is impartial.

Tel: 0171 828 1052
Fax: 0171 932 0747
64 Sussex Street
London SW1V 4RG

Tel: 0171 225 2355
Fax: 0171 225 1119
59a Cadogan Street
London SW3 2QJ

The Good Gap
and Sixth Form Guide

Amanda Atha and Sarah Drummond

MACMILLAN

First published 1995 by Macmillan Reference Books
a division of Macmillan Publishers Limited
London and Basingstoke

Associated companies throughout the world

ISBN 0-333-60927-1

1 3 5 7 9 8 6 4 2

A CIP catalogue record for this book is available from the British Library

Typeset by Spottiswoode Ballantyne Printers Ltd, Colchester
Printed by Cox & Wyman Ltd, Reading, Berkshire

Contents

CONTRIBUTORS

William Hobson

Ralph Lucas

Patrea More Nisbett

ACKNOWLEDGEMENTS

We would like to thank the following people for their help,
support, advice and editing:

Jeremy Carson

Philippa Davenport

Caroline Dawnay

Diana Johnson

Kavita MacLean

Jenny Page

Olivia Reynolds

Monique Riccardi-Cubitt

Dominic Taylor

Shane Winser

and also:

Marcus Beale

Rosemary Allott

Antonia Atha

Richard Calvocoressi

Archie Coulson

Marie-Hélène Gatineau

Ben Gibson

Peter McGarrick

Patrick Morrissey

Rodney Portman

Emily Schmitt

Peter Straker

Martin Walker

Christopher Wood

Laura Wood

List of Abbreviations

ADAR Art and Design Admissions Registry

AEB Associated Examining Board

AI Assistant Instructor (horses)

a.k.a. also known as

ALIS A-Level Information System

AS Advanced Supplementary (public exam equivalent to half an A-level)

ASSI Artificial Slope Ski Instructor

B & b bed and breakfast

BA Bachelor of Arts

BAC British Accreditation Council

BASC British Association of Shooting and Conservation

BASI British Association of Ski Instructors

B.Ed. Bachelor of Education

BHS British Horse Society

BHSI British Horse Society Instructor

B.Lit. Bachelor of Literature

B.Sc. Bachelor of Science

BTEC Business and Technology Education Council (qualification)

CAD Computer-Aided Design

Cantab. Cambridge

Cert. Ed. Certificate of Education

CIFE Conference for Independent Further Education

COSHH Control of Substances Hazardous to Health

c.v. curriculum vitae

DELE Diploma Español como Lengua Extranjera

DfE (government) Department for Education

Dip. Ed. Diploma of Education

Dott. short for *Dottore* (Italian for Doctor)

EFL English as a Foreign Language

FBHS Fellow of the British Horse Society

FCA Fellow of the Institute of Chartered Accountants

List of Abbreviations

FE Further Education

FRHS Fellow of the Royal Horticultural Society

F.I.Agr.M. Fellow of the Institute of Agricultural Management

FIAP Foyer International d'Accueil de Paris

FIHort Fellow of the Institute of Horticulture

F.R.Ag.Ss. Fellow of the Royal Agricultural Societies

FRSA Fellow of the Royal Society of Arts

FSGD Fellow of the Society of Garden Design

Gap a colloquial term for the year between leaving school and going on to university

GCSE General Certificate of Secondary Education (first public exam in UK)

GFL German as a Foreign Language (teaching)

GNVQ General National Vocational Qualification

HDFA Higher Diploma of Fine Art

HND Higher National Diploma

IB International Baccalaureate (a public exam at secondary level)

ISID International Society of Interior Decorators

IT Information Technology

MA Master of Arts

MBE Member of the Order of the British Empire

M.Ed. Master of Education

MHort Master of Horticulture

M.Sc. Master of Science

ND National Diploma

NDD National Diploma of Design

NNEB National Nursery Examination Board

NVQ National Vocational Qualification

OTT Over The Top (i.e. going too far)

Oxbridge short for Oxford and/or Cambridge universities

Oxon. Oxford

Pastoral care care of students on matters not related to their work, e.g. personal and social

p.d.q. pretty damn quick

PGCE Post-Graduate Certificate of Education

Ph.D. Philosophiae Doctor

RCA Royal College of Art

RGS Royal Geographical Society

RSA Royal Society of Arts

SFC Sixth-Form College

suss slang for find out, get to the bottom of, sniff out, investigate

List of Abbreviations

TEFL Teaching English as a Foreign Language
TLC Tender Loving Care
v. Very
V & A Victoria and Albert (Museum)

YHA Youth Hostel Association
ZDaF Zertifikat Deutsch als Fremdsprache – official German as a Foreign Language exam

Introduction

We have written this book – the insider's guide to teenage education after 16 and mainstream schooling – as a sequel to the *Good Schools Guide*. It comes in response to countless inquiries we have had from parents and students seeking information on everything from the best language schools, to sixth-form colleges, garden design courses and how to take part in monitoring an iceberg.

Specialized reference information exists dealing with specific areas, but none we have found – and we spent hours in public libraries and in bookshops – told us either what these places were really like or which ones we should choose. We could find no selective 'bible' for parents of teenagers who have reached this springboard stage in their life, ready for A-levels, 'life skills', and expanding horizons.

We say this with feeling as it is the stage that (some of) our own children are at or coming up to. Schools seem to be surprisingly ignorant about these next steps beyond their gates. Children pick up tantalizing snippets on the grapevine, but it is all so vague and usually too late. Opportunities are constantly missed. Parents are all too often left standing bewildered; willing to help, but not really knowing what the options are or how come they have missed the application date by several months.

On the 'gap' front (whether it's a year or an extended summer), this is a time rich in excitement. It is the moment to dare to enter new fields and try new things. What about learning to cook, restore furniture, be a butler, gamekeep, teach English, save the planet – not to mention making some money to do these things? Being footloose comes as a shock after the narrow tracks of school.

Introduction

('Suddenly you're at school – and suddenly it's all over,' said a recent school-leaver). It is only too easy to fritter away this precious period of life and waste it all, drifting, and not recognize how special it is.

Researching for the book, we found a wonderful diversity of courses and enormous enthusiasm from the people running them. The quality of some was inspiring. Equally, some were ghastly. As a contributor commented on a famous finishing school: 'I wouldn't send a stuffed rabbit here.' We went up heaps of blind alleys and bombed out *countless* courses in our attempt to be truly selective. We were struck over and over again by the vital importance of matching the person to the course. There is, for example, no point in a budding professional portrait painter sitting beside bored housewives dabbling in paint for the first time.

In each section we have included information on contacts, timing, useful questions to ask (e.g. 'What will I actually be doing in Calcutta?'). But above all we hope we have given the flavour and the feel of the courses, establishments and activities we have chosen. We have tried to steer a way through the bewildering amounts of information to be found in the bumf in order to highlight the interesting bits (e.g. a French university may be offering all things to all people, but what *we* want to know is what the language classes for foreign students are like).

We have limited our choice to courses not longer than two years; the majority are under a year, some as little as two days. And, by the way, we notice that courses are often volatile: what we have written is how it was at the time of going to press. Among the state-funded courses, remember that government cuts mean everyone is scrabbling for money and is having to increase the numbers of students, often without increasing the number of staff. Don't be surprised if 50 more students have been stuffed in since we visited.

It has to be admitted that, alas, privately run courses tend to cost a lot, often well into four figures. It is easy to be seduced into false economies, and some of the most expensive are in fact the best value: you may be getting the world's top experts: if you're up to it, this could be an investment for ever.

Introduction

We would like to say a very big thank-you to all the people all over who have helped in so many ways – providing information, thoughts, suggestions (not to mention warning notes), beds for the night, tea and sympathy, strong drinks – and who have helped us through the maze. We are enormously grateful.

Amanda Atha
Sarah Drummond
London 1995

CAN YOU HELP?

We would welcome suggestions you may have for the next edition of the *Good Gap and Sixth Form Guide*, in particular information on courses which you have found to be *really* good. Please write to Amanda Atha and Sarah Drummond, c/o Macmillan Ltd., Cavaye Place, London SW10 9PG

1

Jumping Off

School-leavers and gap-year people, start here. This chapter you may well feel tempted to skip. Nevertheless, here it is, and it could actually be very helpful to you.

The key to getting on with the world is to put yourself in the shoes of the other person, that is, the person from whom you are trying to get the job, the place on the course or expedition. Try to imagine what *they* want, not what you want: they will be sussing *you* out. 'They come here,' said an admissions tutor for a course which has 700 applicants for 25 places, 'without knowing anything about the course or why they want to be on it.' It will *not* score any brownie points if you tell a personnel director that you are only here for the beer or you were too late to get in anywhere else, or you wanted to be beside the sea, or any other of the unfortunate comments we have heard. What they want is a bright, keen applicant who can deliver the goods, e.g. if it's a chalet job, you can cook and speak French and are prepared to work; if it's an art course, that you've really read the prospectus, know what the course offers and want it and will benefit from it; or if you're trying to get to Mexico to look after orphans, that you like children and genuinely want to help and are resilient and aren't looking for a cheap holiday.

Timing and Planning

This is boring, we know, but if you can bear to sit down now and think ahead, it will put you way ahead of most of the competition. Planning and organizing yourself does not mean you are lumbered

1

for ever with your plan, but cancellation is far easier than scrambling and fighting your way, often expensively, at the last minute.

Start backwards. Have you any idea where you want to be in five years' time? Mother of three children? On a yacht in the Caribbean? Still a student? Your own boss? Earning pots of money? You are not going to be held to this, but the exercise of thinking about what comes next will help focus your mind on what happens now. What do you really *like* doing? Don't be shy: if what you enjoy most is watching television, admit it, if only to yourself. It could be you are headed for stardom as a TV commentator, in which case a few months as a gofer on the radio station in the Cook Islands might be a good idea. The experience may suggest other directions for the future, but the important thing is to get stuck in. Expect your thoughts to be influenced by your experiences. Better to have a direction and change it, than drift too long in a mindless and depressing way, spiralling downwards.

Telephoning and telephone manner
Your first step will probably be a telephone call. Points to remember:

1 The telephone directory (business section and Yellow Pages) is the most useful book in the world. It is all there.
2 Call in office hours. Avoid totally lunch-time and the end of the day. All agree that between the hours of 10 and 12 in the morning is the best time to ring, while your prey is awake and not yet thinking of lunch or asleep after it.
3 Think before you call: what are you calling for? More information? If so, what? Application form? Be precise, be clear, and above all, be polite. You may just think you are talking to a disembodied voice, but at the other end, funnily enough, is a human being, who can be wonderful and helpful (e.g. can tell you when the boss is there and put you through to him or her) or can be turned into an obstructive enemy.
4 Sorry, but you really should be efficient. If you're calling a whole row of agencies, for example, it is embarrassing if you call

2

the same one twice (it looks hopeless) and insulting if you forget who you've been talking to. Notebook and pencil come in handy. Also a wallet file for all your 'business' activities.

5 Be available to receive calls if, for example, you are on an agency's list. Otherwise the job will go to the next person who *is* in.

Form-filling

Your telephone call may well result in an application form to be filled in. Form-filling is an art. Read the thing from start to finish before putting pen to paper. Use pencil to start with. Check your spelling – poor spelling loses points. If you are given the slightest opportunity, tell them something which helps pick you out from the herd, e.g. you're grade 8 music, half French, you've just come back from St Petersburg. Check they have everything they need: exam results? Four photographs (signed, perhaps)? Cheque? SAE?

A covering letter never does any harm, and often does good *if done properly*. Find out the name to write to and *spell it right* (another telephone call?). The letter should be short and to the point: you enclose the form, invite them to contact you if there are any queries, say you will telephone them in a few days' time to see if there is any news (unless they specifically tell you not to). From the other side of the fence this sounds on the ball, keen.

Curriculum vitae

This is your big moment to be creative. The first step is to get the story of your life down in black and white for all future reference. This is your blueprint. Write down everything you've done, with dates attached, including exam results, all schools attended, summer schools (if any), courses already done (if any), hobbies, interests (make one up if necessary), sports, music or drama exams taken, Duke of Edinburgh awards (they love that), any successes however humble (school prefect? Member of the choir which was on telly last week? Played for the first fifteen? Solid record of granny-bashing? Played in a band which raised money for charity?), work experience (even if it's only the paper round or local supermarket). And don't lose it.

Now tailor your blueprint to suit the application you are making. This means finding out about the course, company or agency you are 'targeting'. Ask companies for background information, ask friends who know the outfit. As a result of your researches, you will want to emphasize some aspects of your life and maybe play down, even eliminate, others. Make it look as positive as possible; and lively and fun. Blow your own trumpet – nobody else will. Remind yourself that the point of all this is to get your foot in the door. Dare we suggest you ask a beady adult to give it the once-over before you post it.

Interviewing techniques

1 Arrive 10 minutes early. This means looking at the A–Z in advance, finding out train times, giving yourself a wide margin for traffic jams, leaves on the line.

2 Read today's newspaper on the journey. You never know when that news item will come in handy. If you know there's been a change of government or the company you are talking to has just been taken over, you will score.

3 Dress for the part. Appearances really do matter: it's a cliché, but, alas, too true. This usually means skirts for the girls; clean shirt and a tie for boys, and trousers (not jeans). Hair: it must be clean and, if long, tied back (boys and girls). You may feel that they can take you or leave you and you're damned if you're going to conform to 'their' ideas, but if you do have this 'attitude problem', we assure you, you will be left. A little arse-licking in a good cause never hurt anyone. Your family may love you, ripped jeans and all, but why should the outside world? Never underestimate the speed with which the hidden message is picked up.

4 Be aware of your body language. Stand and sit up straight (yes, it sounds military, but believe us, it works, and by the way, anyone can do it for half an hour). Look the person interviewing

4

you in the eye, however awkward it feels. Put it this way: if you shuffle in looking messy, hung-over and half-baked, they will understandably assume that is what you are and how you will be on the job.

5 Be prepared for the questions. For example, they may say:

What are your strengths and weaknesses?

What are your interests?

Why do you want this job/course?

Tell us a little about yourself.

Have you any experience in this field? (Don't forget the time you sold bric-à-brac at the village fête.)

What are you going to do next?

These are all hardy perennials, and you want to go armed with nice crisp thoughts.

Networking

You probably hate the idea of string-pulling, e.g. asking your uncle in Australia for a job on the ranch. It looks like cheating, but it is the way of the world. Look at it from your uncle's point of view. He'd rather have someone whose background and reliability are known (we hope) than some totally unknown body. It's less of a risk and, all things being equal, he'll feel good helping his family.

Don't be shy about asking grown-ups, but be tactful and sensitive about it. The line to take is not to ask straight out if they have a job (this puts them on the spot and can be embarrassing), but to say: 'Do you know anybody who might need a bottle-washer, extra crew member, waiter, etc.?' Be prepared to eat humble pie and remember to be grateful. Another tack is the parents of friends at school. Even your fuddy-duddy old daddy might have a job for you in the packing department if you ask nicely.

Tips for getting on to the next stage

* Allow time. There are no short cuts.
* Do it now – golden rule.
* Don't wait for the ad asking for applicants. Be bold. The (polite) direct approach is flattering. Write a short letter saying what you can offer and asking to be considered for anything suitable. Even if the company hasn't got anything right now, they may well keep your letter on file for next time (advertising is expensive and time-consuming).
* Expect a bit of culture shock after school in the unfamiliarity of the wide world.
* If you feel you're getting nowhere and nobody wants you, offer to do some voluntary work. Some organization would be thrilled to have your help, and it sounds good at your next interview.
* Finally, it doesn't hurt to remember the nun's prayer: Go placidly amidst the noise and the haste . . .

When to Do What

At this point, life can feel like snakes and ladders. Roughly, here is your plan of play – but for heaven's sake check constantly for the exact application dates. It's far, far better to be too early: you can always cancel or change your mind (though read the small print on forfeiting deposits, and always part with money at the last possible moment).

Jumping Off

SPRING

Gap students	January: London board A-level retakes (limited subjects).
Second-year Sixth	Art foundation applications must be got in this term (end of January/February, depending on the college).
First-year Sixth	If you're thinking of applying to an American university, get weaving now, i.e. 18 months ahead of entry.
First- and Second-year Sixth	Start thinking of your summer holiday jobs and work experience.
Second-year Sixth	Apply now for popular post-A-level non-examination courses, e.g. cookery.
Second-year Fifth, First- and Second-year Sixth	Revision courses take place in the Easter hols for GCSE and A-levels.

SUMMER

Second-year Fifth, Second-year Sixth and gap retake students	May and June: exams, all boards (GCSE and A-levels)
Second-year Sixth	Buy your international student card by the end of the term you leave school – see Travel chapter, p. 280.
First-year Sixth	Start planning your gap year/gap summer in the summer holidays, i.e. a year and a bit before you set off.
First-year Sixth	Start thinking hard about which subjects you want to study and which university you want to go to. Start the rounds of visiting now (open days are in term-time).

7

Fifth-year and post-school	Mid-August: GCSE and A-level results come out. Be available regularly, at least on the end of the telephone, to sort out changes, maybe fill in more forms, sort out clearing-house places, etc. from now until October.

AUTUMN

Second-year Fifth	September: apply for sixth-form places if you've got itchy feet for next year (apply earlier if you can).
Gap students	September – A-level retakes: start studying now for AEB and Cambridge board exams in November (limited subjects).
Second-year Sixth	Apply now for your travel scholarship or bursary from your school.
Second-year Sixth	Conditional offers from universities and university interviews begin in October and go on until 31 March.
Second-year Sixth	Look out for and go to open days for art foundation courses.
Second-year Sixth	University applications must be in by the end of December but preferably earlier; before half-term is best. There is a correlation between applying early and being offered that place, say the powers that be.
Second-year Sixth	Now is the time to start applying to organizations offering work and expeditions abroad after you've left school – see Gap Expeditions, etc. chapter, p. 128. They'll want to 'screen' you sometime between now and next April.
Gap students	After A-levels and before you go off on your travels, write to your university and state a preference for a particular hall of residence.

2

Sixth-Form Colleges

Sixth-form colleges are becoming an increasingly useful, often brilliant alternative to fee-paying schools at sixth form and, from every angle, are well worth considering if you are contemplating a move after GCSE.

The term 'sixth-form college' generally means an establishment specializing in A-levels which is large enough to offer a very wide range of subjects as part of the curriculum. One or two genuine sixth-form colleges are private (Atlantic College, for example), but the overwhelming majority are state-run: this is an area in which the state has, for once, had a good measure of success. The majority of students come from local schools but this is gradually changing, as the government will now fund you at this level wherever you are offered a place. Only two sixth-form colleges at present run boarding houses, but if you have set your sights too far to commute, you might consider lodging with a landlady (colleges are increasingly giving help with this), or camping on granny's doorstep.

If you have been in the cosy end of the private sector, you will be hit by some pretty major contrasts; culture shock, even. Sixth-form colleges are *big*. Classes tend to be bigger – up to 20, and often above – rules are more relaxed and the social network is completely different. Also, there is much less of a tradition of students working or playing after hours. Generally, students from fee-paying schools do very well in sixth-form colleges, but you do need to be 'self-motivated', say heads, and reasonably mature.

How to Suss Out a Sixth-Form College

Most of the criteria for a good school also apply to sixth-form colleges, e.g., are the staff bright-eyed and bushy-tailed? However, there are some qs which are particularly pertinent for sixth-form colleges (and, by the way, many could be applied to traditional secondary-school sixth forms should you be considering moving from one to another):

1 How big is the college? Too big, and a student coming out of a cosy convent could get lost and lack TLC, but too small means not enough cash to fund a wide curriculum. As a general rule, under 700 students (i.e. 350 in each year) is too small; over 1,700 and it is getting unwieldy.

2 How wide is the A-level curriculum? It should be rich indeed compared with the average secondary school – 30 to 40 subjects would be usual, including such exotics as Media Studies, Sports Studies. Most sixth-form colleges now also offer GNVQs. These are gradually increasing in popularity. Sixth-form colleges also do GCSE retakes and often offer other qualifications as well.

3 How does the college look in the government A-level league tables which are generally published in November? If the college is 'open access', i.e. not academically selective, a 15-point score is not to be sneezed at.

4 Ask for ALIS. This is a statistical survey being developed by the University of Newcastle which has amassed (statistical) evidence to show a relationship between a student's performance at GCSE and his or her performance at A-level, e.g. (to put it crudely) if she gets five Cs at GCSE, statistically she will get whatever it is at A-level (each subject has a different profile of expected results). The excitement of this is that if a student gets *better* results at A-level than the statistics predict, then it could be the college (or a department of the college) is doing a good job; or, to put it in teacher-speak, it is 'value-added'.

5 What extras are on offer and how enthusiastically are they pursued? Good colleges offer a terrific variety of sports, art and other options. Compared with public school, the standard tends to be disappointing, but it should at least be *happening*. Check the fixtures list, and the college calendar.

6 What is the pastoral side like? Fee-paying schools tend to point to lack of pastoral care as the great weakness of sixth-form colleges. Sixth-form colleges would disagree in spades, however: 'the direction is for getting students to take responsibility for their own lives, rather than directing them,' says a sixth-form college supporter. A good college will have fewer rules than the average school. However, a good college should 'clock in' students, and should know where they are. There will be a terrific and very professional support system, both for pastoral matters (counsellors on tap) and for academic matters, and for sorting out A-level-result agonies.

7 Go to an open evening. This is a great opportunity to wander at will round the college, to talk to the staff *and to the students*. You will find the latter amazingly forthright.

PS Don't expect your fee-paying school to be any help to you in finding a sixth-form college: they are a considerable threat to the private sector, and we found hardly a head brave and/or magnanimous enough to admit even grudgingly that one on his doorstep was good.

Getting In

The minimum entry qualification for doing an A-level course is generally around five Cs at GCSE, but most colleges are prepared to listen to entreaties, or offer other courses for students with lesser or no GCSEs. Colleges generally publish their prospectuses in October, and hold open evenings between November and January. The earlier you make your application the better. Interviews are generally held soon after Easter, with an offer of a definite place a week or two later.

NB Oversubscribed colleges apply a wide variety of selection criteria: make sure you know what they are.

Further Education Colleges and Tertiaries

Not all counties have sixth-form colleges. In which case, don't bomb out further education colleges and tertiary colleges.

Further education colleges are 'grown-up' (i.e., not schooly), with an emphasis on adult students, part-timers, and 'vocational' courses for trades (e.g. catering, hairdressing, the leisure industry, etc.); and always bear in mind that many 'vocational' courses now lead on to university (e.g. electronics). They are usually even *bigger* than sixth-form colleges – i.e., huge. A-level results may well appear worse (there's a broader intake). Rules will be looser: at one college we know – and a good one at that – a student skipped classes consistently for a year before anyone noticed. Links with employers and careers advice, on the other hand, are both likely to be strong.

Broadly speaking, tertiary colleges fall somewhere between sixth-form and further education colleges, both in courses followed and in general ethos.

Contact

Further Education Funding Council: Cheylesmore House, Quinton Road, Coventry CV1 2WT, tel: 01203 863000, fax: 01203 863100.

They will send you a list of the 450 or so sixth-form colleges, and further education colleges.

SIXTH-FORM COLLEGES

ALTON COLLEGE

Old Odiham Road, Alton, Hampshire GU34 2LX, tel: 01420 88118, fax: 01420 80012.

Principal: Mr Michael Gray MA (early 50s) has been at Alton since 1978 (the year the college opened as a sixth form) and is clearly not ready to leave yet. A man with a broad smile, obviously known to, and well liked by, the students.

What it does: Offers A-level and GNVQ courses. There is an excellent GCSE retake option, and intermediate level GNVQs too, plus other practical courses. There's a reasonable range of extracurricular activities, including much music. Type of college: tertiary. Number of students: 1,400 (plus squillions of people at evening classes, etc). Maximum class size: around 18.

What it's like: Good exam results, both A-levels and vocational courses, with a bias to practical subjects, and strong in combinations of practical (e.g. Design and Technology) and academic. A happy spirit reigns throughout the college, and there's a strong pastoral system (and students must clock in). Study areas are located in the various subject areas so that students wishing to revise, bone up, work up, etc. have ready access to a (willing) teacher – and it need not be their own.

No layabouts – you need to be hard-working. This is not a place for the not-yet-independent, of whom there were some when we visited. The college does its best to support these, and will offer discipline to the needy at least for a while.

There are two student canteens, one scruffy and one smart. The scruffy one is v. basic – plastic chairs and tables, etc.

The buildings are largely modern and purpose-built; comfortable, light, roomy and well laid-out. The college is surrounded by the town of middle-class, light-industried Alton, but has enough room for playing-fields and car-parking. Extras are not greatly in evidence, but they haven't disappeared completely. When we visited the library smelt of stand-up scents, and the loos were somewhat noisome. Smoking is permitted, but only behind the bike shed: keeps them from annoying the neighbours.

Getting in and on: To do A-level, you need five C-grades at GCSE, with a bit extra in the subjects to be studied. Students come from a wide area, with about 25 per cent from private schools.

CITY OF STOKE-ON-TRENT SIXTH-FORM COLLEGE
Victoria Road, Fenton, Stoke-on-Trent, Staffordshire ST4 2RR, tel: 01782 48736, fax: 01782 747456.

Principal: Since 1993, Mrs Christina L. Cassidy B.Sc. (50s). Trained and worked as a biotechnologist and a manager before turning to teaching (Warrington Girls' High), then working her way quickly up the sixth-form college ladder. A leader with a slightly shy manner, she is immediately engaging and friendly. Consultation and delegation are definitely her style and she headlines 'care, support and push'.

What it does: Offers A-levels, GCSEs. Breadth of curriculum is provided mainly through a taught (two hours per week) General Studies A-level course, which covers many basic life skills. Number of students: around 1,550.

What it's like: Stoke is a good college that is just waking up to the realization that it could be an even better one. The grammar-school tradition is still strong (the staff Gents features 'The Miss Willis Bequest', a clothes brush for the removal of dandruff from shoulders), but celebration and display of students' successes are beginning to sprout around the college, and the young, enthusiastic staff in Art, Drama and Technology bring a sense of delight to their teaching. Results show the basic strength of the college, but at time of writing there are not enough A-grades – watch out for better things, though. Options are strong and compulsory.

Stoke is a city college, and this shows in the greater discipline and support that it feels are necessary for its students. Attendance and punctuality are kept to employment standards, smoking is not allowed anywhere, and students have to work hard for their first-year exams because failure may prevent them from continuing the course. Student support is particularly strongly emphasized, notably in assisting with applications to university. Friendly and articulate students – many are first-generation sixth-formers. The college is earning itself the nickname of 'Stoke-on-Trend'.

The buildings are in the London South Bank tradition, bare concrete and blood-red brick, seventies, but they feel fine to be in. They form a nice compact group in a pleasantly green setting.

Getting in and on: Stoke is an open-access college, taking all suitable applicants. The basic requirement is four C-grades at GCSE for A-level courses. About 10 students a year go to Oxford.

GODALMING COLLEGE
Tuesley Lane, Godalming, Surrey GU7 1RS, tel: 014834 23526, fax: 014834 17079.

Principal: Since 1987, Mrs Margaret Hobrough (pronounced Hoeboro) BA, M.Ed. (50s). Mrs Hobrough has a history background, with teacher training and the deputy headship of a state comprehensive. A friendly, open, clear headmistress, with a good management team.

What it does: Offers the most popular A-levels, including Media Studies, Fashion and Textiles, and lots of Maths combinations. No General Studies, some AS-levels, and IT for all. GNVQs and GCSE resits are also available. Type of college: sixth-form. Number of students: around 1,300–1,400.

What it's like: Good all-round academic performance here, in a strongly grammar-school atmosphere. The art department is extraordinarily good: of the tutors, Russell Gray hangs in the Tate and Michael Clark was commissioned by Bacon to paint Bacon. Art has had e.g. 45 As, 10 Bs, 4 Cs, 2 Ds, and 0 everything else, this and every year. Good results proliferate in many other subjects, and there have been other patches of high excitement (e.g. in Chemistry, no less). GNVQs are strongly supported and very well taught. Theatre Studies results have been disappointing, but it's lively. Displays of work, etc. are almost absent, purposely, as it is not felt to be needed when everyone knows how well they are doing: a pity.

Godalming is a stricter college than most, with a stricter college contract and tough enforcement of it, which produces a more regulated grammar-school atmosphere that fits in well with the college's intake (large numbers from private schools). Most staff are called 'Mrs' or 'Miss' or 'Mr', some 'Sir'.

There's a strong Christian Union and Christian spirit. Students report that they find the college very friendly and supportive. Good football and rugby, but options on the whole are weakish, not emphasized or appreciated (Japanese conversation is offered, however).

Buildings are 1930s, with stark corridors. The modern additions are good; a compact arrangement with adjacent space (and playing-fields). The college is in *immediate* need of a new building, however, as we write, particularly a new canteen and common-room.

Getting in and on: Five Cs or better are required to do A-levels. The last open evening is in March for 'sweep-ups', and to 'solidify choices'. About 30 students go on to do a gap year and 10 per cent take a year off.

GREENHEAD COLLEGE

Greenhead Road, Huddersfield HD1 4ES, tel: 01484 422032, fax: 01484 518025.

Principal: Since 1986, Dr J. K. (Kevin) Conway (40s) B.Sc., Ph.D. A Belfast-born physicist (first-class honours from Queen's University), Mr Conway is an upbeat, friendly, white-haired, charismatic and very open man; well organized, and much given to praising staff and students, and to measuring their performance. He believes that 'everyone is individual, everyone is valuable'. If you wish to be in his good books, do not call him 'Kev'.

What it does: Offers A-levels, and is particularly rich in practical, down-to-earth subjects (Computing, Accounts, Business Studies, etc.). GNVQs are on the menu in Business, Health, Science. There is a reasonable range of extracurricular offerings (known as 'enrichment'), and good relationships with local companies that allow for the best system of work shadowing and project work that we have seen. Non-examination courses include Rambling. Extra support is available in Maths and English. Type of college: sixth-form. Number of students: 950.

What it's like: Impressive (don't just take our word for it – the inspectors thought so too). Greenhead differs from the general run of sixth-form colleges in many ways: the tutorial system is based on specialist tutors, rather than every teacher playing a part (as happens elsewhere); there are regular assemblies for the whole college (rare elsewhere); new teachers are required to demonstrate (if they are not new to the profession) that the groups they have taught over the past four years have achieved good results (not at all common elsewhere).

The college runs the most sophisticated and complete quality-assessment and control system that we have come across. Teachers – traditionally shy of measurement – have responded enthusiastically to a system which allows them to analyse the reasons for each student's performance, and take specific action to improve it, from halfway through the first term. The students are chatty enough, even in large groups, and in smaller groups, zippy. Seventeen per cent of students are from ethnic minorities. Toffs will do well here if they are brave enough.

The college is particularly strong on sciences and Business Studies. You'll find some useful student comments in the prospectus. Each subject group has a resource area, where teachers are available at all times.

Getting in and on: Demand for places here now exceeds supply. Entrance to A-level courses requires two grade Cs and two grade Ds at GCSE, but more may be required of applicants from schools not linked to Greenhead. About 80 per cent go on to higher education.

HAYWARDS HEATH COLLEGE
Harlands Road, Haywards Heath, West Sussex RH16 1LT, tel: 01444 456281, fax: 01444 417047.

Principal: Since 1982, Mr Brian Derbyshire MA (50s). A Mancunian (he taught at Manchester Grammar School early on in his career), Mr Derbyshire is highly articulate, a good manager who leads from the front, decisive and incisive. English is his subject, and he has taught General Studies here (Mental Hygiene). Both his son and daughter went on to Cambridge from this college. He is not at all bothered that some students describe the college as 'a bit schooly': 'I don't apologize', and he is well aware that liberalizing may lead to erosion.

The college was preparing to expand, at the time of our visit, as per the government's edict, to take on twilight teaching of adults and part-timers, but the head is very proud of its being a sixth-form college, and is keen not to lose all the positive elements of this. Mr Derbyshire is good at marketing, which requires 'effort, not money', to which end he spends time visiting local schools and inviting the public in. (Brighton and Lewes and Horsham are all likely competitors in the sixth-form field.)

What it does: Offers 30 A-levels, 18 AS (fewer and fewer take them); also GCSE (retakes happen often), GNVQ (Intermediate and Advanced) from '94. Type of college: sixth-form. Number of students: just under 1,000. Staff–student ratio: 1–12. Maximum class size: 21, but the average class size is 13.2.

What it's like: There's a 'well-ordered' atmosphere, and in general organization is 'ticketyboo', according to a parent. The college is set in agreeable green playing-fields (and there are more playing-fields across the road), set in a comfortable residential area five minutes' walk up the hill from the railway station. Study areas (with computers) are attached to main subject areas, providing quiet areas to work and, 'if you're lucky', a member of staff too.

There are computers everywhere. The principal and staff are keen on letting students 'have a go' at a subject if they enjoy it, even though this will dip results. The art department is strong. Staff are exceedingly committed, and have a policy of constant meetings, so that there is a good deal of interaction. End-of-term tests, regular reports and self-assessments all feature.

Built as a grammar school in 1958, the college became a comprehensive in '74 before transforming into a sixth-form college in '76. The architecture is functional, of the successive dates, and is well adapted to present use, with good science labs and art rooms. Substantial numbers of 'temporary' teaching huts have been *in situ* for 20 years, and more have been recently built. The college has its own gym, outdoor heated pool, and a big hall (for drama, exams, etc.). A canteen area with round tables doubles as the students' common-room ('we all long for more space here'), where students run their own radio station at the start of the day and after lunch.

There's a good programme of 'extension studies' set in 13-week blocks: students must undertake two per week. There's also a weekly 'element' of sport and fitness. Aerobics, self-defence and weight training are perennially popular. There's an interesting record of visiting speakers. Social life is vigorous – students organize at least one, sometimes three, balls per year. The theatre department is energetic and enthusiastic. Festival week annually involves everyone in fund-raising.

Pastoral care is definitely strong, and is often the reason parents choose this college. A tutor system applies (18 students per group); tutors meet on a brief daily basis, with regular lengthier sessions. 'We aim for the best and hope to please. We don't aim to please and hope for the best', was the principal's slogan for a long time; 'But I said it too often and it's too slick.' It certainly sums up the college's attitude. The principal is fiercely ('obsessively', according to local newspapers) anti-smoking – this applies to staff as well as students – and after much persuasion, has introduced a smoking zone (an unlovely corner of a field) to the delight of local residents who used to complain about students hanging around the entrance smoking.

Good, considerate relationships are enjoyed by staff and students: 'not a problem in this area'. However staff are well aware of the student 'linguistic subculture' (effing and blinding, etc.).

Careful career guidance is given throughout.

Getting in and on: Potential students are interviewed two or three times before they arrive. Figures on college leavers (where known) in 1994: 52·5 per cent went on to higher education, 29 per cent to further education, and 17 per cent went into employment.

HILLS ROAD SIXTH-FORM COLLEGE

Hills Road, Cambridge CB2 2PE, tel: 01223 247251, fax: 01223 416979.

Principal: Since 1984, Mr Colin Greenhalgh MA (50s; pronounced Greenhalge, as in alge(-ebra)). Came from Bradford

Grammar School, then Bullmersh, Reading; then St Bartholomew, Newbury. Friendly and open, Mr Greenhalgh combines the looks and the charm of Clive James and Clive Anderson. The college as it is now is largely his creation. Besides his other talents, Mr Greenhalgh is a masterful fund-raiser.

What it does: Very much an academic shop, including Latin and an unusually popular Religious Studies course (Christianity and Hinduism, principally). GNVQs start in 1995. A good range of extracurricular activities is on offer, with much participation in sports, arts, music and drama. Number of students: around 1,000.

What it's like: Superb all round, and sends shivers down the spine of many a fee-paying school in the area: it ranks as perhaps the most friendly and enthusiastic college in the grammar-school tradition that we have seen. Exam performances at A-level are excellent by any standard, and there are no weak subjects. There are very good results on GCSE retakes. A wonderful place altogether for an academically gifted child – we came across lots of happy little workers. There's no sign of drugs or bullying. The college as a whole, staff and students, is protective and welcoming. Nerds will fit in here. There is a spirit about the place which seems to lift the exam performances of gifted and less able alike.

Very much a city-centre site. A collection of good buildings, old and recent (not to mention some Portakabins), crowded (but not yet overcrowded) on to a long rectangular site. The flag-poles outside are a gift from proud parents. (Next year they might consider giving a clock: there appear to be only two on the whole site.) A new sports centre is under way at time of writing. The loos were smelly when we visited.

Getting in and on: The college is seriously selective. Although its entry criteria for A-level are only a little higher than the average, Hills Road is heavily oversubscribed, and they do choose carefully which students they take. Students are drawn from a number of feeder schools within 15 miles of Cambridge and from the private sector. You'll be lucky to get in if you live more than 15 miles away. Most students go on to university (50 or so to Oxbridge per year).

LONG ROAD SIXTH-FORM COLLEGE

Cambridge CB2 2PX, tel: 01223 247810, fax: 01223 416118.

Principal: Since 1989, Mrs Madeleine Craft B.Sc. (Maths) (early 50s). Mrs Craft came into teaching just 20 years ago after a career in telecommunications and parenthood. A thoughtful and widely respected principal who has helped bring Long Road out of a long period of (relative) neglect, to the point where it has gained one of the most glowing inspection reports yet issued. Her management style is one of consultation and participation.

What it does: Offers a good range of A-levels, an expanding range of GNVQs, and has a very successful GCSE department. Extracurricular activities are numerous and much enjoyed. Number of students: around 1,200.

What it's like: A relaxed and friendly college, with most students on first-name terms with their teachers. For reasons of history (Hills Road Sixth-Form College was formerly the boys' grammar school, Long Road the girls'), there has long been a tendency for the most academically gifted students to gravitate to Hills Road, with Long Road emphasizing its success with the middle of the range. But do not think for a moment that this makes Long Road a second-class place to be: it just makes it different.

The broader ability spectrum at Long Road has led to its becoming less formal, with less emphasis on academic success and more on individual support and responsibility.

The main buildings are a rambling fifties creation, undistinguished in appearance but pleasant to work in. There is a wonderful new arts block, and lots of open space and greenery.

Long Road has a top-class art department, and unusually good results are achieved in Performing Arts and Electronics. Inhabitants of Cambridge have a choice between two fine sixth-form colleges, and can confidently plump for whichever suits their child best.

Getting in and on: This college must be in danger of becoming oversubscribed too. For the moment, though, early applicants should be sure of a place. Most students go on to higher education, with about five a year getting to Oxbridge.

PETER SYMONDS' COLLEGE

Owens Road, Winchester, tel: 01962 852764, fax: 01962 849372.

Principal: Since 1993, Mr Neil Hopkins B.Sc., MA. Mr Hopkins is a mathematician from the University of East Anglia; the Master's degree is from Manchester. He took over from Stuart Nicholls, a keen pioneer of sixth-form colleges and responsible for much of the college's success. Mr Hopkins says modestly that he is 'only doing a housekeeping job', and that he is particularly keen on quoting Mr Nicholls's maxim: 'We count in ones.' Mr Hopkins was previously acting principal of the only other sixth-form college with boarding: Rutland. He has a nice sense of humour, very quick intelligence.

What it does: Offers the usual wide range of academic A-levels, GNVQs, also Performing Arts, etc., and the Hampshire Specialist Music Course, see Music chapter, p. 252. Number of students: around 1,654.

What it's like: This is considered by many to be the best sixth-form college in the country. Strong on all fronts, the college regularly comes top of the Hampshire (state) league tables. The average total point score in the government A-level league tables per top 200 students was better than next-door Winchester College last year. Renowned for strong – wonderful – art department: good lively, original work is constantly emerging, and there is some excellent sculpting. The psychology department is considered outstanding too. The presence of the specialist music course has an electric effect on the college orchestra.

The college was founded in 1607 by mercer Peter Symonds as Christe's Hospital almshouse for six old men and four boys. Links with the Mercers' livery company were recently renewed, and funding from them provides just that little extra for students to do wonderful things like buy a chanter for their Irish bagpipes, or take part in the Tall Ships Race. The present college became a grammar school 100 years ago, then a sixth-form college in the early seventies – one of the pioneers. Sited on a green hill to the north of Winchester, a good main redbrick building provides a focal point, overlooking pleasant playing-fields. Dotted around the campus are the various departments – 'So,' says the principal, 'students are not always falling over each other.'

An unusual feature is the boarding houses right on the campus. There are about ninety boarders in two houses: one coed, girls on one floor, boys on the other, and penalties if you're caught on the wrong floor at the wrong time; one for girls, and at the moment the college is overflowing into the boarding facilities of secondary schools in the area. Go round the girls' boarding house and you will ask yourself why you ever contemplated paying £12K a year for private education. That said, the boarding is not cheap: at time of writing, it costs £1,800 a term. Also, some parents have voiced fears about the lack of supervision in the boarding houses, with tales of students loitering round town. Boarders come from the Forces, from the Channel Islands and the Isle of Wight and, on an interesting note, Peter Symonds' is the official school for Falkland Islanders to study A-levels at – Falkland Islanders who get the requisite five Cs at GCSE are paid for (all twenty or so of them).

There is enthusiastic rugby and football here (the principal is keen on the latter), and a champion hockey team. Facilities for minor sports are not anything like as good as the average public school, however, and the standard on the whole is not so high. The first-class library opens at 8.30 a.m., by which time there is usually a queue of students at the door.

Discipline is 'not a problem,' says the principal. 'The worst we would have to do is call in the parents.' There is one part-time counsellor plus two volunteers on tap. There's one area for smoking: appropriately enough, beside the bicycle shed. Winchester is a slightly druggy area, and the principal admits he couldn't rule out the possibility of their presence, 'though not as far as I am aware of'. The place is imbued with Winchester's middle-class go-and-get-it spirit, though, and the atmosphere is quite purposeful.

Some excellent, dedicated and very professional teachers here.

Getting in and on: There's open access: 'Once a place is offered we won't take it back, whatever the GCSE results.' However a minimum of five Cs are almost always required to study A-level courses. Around half the students come from the local (good) state schools, the rest from 142 different schools all over the place. Around 25 per cent are from the private sector, including a batch from St Swithun's in Winchester. There's a large middle-class contingent. The majority of students go on to university (mainly in the South), including 18, in '94, to Oxbridge. An increasing proportion do a gap year.

QUEEN MARY'S COLLEGE

Cliddesden Road, Basingstoke, Hampshire RG21 3HF, tel: 01256 20861, fax: 01256 26097.

Principal: Since 1990, Mr Ivan Peters BA (40s). Direct, energetic, Mr Peters talks like a captain of industry, clearly coping well with the government's new agenda. He started his career in industry, then taught in a boys' grammar school in Cornwall, before setting up a multi-ethnic sixth-form college in Birmingham. Mr Peters does 'walkabouts', with a member of staff, as a way of keeping his finger on the pulse and getting to know students.

What it does: The majority (75–80 per cent) of students are taking A-levels, though endless other courses and possibilities are on offer with around 50 pupils from local schools doing GCSE languages after school hours (Latin, Italian, etc.); BTEC has recently been introduced, and GNVQs from September '94; also RSAs, City and Guilds vocational modules, secretarial and language courses, etc. Forty A-levels are available (including three different History boards). Results are 'comfortably in the first quarter of sixth-form colleges'. Type of college: sixth-form. Number of students: 1,450, plus some part-time and adult students.

What it's like: This is a well-run college with a deservedly high reputation. There is a clever timetabling system with 'support clinics' for those needing extra help (i.e. the very top end and the very bottom). Teaching groups average 16 students, and there's absolutely no streaming. Students refer to personal study time as 'free time'.

The college was set up in 1972 with 500 students in the sixth form to serve local schools (most Hampshire state schools do not have sixth forms). Numbers have grown to the current bulging-point as more teenagers stay in education longer. 'There are about 100 children here who in other times might be out in the job market,' comments the principal. There is a large number of buildings (and more on the way), mainly well equipped, including a theatre, arts block, etc., though in some areas there's a sense of overcrowding – the Focus, for one, which doubles uncomfortably as canteen and study area. The Street is a broad, linking corridor, with walls used for display and providing an area where students can sit with chums, books, or tutor.

The college is away from the centre of the town, with tennis courts and playing-fields on site. It has its own swimming pool, gym, etc. Facilities include a crèche for the staff's infants.

Every student must undertake some 'complementary studies'. The list is long and various, e.g. start-up Russian, first aid, golf, etc. Hands-on subjects e.g. photography are always the most popular, 'so it's difficult to get to do what you really want,' said a student. For the first year, one afternoon of sport is obligatory.

Also on offer are extremely good, lively, in-demand drama courses, including a foundation course which deals with all aspects of theatre both on-stage and backstage. 'We put a lot of our resources into drama; we're very proud of it.' It's often the reason boys and girls come here in the first place. You find happy and fulfilled students in this department.

Tutor groups of 16 students (ages, levels, subjects, etc. are mixed) meet for pastoral reasons, and tutors have a senior member who shepherds them. However, absenteeism, lateness, etc. would not reach home (via a letter) for three days. Students and parents must sign an agreement before joining the college: this is a sensible list of college and student intentions. Staff and students are all on Christian-name terms.

There's a full-time counsellor (much in demand) for everything from troubles at home to drugs, 'though I still think alcohol is by far the worst problem for this age group,' says the principal.

Getting in and on: There is open access, no special qualifications are required. There is competitive entry via interview for the theatre foundation course. Fifteen per cent of the students come from fee-paying schools. Sixty-three per cent go on to university, between 8 and 14 a year to Oxbridge; art school and drama school are always popular options. There are very strong links with local industries for employment, including the Automobile Association and IBM.

RICHMOND UPON THAMES COLLEGE

Egerton Road, Twickenham TW2 7SJ, tel: 0181 892 6656, fax: 0181 744 9738.

Principal: Since 1987, Mr Eric Kirby B.Sc, M.Sc., FRSA (50s). A degree in Physics was followed by a career in aerospace engineering, an M.Sc. in Solid-State Physics, and then teaching. A nice man.

What it does: As you would expect at a large college, there is a very wide choice of curriculum options. Exotic A- and AS-levels taken by more than one student in '94 include Accounting, Chinese, Dance, Latin, Portuguese and Russian. GCSEs offered also go much wider than the usual range. 'Skill Centres' are available to students who need extra help with particular problems, and dyslexics get one-to-one support. In the vocational area, Richmond has a national reputation for HNDs in Graphic Art, and for Computer-Aided Design training for the petrochemical industry. Type of college: tertiary. Number of students: 5,150, of whom 3,400 is the full-time equivalent and of whom 1,750 are doing A-levels. Maximum class size: aims to have a maximum of 20 'but occasionally this may vary'. Approximately 24 per cent of students are aged over 19.

What it's like: Richmond is about in the middle of the tertiary college spectrum, with a strong A-level tradition and a growing emphasis on vocational courses. A-level results are OK, but GCSEs have shown blips, and at A-level some subjects are way ahead of others.

The music is excellent, and some students leave top-flight private schools to come to Richmond just because music is so good here. Richmond is also a serious and successful sporting college, though all sports are voluntary. *The College Rumour* is the most interesting and well-produced magazine we have seen yet in this sector: it's part of a course.

Richmond College has a large, friendly and quite imposing campus, and is near British Rail (Twickenham), which is handy for the many refugees from central London education. Ample car-parking is available, but the college is short on space considering the area.

Within the context of colleges generally, the pastoral overseeing – despite lots of counsellors, etc. – appears to us to be clearly at the looser end of what is acceptable. Student facilities seem to be dominated by one group of students, who play their kind of music and ignore the smoking ban ('How can we enforce it?' say the staff, 'this is Liberal Richmond and we would never dare to expel a student even for repeated breaches of the rule'); the occasional student appears to be able to get away with extended periods of cutting lessons without effective action being taken. A conventional middle-class parent comments: 'We are a bit alarmed to see our daughter turning into a cockney-speaking lefty.' That said, a mature, responsible and self-motivated student (like the great majority here) should be untroubled by this.

Getting in and on: An open-access college, Richmond guarantees to take all comers from 'partner' schools (about 50 per cent come from these). The college hosts a higher education fair every year, attended by many universities. Support for Oxbridge applications is notably strong and much appreciated; 20 + students go there per year.

ST CHARLES CATHOLIC SIXTH-FORM COLLEGE
74 St Charles Square, London W10 6EY, tel: 0181 968 7755, fax: 0181 968 1060.

Principal: Since 1990, Mr J. F. Rourke MA (50s), previously head of a comprehensive. A John Major look-alike, Mr Rourke is forthright, humorous and efficient. He is also watchful, and stands poised, daily, at break-time in the entrance hall observing and chatting to students, before whizzing up to the staff room 'just to be available'. Commands huge respect from staff and pupils, and, moreover, is liked. His wife has her own teaching career; the Rourkes have three grown-up children. Mr Rourke is a firmly committed Catholic.

What it does: Offers A-levels, also GCSEs (done in combination with other courses: you can't come here just to do GCSEs), GNVQs (at Foundation, Intermediate and Advanced levels). Number of pupils: 750. Staff–student ratio: 1–14. Around 14 per cent of students are non-Catholics.

What it's like: St Charles's takes on a truly comprehensive ability range of students, from Oxbridge candidates (around six aspirants per year, who get special support) to those with learning difficulties. English-as-a-second-language support is bought in from the local authority for around two dozen students. Media Studies, Design and Business Studies are all notably successful subjects at all the various levels. The college is well known for its success at GNVQs (taken by around one-third of the students), about which students and staff are enthusiastic.

A-level results reflect the intake, i.e. they are very mixed, with regular handfuls of A-grades in a wide variety of subjects – it is still early on in the college history to have built up much of a track record, and results are consistently higher than the national average. Excellent advice is given on subjects and further education.

Purpose-built, the college opened in 1990 with four designated contributory Catholic schools (Cardinal Vaughan and the Oratory were originally designated to be among them; however, amid much controversy, both these schools held on to their own sixth forms). The college is well resourced by the local authority, from the DfE and the diocese.

The college is in a fabulous building which has been well set in the square, with plenty of benches, greenery and space for sitting and walking, an oasis of calm not far from the Harrow Road. The main building is large, light, buff-coloured outside and inside, and is kept in smashing order. Matching blue carpet is fitted throughout (posho in the 'best' rooms), and note the lino floor design in the central hall, copied from the Borromeo Palazzo in Rome, i.e. St Charles Borromeo's family *palazzo*; the original version is in marble). The inherited school buildings have been revamped in a similar design and colour scheme as the rest.

There are terrific facilities throughout, with six high-tech labs (run on the university-standard Lab Kit system), a lovely library (book a carrel for private study time), with CD-ROM and Apple Macs everywhere, loads of newspapers, periodicals, etc.

IT is compulsory for everyone on a workshop basis. Also compulsory (one and a quarter hours per week) is Religious Education, to which there is 'no consumer resistance', say the staff. The RC element comes 'in all shapes and sizes', and the non-RCs applying for places must write a letter saying why they want to attend a Catholic sixth-form college.

The college is hot on pastoral care. There is a small chapel, and large reproductions of icons are dotted around the college. Daily lunch-time Masses are held (students sit on the floor), attended by a regular few. The full-time chaplain and his assistant (a nun) are both popular figures, whose chaplaincy is a relaxed meeting-place for students and staff. Retreats and pilgrimages are regularly organized.

There's a keen theatre, with an excellent theatre workshop (professionally equipped).

Around 60 per cent of these inner-city students are first generation in further education, and most of them are appreciative. 'There's no vulgarity, they're not difficult,' say staff. 'I've had to ask a few to leave,' says the principal.

Getting in and on: Via written application, followed by an interview. Large numbers apply. Attitude and commitment count for much. Of the students who leave after A-levels or Advanced GNVQs, about 75 per cent go on to higher education, 25 per cent into employment.

SHREWSBURY SIXTH-FORM COLLEGE

Priory Road, Shrewsbury SY1 1RX, tel: 01743 235491, fax: 01743 242735.

Principal: Since 1993, Mr W. E. (Bill) Dowell, B.Ed. (mid-40s), a teacher of PE and History who came to Shrewsbury from nearby 11–16 Wrockwardine School, Telford. A friendly and open consensus-builder, and a real doer. Should make the college even better over the next five years.

What it does: A-levels on offer include exotics such as Industrial Studies and Theatre Studies (though Geography and History are currently very popular). The standard package is two A-levels plus two AS-levels. Students follow a strong extracurricular programme that includes much IT, and leads up to the General Studies A-level. No vocational subjects are taken. Number of students: around 850 in all.

What it's like: Shrewsbury has what the principal calls a 'commitment to student development', and excellent staff–student relationships. Despite having the 'oldest staff room in Shropshire' (the denizens, not the building), with lots of jerseys and no exotic ties, students report that staff are very helpful, alive and enthusiastic. Academic results are good.

The buildings range from the twenties to the eighties and are crammed into a rather constricted site (could do with acquiring the site next door), but a wide and beautiful park (The Quarry) and a lively town are just outside the gates. Tourists roam everywhere, and the River Severn runs by. The college is well financed, but the money goes on staff rather than buildings and equipment. Students are enthusiastic about the place: 'a great two years,' says one of them. The college was founded in 1981, and is one of the few to have a flourishing Army Cadet Force (around 60 cadets).

Getting in and on: Most students come from nine 'partner' schools; not many are from the private sector. The college is oversubscribed: selection is based on a 'personal statement', school reports and an interview, though C-grades at GCSE are generally expected. Particular efforts are made to provide the right course for each student from the outset. Drop-out rates are very low as a result. Eighty-six per cent go on to higher education, though not many to Oxbridge.

THE SIXTH-FORM COLLEGE
North Hill, Colchester, Essex CO1 1SN, tel: 01206 577266, fax: 01206 573217.

Principal: Since 1987, Mr John A. Edwards B.Sc., Dip. Ed. (early 50s). Mr Edwards read Physics at Imperial College, London, and taught in a state secondary school before moving to sixth-form colleges. His previous post was principal of Barrow-in-Furness Sixth-Form College, and he moved to Colchester to found the sixth-form college here. An excellent administrator: the place seems to run on oiled wheels, with any mistakes and weaknesses acknowledged, monitored and dealt with. Well liked, Mr Edwards believes in an 'open door' policy – people run in and out of his office as though it were the local railway station. Not surprisingly, Mr Edwards has a very efficient secretary, Mrs Borton.

What it does: The usual, also a one-year A-level course; GNVQ Business Studies has been offered since September 1994. The college initially offered the traditional A-level subjects and most of its work is in this field, gradually grafting on new ones: Art, Music, Theatre Studies, etc. Number of students: around 1,750 boys and girls. Staff–student ratio: 1–13.8.

What it's like: Got going from a standing start in 1987 to its present oversubscribed position, vying for supremacy with two very strong local state grammar schools. The college produces good results in most subjects. It's an enthusiastic young staff, all called by their Christian names by the students, 'which,' says a member of staff, 'you may think is a little thing, but it makes all the difference: students really appreciate it'. They also appreciate being able to wear what they like 'providing they are clean and tidy'.

The place feels very like a cosy university campus, but do not be misled by this: there is a very strong structure of classes, register-taking, a tutorial system (weekly sessions, and six-weekly reports). The usual no-drugs-no-drink rules are enforced ruthlessly: 'There is no point in having a rule if you don't enforce it, is there?' says Mr Edwards, almost apologetically.

The college is housed in the old Gilberd School buildings, an imposing façade on a hill overlooking the city's interminable roundabouts, within a stone's throw of the further education college. Good use is made of space and 'infill' of corridors, etc. The general impression is light, roomy, carpeted, with lots of comfy chairs for students to sit around in. Every spare inch of space is used up. There are no expansion plans, says the principal, as there isn't anywhere to expand, though a sports hall is planned for the area behind the car park.

There is lots of evidence of extracurricular activity: all students must do between two and four hours a week, choosing from a huge range of options – Dream Analysis, we were told, is particularly popular at the moment. One ex-public school boy was happily synthesizing music in a recording cubicle as we visited. Blur, the pop group, were at college here and recently returned for a concert.

Students come from Colchester and around; children of yuppies, etc. There are bags of bright brains about but 'you've got to be motivated,' says a student, earnestly. The atmosphere is friendly, and the impression we got is that the gentle and the inarticulate will not be lost. It's also blessed with a top-class caretaker.

Getting in and on: Applications are required by the end of January at the latest. A group of students goes to Third World countries to do a digging project in the summer. Many take a gap year. Twelve to 15 students per year go on to Oxbridge. Job experience opportunities could perhaps be expanded.

WOODHOUSE COLLEGE
Finchley, London N12 9EY, tel: 0181 445 1210, fax: 0181 445 5210.

Principal: Since 1982, Dr Colin Wharton MA, Ph.D. (50s), an English teacher. Dr Wharton has bright, brown eyes, is keen and incisive.

What it does: Offers A-levels and AS-levels (90 per cent of students take two of each) and GCSE retakes in the usual wide range of subjects. All take part in a well-developed work placement programme. Type of college: sixth-form. Number of students: around 700 – i.e., smallish by sixth-form college standards.

What it's like: For those not in the linked schools, the college is highly selective – there's much pressure on places, though, said a local educationalist tartly, 'that's because of lack of [state] competition in the area'. Like the nearby Colney Hatch mental hospital, the buildings are scruffy and run-down – 0 out of 10 to the Council – but they are now being tarted up. Even when tarted up, however, the college could still do with a massive injection of capital for new buildings, equipment, etc. The college got a pat on the back from the inspectors for Languages and Business Studies. There's good, active extracurricular music – classical and jazz, with frequent concerts. Good drama is also a feature.

There was no general IT training at the time of our visit. The teaching is 'old-fashioned,' said a visiting teacher: Woodhouse is in the grammar-school tradition and proud of it. Not much evidence of students' work or achievements on display, the policy being that 'the results speak for themselves'; presumably this accounts for the unexciting prospectus too. Backup for students could be better, some feel, but all this said, the college is a little academic oasis in the north London state scene.

Getting in and on: Woodhouse is an 'open access' college for around half its intake: students from neighbouring schools without sixth forms. For the rest, it's highly selective. Fifteen or so a year go to Oxbridge. Students come from a wide range of backgrounds: 25 per cent of students are from the private sector (Mill Hill, City of London, etc.); over 30 per cent are from ethnic minorities (mainly Asian).

3

Crammers

Crammers originally made their money cramming students for university and for retaking bodged A-levels. However, now that almost anyone can get into *some* university, crammers have had a hard time of it, and are increasingly turning their attention to the great new market: first-time A-levellers, not to mention GCSE-ers. They are also useful for brushing up at the last minute (revision courses are *big* business) and indeed for doing anything in the academic line that you may need in order to get on to the next stage.

Crammers now tend to call themselves 'tutorial colleges' or, muddlingly, sixth-form colleges, but in reality most are now registered as schools. They are by definition private, and (fat) fee-paying. They differ from schools, however, in that they exist to cater to the individual student's needs rather than offering a syllabus which the student must fit in with. Crammers specialize in catering for everything in the A-level line – not just the mainstream subjects offered (often in 'blocks', enforcing limited choice) by most schools. Classes in crammers are, or should be, smaller; the learning more intense (taking place in seminars), with *lots* of exam practice (timed essays, etc.). Extracurricular activities, on the other hand, will be minimal (though again, this is changing). Rules are usually kept to the minimum, and students are treated as grown-ups rather than fledglings.

All of this is alluring to students tiring of the constriction of conventional schooling (prefect duties, boarding, choir and all that). More alluring to parents, however, is the hope that their children will get their heads down and get those good grades. Either way, caveat: a crammer is not necessarily a magical solution.

Crammers

The work comes as a shock (true of A-level work anywhere and particularly so of crammers); the environment comes as another shock (tiny classrooms, no tinies); and the freedom itself can be a bit of a shock as well.

Most crammers are in centres of learning – in the hopes that some of it rubs off, no doubt, and also because such centres are good sources of tutors. Central London, city centres, including Oxbridge, are where they gather. Some belong to CIFE – the Conference for Independent Further Education – a grand-sounding organization set up by the crammers themselves to 'audit' their own performance and watch out for the 'pirates'. Being a member of CIFE does not guarantee good results, but it does mean you should get a straight answer when you ask about them. However, a number of reputable crammers do not belong.

Beware of crammer league tables. There are two sets: retakes, which come out in the *Telegraph* and are supplied by CIFE (and therefore only list their members); and the government league tables, which come out in November (and only apply to DfE-registered schools). The whole question of league tables in this context is fraught with difficulty. Results can be fudged, misprints made, colleges are left off, and in any case results in this sector are very volatile.

Questions to Ask of Crammers

* How big is the maximum class size? Seven is OK for A-levels, 10 is getting to be on the large side.
* How many taught hours are there for each subject per week?
* Ask about studying in their large amounts of 'free' time – are there any quiet study areas on the premises?
* What is their attitude to pastoral care? Do students, for example, have to clock in every morning? (Where students are not living at home, landladies report those not getting up till midday, and one college at least stipulates that landladies must leave the heating on all day in case students want to stay at home.)

* What happens if students don't clock in all day?
* What organization is the crammer accredited to? The main inspection board is the BAC.
* Where do the students live?
* How does the tutorial system work?
* Fees? (It'll cost you two arms and a leg.)
* Ask to see ALIS bar charts (see chapter on Sixth-Form Colleges, p. 10, and NB one crammer we visited hadn't heard of this). Crammers should be able to bump up students' retake results by a level or two. Watch out for crammers so small that any results are meaningless. The larger the numbers taking an exam, the harder it is to achieve an overall high result (and bear in mind that most crammers are academically unselective).
* What are the qualifications of the staff, and their teaching experience? It is *vital* to know this, as it is only too easy to corral someone to help out who though academically qualified has no teaching experience. (Hope to find really dynamic experienced teachers who, for one reason or another, have opted out of mainstream schools.)
* Retake question: which examination boards can the crammer offer? (Only three boards offer exams in winter and then only in some subjects . . . Don't get stuck doing a whole year when a term would have done.)
* What is the policy on taking in students expelled for using illegal drugs? They need to be pinned down closely on this – there cannot be a crammer in the land that has not taken in pot-smoking swingers, but there are degrees of tolerance. How do they regard 'suspicion of taking drugs' cases, for example? Do not necessarily be put off by a crammer which admits to taking (ex)-drug offenders: everything depends on the attitude, both of the school and of the offender (not to mention the parents), and on the quality of pastoral care.

Contact

British Accreditation Council: Suite 401, 27 Marylebone Road, London NW1 5JS, tel: 0171 487 4643, fax: 0171 486 4253. This exists to inspect places of further and higher education. This is voluntary – the school or college requests inspection and pays a fee for it. The Council will send you a list of schools which are members – i.e. they come up to its standards.

Conference for Independent Further Education: Buckhall Farm, Bull Lane, Bethersden, Ashford, Kent TN26 3HB, tel and fax: 01233 820797.

Portman Educational Consultants Ltd.: 3 Harley Gardens, London SW10 9SW, tel: 0171 835 0637, fax: 0171 373 6801. Specialize in advising on tutorial colleges, university entrance and careers.

Trotman & Co. publish a natty and *very* useful collection of guides e.g., *How to Complete Your UCAS Form, Getting into Medical School* – telephone 0181 332 2132.

CRAMMERS

ABBEY TUTORIAL COLLEGE

53–5 Cornwall Street, Birmingham B3 2DH, tel: 0121 236 7474, fax: 0121 236 3937.

Vital statistics: Number of students: 118 (maximum capacity: 150). Ages: 14–20. Maximum teaching group size: eight (average six).

Head: Since 1992, Mr Kevin Byrne (early 30s), educated at Penistone Grammar School near Barnsley, Lancaster, Bangor and the world. Mr Byrne has a degree in Forestry, did his PGCE at Durham, has worked in Canada, Nepal, and for the Forestry Commission, and came to teaching when he discovered how much he enjoyed it. A brilliant hands-on enthusiast – could be one of the best teachers of his generation. Mr Byrne is a great believer in learning being fun, and is 'almost' of the opinion that there is no such thing as a bad student, only bad teaching.

What it does: Twenty-seven A-level subjects, 12 AS plus all the GCSEs. Retakes (currently about 35–40 per cent of students are doing these); all boards are available. Extra tuition is given. Planning to offer Land-based Skills as a GNVQ in 1995.

What it's like: Abbey started in 1992 as a specialist science and maths crammer, one of the Further Education Group (see Davies, Laing & Dick, p. 43), and sister school to Abbey Manchester and Abbey London, but is gradually breaking into other areas e.g. languages and art (new art studio). Music is not on offer at time of writing (but check, as the school is dynamic).

Abbey got off to a standing start, coming top of the crammers' value-added league tables in '92, though, as Mr Byrne modestly pointed out, the school had fewer pupils than some to start with, and that made it easier. However it also came top among crammers in the '93 and '94 tables, with, in '94, a staggering 2.54 *average grade improvement*, and the school is altogether an impressive little performer.

Bursaries undoubtedly help to create this rosy picture. Mr Byrne comments: 'If a student can convince me they want to do A-levels for the right reason, we will get them in.'

The school is housed in what *was*, but is no longer, a scruffy little building tucked in a quietish backstreet in the centre of Birmingham, an eight-minute walk from New Street. Packed with bubble and bounce, though – cheerful-looking students in every corner, and a real feel of zip and the feeling that work is *fun*. Tutors are known by their Christian names 'on good days'. There are regular Law, Environment and Medical seminars with visiting speakers – usually admissions officers from key university departments. Lots of jolly outings are put on, including 'trips to Mars' and the Birmingham Stock Exchange, Outward Bound trips in Wales, and there are activities such as football every Wednesday night. The school uses the city's main central library, which is excellent. There is a new canteen for lunch, or you can get a v. good sandwich from the local corner shop. There is an attendance register 'just like you would have in school'.

Fifty per cent of students come from within a 35-mile radius, the rest from 'all over the country', and indeed some from the Cayman Islands, Barbados and Japan (these last via the university).

Accommodation: There is 'vetted' accommodation for about 25 students: nine in two family homes with children at university; the rest *en famille*, or self-catering within a family home. Accommodation Officer Colum Devine 'sorts them all out', and does the deal, e.g. £35–£55 a week for b&b, or £70 all-in (a bargain compared with, say, Oxford).

Cost: It's on a par with the rest, but around 40 per cent of students are on some sort of bursary, including some on full fees.

BASIL PATERSON ('BP's') COLLEGE FOR ACADEMIC STUDIES

22–3 Abercromby Place, Edinburgh EH3 6QE, tel: 0131 556 7695, fax: 0131 557 8503.

Vital statistics: Number of students: approx. 50. Ages: generally 15–19, but has been known to take younger students. Number of staff: 12 full time for the whole college (see below).

Principal (of all three schools): Since 1991, Mr Robin Mackenzie MA (50s). Mr Mackenzie was educated at Aberdeen University, and has a postgraduate degree in Language and Politics from McMasters in Canada. He worked as a senior English instructor in King Faisal's Air Academy (the Cranwell of the Middle East) before coming to BP's. Laconic but with a great sense of humour and a pragmatic approach. He comments: 'But for our foreign students we wouldn't be here today.'

What it does: BP's is three schools under one roof – English, Secretarial and Business Studies, and Academic Studies. The academic studies school does GCSEs, A-levels and Scottish Highers, also Easter revision courses and private tuition. They are currently looking at offering, among other things, the Diploma of Achievement.

What it's like: This is a famous Edinburgh crammer which has responded to market forces by diversifying into other areas (see Traditional Alternatives – Indoors chapter, p. 176) and the crammer operation is now the poor relation.

The atmosphere is laid-back, and produces a few raised eyebrows among the matrons of Edinburgh, but from parents seeking a solution to real educational problems we have heard nothing but praise. The school is less frenzied than, say, its London counterparts, and feels safer, but do not forget that Edinburgh is one of the drug capitals of Europe.

The school is housed in elegant buildings in New Town, a peaceful location overlooking gardens. There is a cosy, trattoria-type gingham-tableclothed canteen in the basement, where the heaps of foreigners studying English as a foreign language might feel at home. Students 'we try to treat as adults,' says the principal, but 'occasionally I go into the Wally Dug [local pub] and do a sweep'.

Accommodation: Students mostly live in families within a 15-minute bus ride – around £80 a week half board – and there is an accommodation officer on site.

Cost: Approx. £2,000 per A-level (two terms), science subjects approx. £700 extra. Scottish Highers £1,400 each; five GCSEs £5,072; private tuition £18 an hour for BP students, £24 if you come off the street (i.e. much cheaper than London prices).

CCSS

(Cambridge Centre for Sixth-Form Studies), 1 Salisbury Villas, Station Road, Cambridge CB1 2JF, tel: 01223 316890, fax: 01223 358441.

Vital statistics: Number of students: 200+. Number of staff: 25–7 full time, plus 15 part time. Teaching group size: maximum seven. Twenty per cent of students are from overseas (including 15 per cent expatriates).

Principal: Since 1981 Mr P. C. Redhead MA (Cantab.) (40s); a biologist, friendly and bearded, a good manager with an encyclopaedic knowledge of all the ins and outs of higher education. **Co-Principal:** Mr A. M. Dawson MA (Cantab.), a historian.

What it does: A-levels and GCSEs; retakes, one-year and two-year. Various boards, 'depending on the subject and changes to the syllabus'.

What it's like: Definitely not a place to lock up your daughters – or indeed your sons. 'You may think they've got too much freedom,' said one father reflectively, 'and don't give them too much pocket money.'

There are three main teaching houses (including a delightful original almshouse). Good art studio (with photography department), fashion and textiles are also options. Notice-boards are hung with lively info on local concerts, plays, etc., and copy machines whirr. There's a good wodge of option subjects (fairly rare in a tutorial), including computing, guitar, philosophy and French cooking. A-level students must do some (non-examination) general studies, e.g. Psychology, European Studies. 'In practice, the tutor introduces the subject and it's an excuse for students to debate and argue.'

Accommodation: CCSS owns 14 houses in Cambridge (study-bedrooms), each with a live-in member of staff (from twenty-something to sixties), who provides breakfast and supper. Every student has a front-door key; A-level students must be in by 11.30 p.m.

COLLINGHAM BROWN AND BROWN

31 St Giles, Oxford OX1 3LF, tel: 01865 728280, fax: 01865 240126.

Vital statistics: Number of students: 70+ (numbers increase throughout the year). Ages: 14–18. Number of staff: 12 full time, 20 part time. Maximum class size: seven, but four is the norm. The majority of students are doing A-levels.

Principal: Mrs Carolyn Llewlyn MA, who has three school-age children. Mrs Llewlyn was educated at a northern grammar school, and read German and Latin at St Anne's College, Oxford. Has taught at Oxford Brookes University. Founded this college (as

Brown and Brown) in 1971. Mrs Llewlyn is very straightforward, very English.

What it does: GCSEs (one or two years), A-levels (one or two years); also retakes (November, January or the summer). There are Easter revision courses, half-term and summer revision courses. All subjects are catered for, under various boards. (The school also runs pre-boarding courses for (mainly) overseas 13-year-olds.)

What it's like: A medium-size crammer, which is very good on its student care and contact outside study times. 'You need it in Oxford,' commented one mother. Owned by the London Collingham's, but long established in Oxford as Brown and Brown, and shares the same ethos – i.e. hard work, and there's an emphasis on personal guidance. Particularly strong in the humanities; Media Studies (a one-year A-level) was recently introduced and has proved popular and successful. Tests are set every week, grades are given and an individual director of studies helps on the pastoral side, and sees students weekly. By far and away the most popular subsidiary subject (every student must undertake one) is Study Skills.

The main building is above a posh delicatessen; sciences are taught across the way in laboratories and teaching rooms belonging to St Giles Church. The atmosphere is friendly, there are small, bright teaching rooms, a study area, a lived-in common-room, everyone is on their toes. Students have the use of the university students' union (150 yards down the road) for studying, library, etc. – and often take part in games, drama and music via union notice-board announcements.

Accommodation: This is arranged with families recommended by the college (two favourite families have large houses and take 10 students); half board costs from £90 per week.

Cost: Around £980 per subject per term (5 per cent reduction for two subjects, 10 per cent reduction for three subjects. A few scholarships and bursaries are available for GCSE students.

Crammers

COLLINGHAM'S
23 Collingham Gardens, London SW5 0HL, tel: 0171 244 7414, fax: 0171 370 7312.

Co-principals: Mr G. Hattee MA and Mrs G. Green B.Sc. The owners are Dr J. Marsden and Mr N. Browne, who also own Collingham Brown and Brown.

What it does: Offers GCSEs, A-levels, retakes, revision courses. Founded in 1975. Maximum teaching group size for A-levels: eight.

Sarah Drummond is a visitor at time of writing.

DAVIES, LAING & DICK
10 Pembridge Gardens, London W2 4ED, tel: 0171 727 2797, fax: 0171 792 0730.

Vital statistics: Number of students: around 250 at their busiest time. Ages: 15–19. Maximum teaching group size: 8 (10 for GCSE retakes). Contact person for studies: Daphne Morgan (she teaches Physics too).

Principal: Since 1983, Mr Peter Boorman (50s), MA (Cantab.) in Maths and Mechanical Sciences. Mr Boorman is the son of a Norfolk parson. He was formerly headmaster of Aldenham School, and before that a housemaster at King's, Canterbury. He is married to Jo, who helps with the PR and does 'a little nursemaiding'. The Boormans have five grown-up children and two grandchildren between them. Mr Boorman is a good administrator and is good at public relations; he has a nice, reassuring, avuncular manner. Keen on cricket (MCC and Harvester's).

What it does: Aims to package whichever course or board the student wants 'providing it makes sense': be that revision, or A-levels and GCSEs. Easter revision courses are also offered, and private (and v. expensive) tuition with some super staff for e.g. urgent brush-ups.

What it's like: It's a young common-room. The school is housed in a light, quiet building facing on to Pembridge Square in Notting Hill, away from the hurly-burly of Notting Hill but v. near the tube. The college aims to provide something more akin to a school than a crammer, with a very strong emphasis on pastoral care, and a

43

feeling of safety – an atmosphere that is enhanced by the presence of Kensington Park School, which is burgeoning in the basement. The principal has a firm policy of not accepting students who have been hurled out of their previous schools for drugs, and as far as he knows, only one has slipped through the policy net, where the school's report was less than complete. Students clock in for every lesson – absences are reported at the administration office for follow-up.

The school has a canteenlet, a good-sized art studio (by London standards), also chemistry labs. The school is part of a group of crammers and schools, including Abbey (p. 37) – a strength, as staff can move around, there's more flexibility and centralizing on some of the administration. A sound choice of crammer for your tender young customer in need of TLC and some external discipline.

Less fashionable than some crammers and this, to some extent, is its strength. The place to go if you're really looking for a school by any other name.

D'OVERBROECK'S
Beechlawn House, 1 Park Town, Oxford OX2 6SN, tel: 01865 310000, fax: 01865 52296.

Vital statistics: Number of students: around 220 at full strength (in September). Ages: 14+–19. Number of staff: approx. 30 permanent full time and 30 part time. Maximum class size: eight; average group size five to six, also individual tuition.

Co-principals: Mr J. D. G. Noel BA (early 40s); was educated at Downside, London University (Goldsmith's); an international fencer and unmarried.

Dr R. M. Knowles MA, D.Phil. (early 40s); was educated at Leeds Grammar and Oxford – read PPE. Seriously brainy and looks it; married with five children.

Mr Noel is also co-owner of the school with the admin director Dr Tom Mills and with Mr M. D. van Biervliet (pronounced *beerfleet*) alias d'Overbroeck, who teaches full time (French and Spanish).

What it does: 'All boards to all people.' GCSEs, A-levels, including one-year A-levels, Scottish Highers; GCSE and A-level retakes (around 30 per cent of students are currently doing these); it also offers Oxbridge entrance. There's a new information technology centre.

What it's like: A large and famous lifeline for A-level retakes, but increasingly now, like everywhere else, the school is emphasizing its role as an 'independent sixth-form college'. There is a wonderful wide range of rather wild-looking students: 50 per cent are from round about (e.g. St Edward's), the rest are from all sorts of establishments: the German/Swiss International School, Hong Kong, Sibford, Marlborough (a name which pops up regularly here), Ilkley Grammar, Bryanston, St Leonard's, Fife – almost every school you've ever heard of.

The college was started in '77 (one of the new wave of crammers) and expanded in '89 to swallow up the sixth-form school for young ladies, Beechlawn (it took on the head of Beechlawn as well). It is split into several sites – the science block is, as we write, being moved from down over Magdalen bridge to a site in Summertown. Arts are up the Woodstock Road and round the corner by the old Beechlawn building – where there are cosy rugs, a friendly atmosphere, and the rooms feel more like home than school; it's untidy, and there are bookcases around. The college uses the canteen of the language school in Bardwell Road (otherwise it's snack lunches).

This is a particularly good place for helping would-be medics, and, when we spoke, could boast that it hadn't failed a would-be vet in 15 years. The music is a bit rudimentary. The 'in' A-level – Communication Studies – is much patronized, if that's the word. Very good 'value-added' record (of students improving exam grades).

The place does not reckon to guard students the way a traditional school would. It is an efficient, well-run, buoyant place, and its *Guide for Students in the Sixth Form* is a wonderfully useful document, listing everything down to the launderettes. Being expelled from school for drug-taking is 'not in itself a bar – it depends on the circumstances,' says Mr Noel, but, he adds, it would be instant sack if students were caught taking drugs in the college.

Many of the students go on to ex-polys. Mr Noel comments that they practically 'feed' Oxford Brookes. Two or three go on to Oxford, a good clutch to the old established universities such as Bristol and Exeter, some to agricultural college.

Accommodation: The college has a hall of residence with places for around 30, but the majority of students are in digs – these cost around £90–£110 as we write for b&b plus supper per week.

MANDER PORTMAN WOODWARD (Cambridge)

3–4 Brookside, Cambridge CB2 1JE, tel: 01223 350158, fax: 01223 366429.

Vital statistics: Number of students: approx. 100. Ages: 15–18. Number of staff: 34, of whom 13 are full time. Maximum class size: seven (but three on average). The bulk of the students are doing A-levels over two years.

Principal: Since 1993, Ms Daphne Bigmore MA. Ms Bigmore is bright, articulate, direct, firm, fun, has taught in schools (e.g. St Edward's, Oxford), previously ran Duff-Millar's tutorial college in London. Lives at Newmarket, and is keen on horses.

What it does: One-year GCSEs. A-levels: retakes (one year or one term). A-levels – two-year courses, also a one-year course. Easter revision courses are offered. A huge variety of subjects is available, under various boards.

What it's like: A place you could confidently send your son or daughter to, despite its faintly impersonal attitude (the side-effect of being part of a chain and a public company?). It is situated opposite the Leys school, slightly away from the centre of Cambridge, in a large terraced house. You sense an air of efficiency and competence the moment you walk in. It's very spruce; the pretty pale walls are hung with repros of great paintings, and the place is brightened with flowers. Bushy-tailed staff who clearly enjoy their work and excellent relations with the students.

Students are encouraged to be here from 9 a.m. till 6 p.m.: there are good rooms and a library for private studying. Work and progress are very closely monitored by staff *'all'* the time', said a student; 'it wasn't at my school'. One-hour timed assignments set per subject per week give plenty of practice. Students are expected to work hard. The school is open on Saturday mornings (but there are no tutorials).

There's a student counsellor on tap. The canteen is in the basement, offering a sensible baked potato and salads menu, and is open from 8.30 a.m. The ground floor is shared with Brookside Secretarial College (see Traditional Alternatives – Indoors chapter, p. 177). A-levellers sometimes join in GCSE students' sports programmes. Students come here mainly from fee-paying schools (e.g. Uppingham).

Accommodation: MPW recommends landladies (and inspects and briefs them very thoroughly), and families with a spare room (or three), which costs approximately £85 per week (half board).

Cost: A-levels per term: one subject: £1,100 (two-year course); £1,150 (one-year course); three subjects: £2,580 (two-year course); £2,709 (one-year course).

MANDER PORTMAN WOODWARD (London)

Arts Department: 108 Cromwell Road, London SW7 4ES, tel: 0171 835 1355, fax: 0171 259 2705.
Science Department: 24 Elvaston Place, London SW7 5NL, tel: 0171 584 8555, fax: 0171 225 2953.

Vital statistics: Number of students: about 400 a year. Ages: 14ish–18ish. Maximum teaching group size: seven.

Chairman of MPW Group: To be found in Elvaston Place: Mr Joe Ruston, educated at Eton and Cambridge (Mechanical Sciences). Mr Ruston was an officer in the Royal Navy before setting up the science department of MPW in 1977, which has gone from strength to strength. He now interfaces with the shareholders of BPP Holdings plc, which bought MPW in 1988, and which owns, among many other things, Letts Educational Publishing. Ruston is a super friendly chap and a general good egg.

Principal of Arts Department: Since 1992, Fiona Dowding MA (30s). Read English at Somerville, and joined MPW in 1984. Ms Dowding aspires to eventing in her spare time and looks about the same age as her students. Enthusiastic, competent, friendly – and glamorous.

Principal of Science Department: Since 1992, Dr Nigel Stout MA, Ph.D. (30s), educated at Magdalen College School and St Cat.'s, Oxford (read Psychology and Philosophy for his first degree, Applied Maths for the doctorate). Was a lecturer at Worcester College, Oxford, for a year before disappearing into crammers. Came to MPW in 1987 and helped set up the Cambridge and Bristol branches. Stout is seriously over-endowed with brains but with-it. Reads twentieth-century German literature in his spare moments; need we say more? He is very nice, though. Dr Stout became chairman of CIFE – the 'independent' further education propaganda arm – in 1993, and comments that he is 'dedicated to throwing out the cowboys'.

What it does: The college can handle most A-level subjects in most boards, and is good at playing the system. Individual tuition also on tap *and* practice in university interview technique – a snip at time of writing.

What it's like: The friendly, fashionable place to send students flying through A-levels at second, or indeed at first time of asking. MPW is particularly competent and experienced at university entrance, although increasingly known for its A-level courses (both two-year, one-year, and intensive retakes). Flagship of the MPW empire, which was set up in 1973 in a shed at the back end of Chelsea by Robert Woodward and Rodney Portman (the M 'didn't even make it to the launch party'), as crammer to toffs with the philosophy that providing the students did the work, they could come in with green hair, swing from the chandeliers every night, etc. etc.

Nowadays, Dr Stout says he can spend up to one and a half hours a day telephoning parents of truants in Timbuktu if necessary. Each student is assigned a 'personal tutor' and all GCSE students get sex and drugs 'health education talks' (expulsion for drugs, taking of). There is a very serious hard-work ethic and this can take students by surprise if, as is often the case, they are expecting a soft option. Academic subjects are the main thrust, but the recently acquired lease of a third building near by will give the college a stage, a sports hall, a larger art studio and the ability to offer Theatre Studies, Photography, etc., to the envy of lesser crammers. Some students are even doing Music.

The buildings are big and light (there is a small library and canteen on the Cromwell Road site, and another canteen on the new site) in a location v. convenient for Knightsbridge. The houses are divided into small cells, with a rather airless feel, no distractions, just chairs round a central table, pitiless overhead lighting and hard graft. The staff are charming and high-powered (and, by the way, some are A-level and/or GCSE examiners), and results – as audited by CIFE – are good: 47 per cent A and B A-levels out of 274 entries (don't expect the impossible, though – 30 per cent were D–U).

Students come mainly from famous public schools, with Marlborough and Eton heading the list, but also largish numbers from Wycombe Abbey, St Paul's Girls and Boys, Harrow, Stowe, etc. etc. – there's hardly a major school unrepresented. 'It's very often the pressure of these schools,' says Dr Stout, but we have noticed this ain't necessarily so . . .

Cost: Around £1,000 per A-level per term and nearly £3,000 for 6 GCSEs.

NB The college offers one scholarship completely free for a student from the state sector, and there are also some hardship bursaries.

MODES STUDY CENTRE
73–75 George Street, Oxford OX1 2BQ, tel: 01865 245172, fax: 01865 722443.

Vital statistics: Numbers of students: around 70 (numbers drop to 50 post-winter retakes). Staff–student ratio is almost 7–1, and drops to around 3–1 after the January retake students have left. Average class size: 8 (maximum is 10), except for lectures (28). For practicals, six is the maximum class size.

Principal: Mr Stephen Moore MA, one of the co-founders: previously taught at a tutorial college where he was dismayed at the 'shambles' of science teaching. Hot on the subject of GCSEs as a poor preparation for A-levels, particularly the sciences.

The Good Gap and Sixth Form Guide

What it does: One-year A-level courses, also retakes. A-level Science and Mathematics. Also (since September '94) Geography and Economics. Intensive revision courses are also offered. Forty-five per cent of the students do January retakes (two subjects only – never three). One-year A-level courses are undertaken by 55 per cent of the students, of whom the majority are doing retakes; some students have completed one year of sixth-form study elsewhere.

What it's like: Highly successful specialists (regarded with some envy and misgiving by other establishments). Modes makes no bones about the nose-to-the-grindstone aspect. 'We don't offer sport, or social life,' says a tutor cheerfully and frankly – though they can advise on where to find it. This crammer only takes motivated students, and bearing in mind that they are all here because they want to go on to take degrees and follow careers in various branches of the medical profession, motivation is much in evidence. The school claims not to be highly selective, but gets some astonishing results. There is an initial beady interview (students plus parents) and assessment tests, 'to reveal any problems and learn what's gone wrong before'.

Workloads are definitely heavy: hence only two subjects are allowed on the intensive revision courses. Modes is exacting over students' attendance, work is set to be attempted and handed in. Students are setted. Textbooks are very rarely (if ever) referred to: there's a huge emphasis on teaching students to understand principles and to use their knowledge effectively.

Modes was set up in 1978 by three science teachers who were discontented with existing science teaching, and who recognized the need for a college specializing in science and maths. Most staff are full time and have worked in other tutorial colleges and schools and are widely consulted by students outside of class time: a purposeful open-door policy. Thursday evenings staff are available until 10 p.m. Two mock exams are held every term in each subject. The college is open on Saturdays and Sundays as exams approach. Extremely good advice is available – from the start – on medical schools and careers.

Crammers

Housed in the centre of Oxford, and recently extended to take in a neighbouring house, Modes has smallish, sparse rooms and largish lecture rooms, all clean and workmanlike, in a warren of a layout. The three laboratories – surprisingly small and unimpressive – are an interesting demonstration that teaching, not facilities, is the key to success. There's a good library.

'The best thing here,' said an ex-public school boy, 'is getting your homework back so fast.' Another considered the teaching 'quite different from what I had at school – now I *understand* what I am learning about'. 'Studying off the premises is discouraged,' said a parent, worrying that her son was taking his work too seriously. Which said, Modes produces hordes of successful students and relieved parents.

Accommodation: This is arranged with families (single study-bedrooms for each student), but the college opens its doors daily at 8 a.m. and closes at 6 p.m.

Cost: A lot – i.e. approximately £2,345 per subject for intensive revision courses ($17\frac{1}{2}$ weeks); around £1,050 per subject per term for one-year courses.

4

Alternative Sixth Forms

Moving on at sixth-form stage has become so fashionable that we sometimes wonder whether the old school sixth form will continue to exist. Sixth-form colleges and crammers are the traditional caterers to this mobile market (see Sixth-Form Colleges chapter, p. 9, and Crammers chapter, p. 34). It appears that more girls than boys get itchy feet at this point (they have usually been at their senior school since they were 11 or earlier, boys since 13) and we wonder if the growing number of schools offering their services from kindergarten to A-level will further this trend.

We are not at all sure how wise it is to move after GCSEs unless circumstances (finances, choice of subjects, etc.) dictate: several have lived to regret it, not least because it is an upheaval at just the moment you should perhaps be thinking of getting your head down. 'It generally takes the whole of the first term to settle down,' said the honest head of a pioneering school taking girls in at sixth form. Some say it takes two terms. Moving from a single-sex school to coeducation adds a whole new dimension which the students have to get to grips with. Beware of moving to cosy, cliquey places where a stranger may be regarded as an outsider to be tested. If you must move, pick somewhere used to grafting on reasonable numbers at sixth form. Choose a school with a healthy-sized sixth form, a broad range of subjects and good facilities – and, of course, you will pick somewhere with a track record of good teaching reflected in respectable results.

Children will start making noises about moving elsewhere for A-levels well before GCSE. *'Everybody's* leaving', will be the cry. Freedom, fewer rules, a change of scene, a more dynamic academic atmosphere will be some of the reasons they ply you with. Sex could well be on the hidden agenda. (NB to students: have some hotshot serious reasons for leaving up your sleeve.) Parents: don't panic. Ring around to drum up parental solidarity. Be prepared to use blackmail if you truly think it's a mistake.

When and How to Apply

The popular schools get full early. Ring up the school a good year (even 18 months) in advance, and say you want a sixth-form place. You will be sent a prospectus, an application form, and you will very probably be socked a stiffish registration fee (expect to pay out £50–£200 +). Parents and children are usually called for interview: this is important, since your provisional place depends on it and on your GCSE results, as well as (usually) the school's own entrance exam. The report from your child's school also plays a key part. This is where it can get awkward. Be ready with charming and tactful reasons about why you are looking elsewhere: you're in quest of an exotic subject, moving house, and so on. Be prepared for them to try to dissuade you. Schools have been known to offer scholarships to ringleaders of a general exodus. You will of course be investigating scholarships on offer to incoming sixth-formers at the school you are interested in – often there are quite tempting lures. Remember that many public schools have made an agreement in recent years, for political reasons, to offer a maximum of 50 per cent of the fees; however, this can often be topped up by 'bursaries'. If you are skint, it is *well* worth asking. Scholarships will probably involve a special exam (and NB this may be disruptive to the GCSE work in hand).

However, many schools may be able to 'squeeze you in' on later application: it's always worth a try. And some of the boys' schools with girls in the sixth form have been short of girls in recent years. At public schools, boys will usually find it easier to get a place.

There follow some tried and tested schools, all of them fee-paying. Others you might want to consider are: Gordonstoun (for getting away from the pressure of the South, and all that Outward

Bound stuff); Millfield (which has a large sixth-form intake, and offers a *really* wide variety of subjects; it has already introduced GNVQs, and is famous for sports of all kinds – and is good on scholarships); Howell's Denbigh (Assisted Places, and a lovely setting); Bradfield (bathrooms *en suite* for girls and a wonderful Greek theatre); Haileybury (near London, distinguished and traditional with imposing buildings), the French Lycée in London (does international baccalaureate) and A-levels and is the bargain of London schools).

Contact

Gabbitas Truman and Thring: 6 Sackville Street, London W1X 2BR, tel: 0171 734 0161, fax: 0171 437 1764. Provides lists of schools that have places to fill (and gets paid commission by those schools).

Independent Schools Information Service: 56 Buckingham Gate, London SW1E 6AG, tel: 0171 630 8795, fax: 0171 630 50133, press office, tel: 0171 630 8795. Very useful for names and addresses. However ISIS cannot be selective, since it is funded by members (i.e. most of the fee-paying sector).

PRIVATE SIXTH-FORM COLLEGES

ATLANTIC COLLEGE
St Donat's Castle, Llantwit Major, South Glamorgan, Wales CF61 1WF, tel: 01446 792530, fax: 01446 794163.

Vital statistics: Number of students: 350, half boys, half girls. Ages: 16–19. Non-denominational.

Principal: Since 1990, Mr Colin Jenkins B.Sc., Dip. Ed. (50s), who is a marine biologist and geologist. A Welshman, he was previously a leading light in the international baccalaureate world in the UK. He admits to being totally committed to Kurt Hahn's belief that the college should provide an atmosphere 'that would draw out of students a greater range of talents than they knew they possessed', and adds, 'We are constantly asking ourselves here, "Can we make a better world?" – and we're our own strongest critics.'

What it does: Offers the international baccalaureate.

What it's like: Founded in 1962 by Kurt Hahn, the German educationalist, as one of the United World Colleges, aiming to foster international understanding and cooperation. This is the largest of the UWCs: the others are in British Columbia, Singapore, Swaziland, Trieste, New Mexico, Hong Kong and Venezuela (this latter offers only vocational skills, not the IB), and opening in '95, Norway. Most are for students of 16+.

The college is in a superbly dramatic setting – a stupendous grey stone castle (parts date back to 1150) perched on the edge of the Bristol Channel. Once the property of Randolph Hearst, it comes complete with dry moat, portcullis (in working order), ghost, turrets, twisty staircases, etc. There's a vast dining hall with a finely plastered ceiling, and a magnificent assembly hall; the whole thing is set in 150 acres, with woodland and a farm, miles from anywhere.

The international baccalaureate is the qualification taken by all students, and it comes as quite a shock for many (everyone takes 6 subjects: 3 higher, 3 subsidiary). All scientists must undertake some humanities and vice versa, i.e. breadth is the big strength here. Ninety-four per cent of students get the international baccalaureate diploma. The college, however, openly 'abhors' league tables, but is known to be a good performer.

All teaching is in English, except modern languages, which are invariably taught by a native speaker: at the time of our visit the principal was endeavouring to get a work permit for a very highly qualified Russian from Moscow. Substantial numbers of ex-United World College students come back to teach.

Many subjects are taught in purpose-built blocks, with good facilities, others are up in turrets and towers. A very strong work ethic pervades. Lessons are from 8 a.m. until 1.20 p.m. on weekdays. There's a large well-stocked library (in the main building) which has newspapers and periodicals from all over the world.

Acquiring skills and performing services are essentially part of the ethos. Initially, students try out everything, and then choose which 'service' to spend more time in (social, arts service, rescue service – the college has a lifeboat – cliff rescue, coastguard etc.). 'It can be gruesome,' warn students. Also on offer are environmental and estate services (farming and forestry): 'lamb watch' rotas are pinned up on dormitory walls at lambing time with midnight, 3 a.m. and 6 a.m. watches.

With at least 103 activities on offer, students are kept incredibly busy. 'It's very difficult for Orientals and some Eastern Europeans to adapt,' commented a Welsh–Egyptian student. 'They have been trained to put academic work as number one, and it's hard for them to learn that everything else is equally important.'

Weekly lectures are given on Friday evenings (by Sir Crispin Tickell, Tony Benn, for instance) and are followed by terrific debates.

Social life is very lively, with discos and music galore.

An international flavour characterizes the college, with 76 different nationalities represented including students from North America, Australia and New Zealand, bringing native English-speakers up to 25 per cent. The rest come from Germany, Norway, Sweden, Japan, Hong Kong, Poland, Kenya, Zimbabwe, Bosnia, etc., etc. It's a rich mix of backgrounds: from inner cities and refugee camps as well as the affluent and privileged. A religious conference lasting three days is held annually for second-year students; swamis, Buddhist masters, Catholic priests, mullahs, rabbis, etc. are all regular visitors.

Hugely supportive of one another, students are often fascinated by the others' cultures. 'There was a terrific debate in our house last night,' said a German girl, 'on terrorism: there were views from a Brazilian, an Italian, an Arab . . .' 'Friends from my old school,' commented an English student, 'seem tunnel-visioned by comparison.' This environment sets students up for a life with a network of friends and connections all over the world. UK parents comment on the constant stream of friends coming to stay during the holidays (there are two terms per year with a long break in the summer and four or five weeks at Christmas).

Getting in and on: Tricky: *huge* numbers apply. Around 20 places are available for British students here each year, but many others are placed (via Atlantic) in sister colleges overseas.

(Hampshire and Jersey provide county scholarships.) Applications must be in by 1 March for entry in September. Lengthy interviews are conducted for short-listed students. Exit: to university (including Oxbridge), with most Europeans returning to universities in their own countries. Careers students often go on from here to international posts e.g. in the diplomatic service, also journalism, translation, the Red Cross, medicine.

Accommodation: Living conditions are comfortably scruffy and homely. (Forty-eight to a house, with house-parents attached; house tutors visit regularly. Boys live on the ground floor, girls are upstairs.) Students are four to a bedroom: there's an international mix, two first-years and two seniors, always inclusive of one native English-speaker: 'the only social engineering we go in for,' said a member of staff. Students are responsible (a word you hear a lot) for basic cleaning of their rooms; professional domestic help does the rest. There's only one television on site, in the castle's main common-room, and the news is watched here.

A truly remarkable place.

Cost: Eighty-five per cent of students are on scholarships of one sort or another. No means-testing is employed, but students and parents are asked what they can afford (are they always honest?), and all parents are 'invited to contribute'. Sponsorship comes from national and regional government in the UK, from industry, trusts, foundations, individuals – and more is needed, please.

HURTWOOD HOUSE
Holmbury St Mary, Dorking, Surrey RH5 6NU, tel: 01483 277416, fax: 01483 267586.

Vital statistics: Around 280 students, half boys, half girls. Ages: mainly 16–18, but there are about 25 at 14+. Almost all students board. Some scholarships are available. Average class size: 8–10 students.

Head: Mr K. R. B. Jackson MA (mid-50s), educated at Cranleigh (just down the road) and Corpus, Cambridge; read History. With a beard and paunch, Mr Jackson is avuncular and easy to communicate with – for both staff and students – and his jolly exterior hides a sharp business brain. This school is his 'baby' (i.e. he owns it), which he runs jointly with his wife, Linda, whom we did not meet. Jackson says his aim is twofold: to make sure that students feel they are in the 'most exciting place imaginable', and that parents feel their children are in the 'safest place'. It is no coincidence that Mr Jackson started life, very successfully, in marketing (Crawford's).

What it does: The A-level syllabus, particularly those subjects which public schools tend to pooh-pooh, e.g. Media Studies, Communication Studies, Theatre Studies (the school is very hot on these). They get consistently good Maths results. GCSEs are offered as a rescue operation for students who have come unstuck elsewhere – the school can offer all boards. NB Detailed results are not published.

What it's like: A cosy alternative sixth-form education for students who for one reason or another ('I wanted a change', is the usual reason given) want out of their existing school. Many come from single-sex boarding schools (Benenden, Queen Anne's Caversham, Worth, etc.) and appear thrilled to be here – the atmosphere is consequently electric, and the cosiness of most of the houses makes a good environment to enjoy work in.

The school is tucked away in one of the prettier parts of Surrey, miles from the bright lights, and good from the security point of view (it's near Sutton Place. Buildings are a mix of National Trust and institutional, scattered on a steep leafy slope.

The school gives students an illusion of freedom; in actual fact, the place is run like a cosy prep school (Mr Jackson was inspired to open Hurtwood in 1969 following his experiences in the now defunct prep school, Heatherdown). The pastoral care is all-enveloping: the school holds random drug tests, alcohol is not allowed; sex: 'no kissing and cuddling in public, though we're quite relaxed about it'. No uniform is worn, but students are expected to look neat and clean. Staff are all called by their Christian names. There's one jolly history teacher who looks like Jilly Cooper. Music, at time of writing, is more or less non-existent, though Music Technology is a 'new' A-level for '94–5. Hurtwood is *the* popular place for Theatre Studies – everyone is allowed to join in:

rehearsals take place in a big room with a stage at one end. One of the most popular subjects here is Drama: imagine 30 students packed into the auditorium of the small theatre, getting in touch with their emotions.

The art department is small and its students are perhaps less dynamic. Games take place every day (it looks like one of those places where games does not feature at all but in fact Hurtwood are SE England netball champions at time of writing, and when we were visiting the local sixth-form college arrived to play a match.

The whole place is an object-lesson in giving the punter what he/she wants, so much so that one public school head actually came to visit to see what he could learn from Hurtwood. Entrance at present is non-selective, though our impression is that it will become so as the popularity of the place snowballs. Girls need to apply earlier than boys (a year ahead, to be safe). Old boys sound less enthusiastic about the place than girls: 'Oh fine,' said one OB we talked to; 'Fabulous,' said an OG. Students now all go on to university, says Mr Jackson, though the first recent OG we talked to had done a domestic science course and gone straight into a job.

All faiths are welcome – Muslims have the opportunity to pray the requisite five times a day and halal meat, etc. is provided. Fee-paying – fees are in line with major public schools. The school is currently changing status from a sixth-form college to a school: 'It sounds more solid,' says the head.

ST CLARE'S
139 Banbury Road, Oxford OX2 7AL, tel: 01865 52031, fax: 01865 310002.

Vital statistics: Number of students: just under 300. A boarding and day coeducational college. Ages: 15–19. Fee-paying. Scholarships: there are five 'full' scholarships (the exam is sat at the college in January).

Principal: Ms Margaret Skarland BA, Cert. Ed.

What it does: There are three separate courses: the international baccalaureate (the majority of students take this), English as a

Foreign Language (90–100 students), and 40–50 American university students in their 'junior' year.

What it's like: St Clare's is located in 18 buildings up and down the Banbury Road; the HQ is in a turrety Victorian Gothic pile. Founded in 1953, it is one of the many 'fringe' educational establishments operating in Oxford, which benefits from the proximity of museums, libraries, sports facilities, etc. in the city.

Considered a competent establishment; students go on to a huge spread of universities, lots to London, Edinburgh, a scattering to Oxbridge, and also (reflecting the international intake of students) to American and Continental universities. Most students live in the college's own accommodation.

Cost: On a par with the top end of the public school market.

SOME POPULAR PUBLIC SCHOOL OPTIONS

CHARTERHOUSE
Godalming, Surrey GU7 2DJ, tel: 01483 291600, fax: 01483 291647.

Vital statistics: Boys' school with girls in the sixth form (definitely a minority, between 70 and 80). Number of students: 310 in the sixth form (size of the whole school: 700, mainly boarding). Sixth-form scholarships: three, worth one-third of the fees, plus exhibitions; also two music, two art, plus four full-fee Peter Newton scholarships for students who could not afford to come without a scholarship. The requisite entry exam plus interviews are all held at the school.

Head: Since 1993, Mr Peter Hobson MA.

What it's like: A strong school which does most things well, and gets jolly good A-level results. There's heaps on offer – little possibility of doing just your three As. It's seriously strong on Politics, and fascinating speakers visit. The library is glorious and mellow, well resourced, as indeed is the whole school: smashing facilities. Music, sport, theatre, are all notably good. It's very gamesy. It's also hot on the technological front and full of tradition. There are Surrey overtones. A rich, powerful and friendly school.

Accommodation: There are mixed houses for everything except sleeping, but girls sleep in the girls' houses on the campus (they only get 'home' at 10.30 p.m.) and in their second year they live in very small groups with members of the common-room and their families in their houses.

LANCING COLLEGE
Lancing, Sussex BN15 0RW, tel: 01273 452213, fax: 01273 464720.

Vital statistics: Boys' public school with around 76 girls in the sixth form. Numbers of students: around 250 in the sixth form (size of whole school: around 540), boarding and day students. There are some scholarships available at sixth form, including art and music.

Head: Since 1993, Mr Christopher Saunders MA.

What it's like: Rather a good choice for a sixth form for both sexes. The school does not suffer from being fashionable, and has an ethos throughout of live and let live, which is appealing. The music and art departments are great; also on offer is Design and Technology. There's lots to do ('*Too* much!' commented an incomer from a single-sex girls' school) and if the stress of A-levels gets too much, you can always commune with Brian the pig on the school farm, or slip into the cloisters of the towering chapel for spiritual succour. Muscular Christianity is practised here. The site is freezing in winter. Traditionally arts have been stronger than sciences.

MALVERN COLLEGE
Malvern, Worcestershire WR14 3DF, tel: 01684 892333, fax: 01684 572398.

Vital statistics: Number of students: 332 in the sixth form (size of whole school: around 670). Ages: 13–18, more boys than girls, mainly boarding. There are around 60 entrants at sixth form. Sixth-form scholarships: various academic and sports awards are on offer.

Head: Since 1994, Mr Roy Chapman MA.

What it's like: Famous boys' public school which went fully coed in 1992. Does both A-levels and the international baccalaureate; this latter has caught on in popularity, under the French Dr

René Filho, who has taught here for 20 years. He introduced the IB in 1992 with an initial batch of six pupils; at the time of writing, 40 candidates are taking the IB, the rest of the sixth foi.m are taking A-levels. Limited IB results so far, but they're definitely good (including three IB students going to Oxbridge).

One of the increasing breed of schools that now offers education from the age of 3 via its own feeder pre-prep and prep (near by). This is a traditional and all-round school, and strong with it.

RUGBY SCHOOL
Rugby, Warwickshire CV22 5EH, tel: 01788 543465, fax: 01788 569124.

Vital statistics: Public school going coed throughout (the first junior girls joined in '93). Number of students: around 300 in the sixth form (takes in approximately 12–14 outside students at sixth form; size of whole school: pushing 700). Ages: 12–18. Sixth-form scholarships: general and music, providing up to 50 per cent of fees (more is available via a bursary in case of need).

Head: Since 1990, Mr M. B. Mavor CVO, MA. Previously head of Gordonstoun.

What it's like: A famous school, coming back on track, and well worth a look. Numbers are burgeoning (one of the few schools which has actually grown over the past five years), and A-level results are looking good. There is a strong language department being carefully nurtured. The school's mellow redbrick buildings are surrounded by the town of Rugby. Bags of tradition (Dr Arnold of *Tom Brown's Schooldays* was here), and the school is gradually metamorphosing from a very macho, traditional, sporty Boys' Own school into something gentler and altogether nicer (though some OBs would disagree).

Accommodation: There are four boarding houses for girls – v. civilized. Meals are taken in houses (not in a central trough).

ST PAUL'S GIRLS' SCHOOL
Brook Green, London W6 7BS, tel: 0171 603 2288, fax: 0171 602 9932.

Vital statistics: Girls' day school. Number of students: around 214 in the sixth form (known as 'seventh' and 'eighth' forms – size of whole school: around 620). There are five Assisted Places into the sixth form. Means-tested bursaries are available for those in need, and art and music scholarships. Academic scholarships may be awarded once students are in the sixth form, backdated for the 2 years.

Head: Since 1991, Miss Janet Gough MA.

What it's like: St Paul's is the number one academic girls' school in London; dynamic and, for the right students, inspiring. The school takes in around 25 *extra* students at sixth form, so it is well worth considering at this level if you are bright.

The school holds its own entry exam (currently in November for the following September); you do not need to register in advance, but the sixth form admissions tutor, Mrs Parsons, suggests you contact the school in the summer of your fourth year (i.e. one year before GCSE). Places are offered on condition you get a minimum of five Cs at GCSE in mainstream subjects such as English, but if you get through the school's exam this will be a doddle.

The school has a good big site (by London standards) behind Hammersmith. Some of the old girls are very distinguished. There's a slightly cloistered atmosphere. Students come in at sixth form from the state sector, from boarding schools and from London day schools. Paulinas mostly go on to be doctors, lawyers, scientists, civil servants, and there are a few in high-profile media.

SEVENOAKS SCHOOL
Sevenoaks, Kent TN13 1HU, tel: 01732 455133, fax: 01732 456143.

Vital statistics: Number of students: large – around 400 in the sixth form (size of whole school: around 940. Ages: 11–18, mainly day students). Numbers taking IB: creeping towards half the sixth form. Scholarships at sixth form: a 'good' range of academic, sporting and music scholarships are available (the biggest would normally be only half of the day fees, however).

Head: Since 1981, Mr Richard Barker MA, leaving in summer 1996.

What it's like: This is the top choice for doing the international baccalaureate in a traditional school setting. It's a very popular school, great success story, parents have even been known to try bribes to get in at sixth form! Apply early to stand a chance of getting a place; at least a year ahead, preferably two. Minimum entry qualifications: 16 GCSE points; an interview is essential (special dispensation is possible if, for example, you are in the Far East).

The site is located in the town, and is a bit cramped, but buzzing with energy. The technical equipment is outstandingly good, with its own television studios, etc. It's very international at sixth-form level. Around 80 students come in at this stage: expats, 'genuine' overseas students, and lots of girls from single-sex schools.

STOWE SCHOOL

Stowe, Buckinghamshire MK18 5EH, tel: 01280 813164, fax: 01280 822769.

Vital statistics: A boys' school with girls in the sixth form (roughly half-and-half). Number of students: around 240 in the sixth form (size of the whole school: around 545). Sixth-form scholarships: there's a 'range' of these, plus some Assisted Places.

Head: Since 1989, Mr Jeremy Nichols MA.

What it's like: Stowe has been a perennially popular choice for girls for several years. The drama department is good. Some spiffing Grade 1 buildings (it is worth going to Stowe for these alone, as we have said before). This is not an academic hothouse; it's traditionally for toffs but now takes all sorts. The school comes out well in ALIS charts.

Accommodation: Girls are in smart houses.

UPPINGHAM SCHOOL

Rutland LE15 9QE, tel: 01572 822216, fax: 01572 822332.

Vital statistics: A boys' boarding school with approximately 130 girls in the sixth form. Number of students: approximately 320 in the sixth form (size of whole school: around 605). Ages: 11–18, mostly boarding. Scholarships at sixth form: these are on offer for 'almost anything you can think of', including general academic, music (lots of these), art and IT.

Head: Since 1991, Dr S. C. Winkley MA, who was previously Second Master at Winchester.

What it's like: Uppingham is a favourite choice for girls at sixth form who want out of their current school but not out of a traditional school environment. Here you will find good pastoral care, kind staff (some nice furry ones), mellow buildings and altogether a good atmosphere. Outstanding art and music departments, and academic performance is also creditable, though this is emphatically *not* a hothouse. Girls come from 40–50 different schools, including the state sector.

Accommodation: Cosy houses (there are three for girls) – and you can have a friend to stay at the weekend.

WELLINGTON COLLEGE
Crowthorne, Berkshire RG11 7PU, tel: 01344 772261, fax: 01344 771725.

Vital statistics: A public school with girls in the sixth form. Number of students: approximately 350 in the sixth form (size of whole school: around 803), mainly boarding. Ages: 12–19. Sixth-form scholarships: for girls only, music and academic. Five Assisted Places are available at 16. Proper bursaries are on offer for the children of deceased officers (originally army, now other services as well). Bursaries 'are always worth asking about,' says a spokesman.

Head (the Master): Since 1989, Mr C. J. Driver BA, B.Ed., M. Phil., FRSA.

What it's like: This school has a long track record of successfully grafting on girls at sixth form – there are lots of happy reports from girls. Founded in the last century in memory of the Iron Duke, in general the place still has a traditional, military feel about it. About a dozen boys come into the sixth form, and 25 girls, from 'all over the place'.

Accommodation: The girls' houses are warm and friendly (to the envy of some of the boys).

WESTMINSTER SCHOOL
17 Dean's Yard, London SW1P 3PB, tel: 0171 963 1041, fax: 0171 233 0128.

Vital statistics: Number of students: 300 in the sixth form, 70 girls and 230 boys (size of whole school: 670, boarding and day). There is a variable number of sixth-form scholarships. Entrance is gained via the school's own competitive exam (plus a minimum of five Bs at GCSE) and an interview. A few boys also come in at sixth form.

Head: Since 1986, Mr David Summerscale MA.

What it's like: An obvious choice for *very* bright girls, and indeed boys from elsewhere, who need an academic hothouse in which to do A-levels. Don't consider it unless you're robust and self-confident: being clever is not enough here. The teaching is challenging and demanding; so are the staff and some of the students. NB For day students and boarders: there is Saturday morning school. It's very high-powered on the academic front, and it can be a terrific shock after an all-girls' school. A-level results are consistently brilliant, and huge numbers go on to Oxbridge. It's cramped, and there's a slight sense of the lid being held on tight.

Accommodation: There's one girls-only house: the rest are housed in two of the boys' houses.

One-year Sixth-form Courses

If A-levels are not for you, or not yet anyway, here are some fee-paying schools to consider which do one-year sixth-form studies as well as the usual two-year A-level courses. A one-year course probably consists of general academic subjects, plus Business Studies, 'vocational' and practical skills (e.g. word processing) and general knowledge such as how Parliament works. This can make a good stepping-stone for late developers (who may want to do A-levels or an IB later), for foreigners and those who are not quite ready to leave a school environment for whatever reason. There are not many one-year sixth courses like this, but they may be on the increase, if GNVQs continue their march forward.

Giggleswick School: Settle, North Yorkshire BD24 0DE, tel: 01729 823 545, fax: 01729 824 187. *Head*: Mr Anthony Millard B.Sc.

This is a coed school (more boys than girls), mainly boarding. Ages: 13–18. Number of students: approx. 122 in the sixth form. The one-year sixth course, called 'Developmental Sixth', was set up here by the present head who came from Wycliffe (see below). The school is well regarded, and gets very respectable A-level results. There's a happy atmosphere; it's isolated geographically, however.

Queen Margaret's School: Escrick Park, York YO4 6EU, tel: 01904 728261, fax: 01904 728150. *Head*: Dr Geoffrey Chapman MA.

A small (360ish) up-market rural girls' boarding school. Lovely setting – the school is in a Palladian house (plus extensions) in 50 acres of parkland. Very uninstitutional – with chintz, carpets, flowers. The intake is broad, with respectable results produced (GCSE and A-levels), and all types are well catered for. There's lots of games, cooking, dressmaking, good art and design and technology, keen choral music and drama. Enthusiasm all round, morale is currently high. Queen Margaret's has been offering one-year sixth courses to non-A-levellers for over ten years.

Wycliffe College: Stonehouse, Gloucestershire GL10 2JQ, tel: 01453 82 2432, fax: 01453 82 7634. *Head*: Mr David Prichard MA.

A small coed school (325), two-thirds boys, one-third girls, with two-thirds boarding, one-third day, and around 150 students in the sixth form. The dynamic (some say controversial) head is busy injecting eye-catching features, e.g. jacuzzi, sauna, fax machines, the school's own bakery. Some unusual awards and scholarships are on offer including squash, rowing and drama.

SIXTH-FORM OPTIONS OUTSIDE THE UK

AIGLON COLLEGE

1885 Chesières-Villars, Switzerland, tel: 00 41 25 352721, fax: 00 41 25 352811.

Vital statistics: Number of students: 95 in the sixth form (size of whole school: 280, with 158 boys, 122 girls). Ages: 11–18.

The Good Gap and Sixth Form Guide

Head: Since September 1994, Mr Richard McDonald MA (Oxon.) (30s). Educated at Christ's Hospital, Mr McDonald read French and German at Lincoln. He previously taught at Charterhouse before becoming senior housemaster at Christ's Hospital. His wife, Michèle, is a French Canadian-born American, and they have a five-year-old son Howard (who is bilingual). A passionate skier, Mr McDonald is also a karate brown belt, a keen saxophonist, writes and directs plays and is a talented illustrator.

What it does: A-levels, GCSEs, also IGCSEs.

What it's like: A seriously exciting and challenging coed school of the best international kind. Perched 4,000 feet on the south-facing slope of Chesières (just below Villars proper), the school is housed in a delightful collection of Swiss-style chalets and modern buildings.

All the teaching is in English. Sixth-formers do three A-levels plus two subsidiary subjects (non-examination unless you choose to do, for instance, another GCSE). French is a core subject for all, 'But don't expect them to come out bilingual unless they've been here since they were 11 or 13,' says a member of staff. French usually gets the strongest A-level results, followed by Art and Spanish. There's good career guidance and good help is offered for dyslexic children. There's a fair selection of regular games: basketball, soccer, athletics, tennis, swimming and volleyball, but a slightly limited number of other schools to play against.

The skiing is superb (this could well be your reason for coming here) – daily in winter – with masses of expeditions and quite serious climbing.

A more traditional school than you would expect, Aiglon has a strong house system. One of the Round Square schools, founded in 1949, this is an English-speaking school (with extra English language teaching if needed).

The children are charmingly self-confident. Discipline is strong: 'drinking privileges' – small amounts of wine or beer at selected restaurants – are allowed for senior students, who have slightly more freedom and a less strict dress code. Social and academic 'trials' are imposed for slackers. Forty-seven different nationalities are represented at Aiglon, with about 20 per cent British, 14 per cent American, plus Western Europeans and, currently, a dozen Muscovites. There are a fair amount of first-time buyers.

Getting in and on: Sixth-form entrance: not a problem. Exit: most students go on to university, with a bias to the States (Boston, Princeton, Wellesley and Stanford et al.), occasionally Cambridge, as well as LSE, Bristol, Edinburgh, Exeter, etc., plus a smattering to Madrid, Geneva, Wittenberg.

Accommodation: There's a chalet for sixth-form girls, otherwise 'proper' boarding houses operate, with boys and girls strictly segregated.

Cost: It's *very* expensive: current fees are around £25,000 a year.

THE BRITISH INSTITUTE OF FLORENCE
Offers a one-year A-level course in Italian and History of Art. Perfect for arty, not-very-academic types. See main entry in the Languages chapter, p. 109.

LAURENTIAN INTERNATIONAL COLLEGE
CP/PO box 235, Ste Agathe des Monts, Quebec, Canada J8C 3A3, tel: 0101 819 326 3347, fax: 0101 819 326 5980.

Vital statistics: Number of students: 25 in total. Ages: 16–18.

Principal: Since 1983, Mrs Beryl Puddifer MA (early 40s), a delightful and shrewd Liverpudlian ('She has her head screwed on,' said a father); grammar-school educated.

What it does: A-levels.

What it's like: A tiny, private sixth-form college in glorious surroundings up in the Laurentian mountains (floodlit ski-slopes not far off), with fabulous views. There are lots of outings (including trips to the Gulf of Mexico), Duke of Edinburgh, white-water rafting, *loads* of skiing – many students take the Canadian Ski Instructors' Association examinations. Staff are reported to be young and bouncy. Thirteen A-level subjects are on offer. There's good pastoral care. 'Living in a small community can be quite claustrophobic,' warns one English boy who came here from a large English public school.

Laurentian works best for late developers.

Cost: Fees are on a par with the very top end of the public school market.

LE ROSEY

CH-1180 Rolle, Switzerland, tel: 0121 825 4721, fax: 0121 825 2056.

Directeurs généraux: M and Mme Philippe Gudin.

What it does: Le Rosey prepares 10- to 18-year-olds for British public exams (IGCSE and GCSE) and the American equivalent. It also does the French *baccalauréat*.

What it's like: Once famous as a very expensive finishing school, Le Rosey is now more of an academic international one. 'Full of rich international "gypsies" with homes in e.g. Palm Beach, the South of France and Paris,' says an ex-student, 'and the students shuttle about – you have everything and belong nowhere.' It is very good for languages. The whole school migrates to its 12 chalets in Gstaad from January to March – there's 2 hours' skiing, etc. a day. Le Rosey is packed with staff. The main buildings are a bit (Swiss) barrack-like.

Cost: Fees are from around 16,000 Swiss francs a term (a deposit of 5,000 francs is required).

ST GEORGE'S ENGLISH SCHOOL

Via Cassia KM 16, 00123 Rome, tel: 00 39 3790141/2/3, fax: 00 39 3792490.

Principal: Since 1994, Mrs Brigid Gardner MA. Previously head of London's James Allen's Girls' School, where she was known as Mrs Brigid Davies. An interesting move.

What it does: St George's offers the IB for all those coming into the school in 1996 and thereafter (A-level courses are on offer until then). There is a History of Art course based on works on show in Rome. St George's could be a good way to learn Italian, living as a paying guest in a family (the school will help you with this).

What it's like: The school occupies a 27-acre site on the north side of Rome. Ages: 3–18. There are 680 pupils at time of writing, from 60 countries.

5

Languages

Learning a foreign language should be fun. You are absorbing a whole new culture – the feel, the sound, the smells, the food, the people. And when you're looking for a job these days, having a second language is more help than you can possibly imagine. Even pre-prep schools are cottoning on to the fact that French at four is fun and useful. Some schools do regular swaps with schools abroad – does your child pass on the vital information from school? They might also find pen-pals. Check with the language teachers.

An 'exchange' is still the most effective (and cheapest) method of learning a language. Of course it's hit or miss, and all too commonly the children don't get on. When you are choosing a family, remember that aristos everywhere tend to speak English and are used to having English-speaking nannies. Go for big bourgeois families where plenty is going on (it can be soothing to chat with younger children, not to mention dogs and cats, before working up to strength with the peer group). It's usually pretty hard work for the whole family. Hobbies and interests can help, and if you can persuade your pony club to take in little Françoise and find her a pony, *tant mieux*. If you are very lucky, your child's school may be happy to take his or her exchange for a week or two. This lets you off the hook (particularly if it is a boarding school), but you may of course have to pay.

When it's the turn of your child to go abroad, brief him/her first (a) to ask questions, show curiosity; (b) to take part in life on the spot (there's nothing worse than little ones sitting around moping in their bedroom while everyone else is out riding bikes); (c) to smile and look lively as this breaks through all language barriers.

The alternative to doing an exchange with a family is to clock into a language school abroad. They vary greatly. The selection we have chosen run from the gentle to the 'intensive', with many degrees in between. Meanwhile, here are some thoughts.

* Winter can be a wonderful time from the learning point of view. Peace, time, and the staff can concentrate on you, and it is often cheaper. The danger of going during the summer holidays is that natives often flee to their own summer resorts; and beware the pitfalls of mingling with polyglot peer groups.
* Do not share a room or flat with a fellow national or with another English-speaker. If you do, half the point of being abroad is lost.
* If you've never done grammar – and according to the Continentals a lot of us haven't – it will save acres of puzzlement if you learn a few basics in your own language, e.g. what is an infinitive, noun, preposition, etc., before you go.
* Don't be shy of making mistakes: it is better to spit it out wrong than not at all. Language is meant to be about communication.
* Do not be dismayed by the speed with which Scandinavians learn languages. 'They leave everyone gasping,' said a teacher.
* Watch out for courses with too many students from radically different cultural backgrounds who may be struggling to get to grips with *everything*. With the best will in the world, this can hold a class up.
* Don't buy any local travel deals, e.g. bus passes, until you get to the school. They will almost certainly have negotiated a better rate for you.
* Expect to learn a hundred per cent faster than you have been learning in school.
* We think two weeks is the absolute minimum, unless you are under 16. Younger children can get very homesick, and money permitting, two short courses, says one experienced language teacher, are a great deal more productive than one long one.
* A language will not get you a job. A skill plus a language will.

* Once you've learned one Romance language (i.e. a European language descended from Latin), the next should follow much less painfully.
* The best way to learn a language in Eastern Europe at the moment is to go to a university and flush out a native speaker who is prepared to teach on a one-to-one basis. This is very cheap and usually very effective.
* Beware of all those foreigners who want to practise their English on you. At the very least, trade it for conversation in the language you're meant to be learning.
* Universities all over Europe offer copious language courses for foreign students, who perceive them as being where the action is. A slight warning note, however: they may not provide the

---

Tips for boosting a foreign language at home

* Listen to Continental radio stations (especially to advertisements and news).
* Practise role-play situations – shopping, buying tickets (*aller-retour*), travelling, ordering food in a restaurant.
* Get friends to video favourite programmes (*Neighbours* dubbed in French 'really works a treat', comment students and parents).
* Buy *Marie Claire, Elle* ('magic,' said a mother), *Paris Match, ABC, Uomo.* Lay your hands on favourite books in the foreign lingo (*Tin Tin* or *Peter Rabbit* is in most languages, so is *Il Palloncino di Winny Puh*), borrow children's story books and classics from foreign friends.
* Befriend Italian waiters, your Spanish lodger, an Austrian music student; employ an au pair in the language of your choice.

---

easiest environment to learn in. They tend to be big, impersonal, and you need to be self-propelled. And English is all too often the lingua franca.

* English is the world's number one mother tongue (for around 450 million people), and the second language of almost the same number again. However this does not mean that we should be complacent.
* When negotiating fees for courses, schools and staying as paying guests with families, don't be British about it but *negotiate*.
* Last but not least, having a beloved whose mother tongue is the one you are learning, is still a brilliant way to learn.

How to Recognize a Good Language School

Before you start looking, consider what you actually want out of the course. Do you want to learn the language as fast as possible? Do you need to write it, or just speak it? – there's a big difference. Are you buffing up for exam purposes? Do you want to have a holiday with a bit of learning? Do you want the whole cultural bit?

Points to think about (e.g. when talking to contacts, ex-students, etc.):

* Is this going to be fun? Are you likely to become *keen* on the country and language you are learning? (You won't learn much if you're not.)
* What is the location like? Is it a place you want to spend time in? If the school is in a town, is it central and convenient? Is it going to be easy to meet the natives?
* Who are the teachers? Where do they come from? Can they really teach? Are they experienced? It goes without saying that they must be native speakers. Bear in mind that summer courses often import inexperienced staff.
* What is the maximum–minimum size of the classes? Too large and you learn too slowly; too small and learning can be too concentrated – too small is better than too large, however.

Languages

* Is the teaching all in the foreign language? Is there a moment in the day to have something calmly explained to you in your own language?

* Is there a variety of teaching methods? Do the classes include grammar, linguistics and communication? Is there lots of role play, games, diversity? Does the school have a bias to e.g. business language? Whatever their methods, everyone should be on their toes.

* Extracurricular activities: what else is there? Local history? Wine-tasting? Visits? Excursions (be careful – these can be ludicrously overpriced)? Sport? Trips to the theatre? Beware a school offering *too* much outside of mainstream classes – it may be spreading itself and its staff too thin.

* What part does culture play in the set lessons? Can you learn something of the country's literature, music, customs, history, politics?

* How old are the staff? Youth may respond better to younger teachers, more on their own wavelength. But when the chips are down, a cuddly oldie is welcome. Ideally, you want a mixture.

* How much time do staff spend with students outside the classroom? Do they come on excursions? Are coffee breaks shared? Are staff regularly available to keen students? Do they befriend students – who may well be abroad alone for the first time?

* Is there homework? Daily? Written, oral, learning? (Practising subjunctives in a café will do.) What kinds of tests are there, and how often are students tested?

* What emphasis is there on reading? Does the school have a library where you can read magazines and newspapers, and from which you can borrow books? Failing that, is there a library near by?

* What kind of pastoral care is there? Is there someone on the staff to whom you could turn?

* If the school is providing your accommodation, how long will it take you to get to the school in the morning? If they are finding you a family, have they used this family before?

Contact

The Cambridge Advisory Service for Language Courses Abroad: Gives personal advice on a limited number of courses. Contact: P. M. L. Bingley, Rectory Lane, Kingston, Cambridge, CB3 7NL, tel: 01223 264089, fax: 01223 264188.

Grant and Cutler: 55 Great Marlborough Street, London W1V 1DD, tel: 0171 734 2012, fax: 0171 734 9272. Specialists in foreign books – and very often they sell English translations as well.

EF International Language Schools: 74 Roupell Street, London SE1 8SS, tel: 0171 795 6675, fax: 0171 795 6635.

EF was started in the sixties by a Swede who brought a bunch of Swedish students over to England to learn English. The group has now mushroomed into France, Spain, Italy and Germany.

International House: 106 Piccadilly, London W1V 8HJ, tel: 0171 491 2598, fax: 0171 409 0959.

This was founded in the early fifties in London and was the first EFL (English as a Foreign Language) venture. It now has approximately 100 schools all over the world. Each IH school has its own owner, who pays a percentage to the group, which covers, for example, conferences and training and a newsletter. The schools do their own marketing, but the London centre is helpful to anyone needing information on sister schools abroad. Has its own bookshop.

The Earls Guide to Language Schools in Europe: Published by Cassell, price £14·99. This lists around two hundred language schools in Europe, and is the only reference book of its kind. It is selective, and gives useful basic information plus some comment. All the schools have been vetted.

The author of this book also runs an advisory service (free) to help people with specific questions on schools which he writes about. Well worth buying the book for this alone.

EXCHANGES *EN FAMILLE*

DRAGONS INTERNATIONAL

Godswell House, Bloxham, Banbury, Oxfordshire OX15 4ES, tel:
01295 721717, fax: 01295 721991.

Director: Mr Colin Galloway

What it does: This large and successful agency (set up in 1975)
might be useful if you or your school *really* can't find a family for
your child to do an exchange with in France or Germany. The cost
covers accompanied travel (by coach from London and the South,
Manchester, Leeds, Preston, Scotch Corner – set-off points are all
over the shop) over to a French family and back again, also
insurance. There is a fairly basic form for 'matching' purposes, non-
refundable unless the agency cannot find a partner for your
offspring.

EN FAMILLE OVERSEAS

The Old Stables, 60b Maltravers Street, Arundel, West Sussex
BN18 9BG, tel: 01903 883266, fax: 01903 883582.

Directors: Mrs Susan Baxendale, Mrs Lindy Owen-Ellis, Mrs
Jane Tourell; a trio who recently bought up this well-established
efficient agency ('We're not particularly commercially minded, to
tell the truth'), all of whom have worked for the establishment for
around ten years.

What it does: Finds you a host family – at any time – where
teenagers (or adults or indeed whole families) can be paying guests
and learn to speak the language, mainly in France; a few families in
Germany. Private language tuition may be an option. Also
available are summer language courses, where you attend daily
and stay with a family.

What it's like: Long established, this agency was set up just after
the war by a British parachutist whose original contact families are
still involved. Very efficient, and a very personal service. Two-thirds
of students choose to stay as paying guests with families, the
rest go for a language course. Most popular of all in the summer

holidays with students who have just finished their first year of A-levels 'and suddenly realize with a jump just how much there is to learn', as one such put it.

Language-course holidays (one (very intensive), two or three weeks) are organized at la Rochelle, St Germain en Laye (a suburb west of Paris) and at Tours. Age groups are divided into juniors (13 and 14) and seniors (14/15 to 18), i.e. these are pre-GCSE and pre-A-level students needing a boost. The teenagers – from a wide mix of mainly public schools – either meet up on the way over (boat and bus) or they may make their own way out and meet up at the language school where they have two or three hours' tuition in the morning ('lots of the old grammar') every weekday. Some afternoons and occasionally in the evenings the English students are taken on outings with the En Famille organizer, or they may go home and integrate with their host French family. The set-up is structured enough to ensure that the Brits do not spend too much time together. The agency gives sensible advice on pocket money and discusses curfew times with parents and host families.

Host families vary considerably from very formal to very informal ('We never all sat down for a meal together,' said one English girl). En Famille have a very long list of French families (carefully vetted by their French connection) who take English students as paying guests. They all come via word of mouth – the agency never advertises in France for 'host families' – and this is most unusual.

You decide where you want your child to be (country, seaside or city), and what sort of a set-up you would ideally want, e.g. heaps of children plus a tennis court and swimming pool, with no other English for many kilometres. You then receive typed particulars with photographs in plastic wallets (and a sharp reminder to return these p.d.q.) from which you make your choice. Fascinating documents, showing grand but down-at-heel aristos outside the crumbling château and modest families grouped outside the bungalow. Prices vary a good deal accordingly. All without exception claim to be glad to 'introduce their English guests to their many friends and family' and to take them on excursions. Time will tell. It can work wonderfully – provided you've chosen the right family.

Cost: You pay the agency a modest registration fee, then you pay the family direct.

INTERNATIONAL LINKS
145 Manygate Lane, Shepperton, Middlesex TW17 9EP, tel: 01932 229300, fax: 01932 222294.

Director and founder: The voluble Mrs Eve Moody, cosy and reliable, who has contacts in Germany (Cologne, Münster, Bocholt, Bergen and Celle), Spain (Puerto de Santa Maria, Cadiz, Alicante and Zaragoza), France (Paris, Tours, St Malo, Rennes, Dinan, Dinard, Le Luc en Provence), Italy (Siena), and – most unusually – Russia (St Petersburg, Moscow, Minsk) and Japan (Osaka and Ise City).

What it does: Specializes for teenagers in what Mrs Moody politely refers to as 'homestays on a non-reciprocal basis' – i.e. paying guests for small groups or individuals. Formal language lessons are an option, including summer language schools in Brittany and St Petersburg. Occasionally friendships blossom and return visits are made. Most of Mrs Moody's European contacts are teachers.

What it's like: Well run, and just the ticket if you don't want to be tied to hostmanship later and can afford it. Host families are likely to be friendly and welcoming, suburban and unpretentious. 'So much the better,' said one parent, after her pre-A-level daughter did a two-week stint in Puerto de Santa Maria, 'because it meant the family spoke absolutely no English.' This is total immersion in ordinary life. Private tuition can be laid on, and paying guests can spend time in the local schools (very useful for listening purposes), bearing in mind that English and Continental term times are often different.

Timing can generally be made to measure (you are not stuck to starting the stay on a Saturday; a family will take students for two and a half weeks if that's what is needed). You must insist that there are no other foreign students staying at the same time. Go for a family with several children, and for half-term placement; book early. Obviously, the earlier you book, the more choice of family there is. You must rely on Mrs Moody and her contacts' descriptions of host families, all of them thoroughly checked out and well-known to Mrs Moody's on-the-spot contact. Beady questionnaires are first filled out by the English student (with photograph).

You make your own travel arrangements: local contacts can collect students from airports and deliver them to the host family for a fee; on the other hand, it will be cheaper and far more of an adventure for a teenager to take a bus or train from the airport to the family's nearest meeting point (provided you are confident he or she will not become parted from their luggage and travellers' cheques *en route*), and bearing in mind that the examining boards never fail to have questions on travel and *aller-retour* tickets, etc. This is the real-life situation.

Cost: Full-board homestay costs around £180 per week, plus registration fee with the agency of approximately £20. Deposit with application is required, and is deducted from the final total.

FRENCH

French children tend to be more traditional, more family-focused, more serious and on the whole less sports-oriented. When your child goes off to France alone, explain the importance of handshaking (morning and night); explain also that the possible lack of knives and forks on the table doesn't mean little Jamie will starve; and that vegetables may be served as a separate course from the meat. By the way, French and English school holidays rarely link up date-wise: it's worth checking on.

Languages

Location: think carefully. There is a school of thought which considers Paris not to be the best place to learn French as it's full of English-speakers, and cosmopolitan, and it's particularly difficult to find a suitable family there who will really take you to their bosom, let alone anywhere near the centre. However, for streetwise 18-year-olds, Paris may be just the place to acquire some extra polish, including dress sense, a sense of style and self-confidence. It's an incredibly beautiful city, full of history and glorious for art lovers.

Most famous of the teaching establishments is of course the Sorbonne, but this university is probably best for *les anglais* acquiring a postgraduate degree, when they are already fluent. There is also the Alliance Française, which comes with a hefty reputation and 2,000 students. *'C'est une usine,'* said a French educationalist, 'and it's easy to be *perdu.'* Try a small school (see the selection below).

The South of France sounds wonderful but bear in mind that it's very expensive and very crowded in summer, full of international Nescafé society. Also bear in mind the question of regional accents: they can be difficult to understand. The accent in and around Tours is considered the purest.

Reminder to parents on writing to Madame – top: Madame (or Chère Madame if you know her) . . .

. . . and tail:

Je vous prie, (chère) Madame, de croire à mes sentiments distingués – this is the equivalent to Yours sincerely.

Contact

Centre d'Echanges Internationaux (CEI): 61–9 Chepstow Place, London W2 4TR, tel: 0171 221 8134, fax: 0171 221 0642.

This is the London branch of a nationwide French charitable trust whose aim is to promote understanding and communication between countries. It is an excellent meeting-place for young francophiles, and offers heaps of help and information on all that might be of interest for *les frogs* in London, including jobs – this would be a good place to advertise for an au pair. Recommends French classes for the English, and is linked in London with the Alliance Française.

CEI can advise English parents on choosing courses for their children in France, and (for a small fee) can book and arrange payment, etc. for you. Students are assessed in England, a time-saver so that they can move straight into the right level of class the moment they arrive in France.

The director, Monsieur André de Bussy, a charming anglophile who has lived in London since 1981, regularly visits language schools in France and is a fount of knowledge. He produces an annual booklet (free, apply by post) giving details of around 14 language schools which he considers particularly good and best suited to English students. He only selects schools which are small and teach small groups; he also takes into account the location, plus the interest of the region. Some of the schools offer programmes all year round; others specialize in three- or four-week summer courses.

Château de Sauveterre (near Toulouse): Contact the headmaster, Mr Adrian Richardson, Cothill House, Nr. Abingdon, Oxfordshire OX13 6JL, tel: 01865 390800, fax: 01865 390205.

Cothill House was a pioneer in acquiring a château in France (and sends its own students out on a regular basis). In the summer term Sauveterre is available to girls who have done their Common Entrance at 11 + (though this may be fiercely frowned on by your daughter's school). A maximum of 50 girls go for the whole term, never more than two girls from the same school. This is terrifically popular, and it is essential to book well ahead. Mostly French staff are employed, and a great deal of fun is had, as well as good groundwork done.

Cost: Around £3,000 per term.

Club Med: 106–10 Brompton Road, London SW3 1JJ, tel: 0171 581 1161, fax: 0171 581 4769.

Excellent place to pick up the French language *en famille*: ski holidays with a hidden agenda – good for all ages, and all the

family at once. Choose a French or Swiss resort – make *sure* it is
'international' (or your five-year-old will dissolve into tears as
French try to shout French at her) and *check* it is not one of Club
Med's swing-from-the-chandelier places (these are well known to
employees). Experiences in these last have been disastrous.

Go with an even number of people if possible – if you don't, you
may be forced to share a room with someone (part of the Club Med
philosophy). Don't be alarmed if the door has not got a lock – the
idea is to stop worrying about money – hand everything over to the
caisse: it really works. In a couple of weeks, the children will
emerge with more spoken French under their belt than you could
manage any other way, through sheer desire to communicate with
their (French) peers. This is expensive, but it's good value as it is
all-in.

NB to parents: you will hardly see your children from morning
to night – *après ski* they rock on into entertainments, shows, discos
– joy!

The French Bookshop: 28 Bute Street, London SW7 3EX, tel:
0171 584 2840, fax: 0171 823 9259.

French Embassy: Cultural Counsellor, 23 Cromwell Road,
London SW7 2DQ, tel: 0171 838 2055, fax: 0171 838 2088.

Institut Français: 17 Queensberry Place, London SW7 2JR, tel:
0171 589 6211, fax: 0171 581 5127.

A very useful place to plug into the atmosphere of France via its
café/restaurant (attractive students, offhand staff, the smell of
fresh coffee, French posters and French chatter all around). They
run lively programmes of high-quality films (old favourites, e.g. *Au
revoir les Enfants*, classics with Jean-Paul Belmondo, all Jean
Renoir's movies), also theatre: this is the nerve-centre for cultural
activities in England. The Institut also runs a large number of
language courses throughout the year. Next door is the French
Lycée and down the road is the French bookshop, also mouth-
watering patisserie, butcher's, etc.

French Language Schools

CILS

Centre International Linguistique et Sportif (CILS), 1 Route de Paris, BP 36-51700 Troissy, tel: 00 33 26 52 73 08, fax: 00 33 26 52 72 07.

Vital statistics: Number of students: takes a maximum of 120 per session. Ages: 7–18. Number of staff: 30 teachers, most of them young, some Olympic-standard sportsmen and women. Maximum teaching group size: 8–12. Children come here from America, Germany, Scandinavia, England, Middle East and Far East.

Director: M Guy Sénée, who runs the school with his wife.

What it does: This is a residential summer school with lessons in the morning and sports in the afternoon; three-week or two-week sessions are offered (from mid-June until early September).

What it's like: Extremely jolly. The château is in lovely Champagne country, 110 km from Paris. French children can come at other times and have 'support lessons' in their normal school subjects, plus the sporting programme. Three hours of lessons in the morning are followed by lunch. 'The food is absolutely yummy,' said an English 14-year-old. Language teaching is very much geared to communication and interaction (they're dead keen on role play here). Well-structured teaching with daily written work and grammar, but never any written homework. Staff send parents detailed reports of language progress at the end.

Afternoons are devoted to sports, with brilliant coaching: 20 different options on offer, including riding, archery, tennis, fencing, golf, water-skiing, canoeing. Most activities take place around the château, and *moniteurs* chase the children to ensure they speak French. Children rush around, uninhibited, enthusiastic. 'Unlike lessons at school in England,' commented a mother, 'children don't consider this work: as far as Charlotte was concerned, she was doing ponies and just happened to be talking about curry-combs in French.' 'Go two years running,' said a father, 'and they'll probably be almost fluent.'

Book early: this is popular. It is huge fun: not a moment to be bored, children are kept on the go incessantly, and most of them love forming groups and gangs for their own games. Probably works best for the young, and obviously the dream place for active and sporting children. Sophisticated, reflective, or intellectual 17-year-olds might prefer the intimacy of smaller-scale family life.

Accommodation: Staff and students all live in the château, in the exuberant atmosphere of a huge extended family.

Cost: Not cheap, but all expenses are included.

INSTITUT D'ETUDES FRANÇAISES DE TOURAINE

1 rue de la Grandière, 37030 Tours, tel: 00 33 47 05 76 83, fax: 00 33 47 20 48 98.

Vital statistics: Number of students: around 3,000 per year (staying anything from two weeks to a full year). Age: minimum 16, but most are over 20. Number of staff: 1½ teachers per group. Maximum teaching group size: 20, but 17 is the norm, with 9–10 for both lab and conversation work.

Studies director: Mlle J. Launay, a charming, very correct, old-fashioned anglophile, bilingual in French and English. High-powered, she heads the Department of American Literature at Tours University, and teaches and administrates at the Institut.

What it does: There are three 11-week terms (starting in October, January and April); also four-week summer sessions in July, August and September (between 500 and 700 students for each session). French is taught at seven basic levels (nine for summer sessions). There is daily homework, and grading is by continuous assessment. There are 20 specialist teachers, all extremely highly motivated.

What it's like: Long established (80 years old) and highly professional. 'And you get your money's worth,' commented a parent. Pleasant setting in a series of rather grand *hôtels particuliers*: do not be put off by the slick entry hall (looks like an advertising agency, this 'refurbishment' a gift from the town council). Despite the odd chandelier, fine panelling and parquet flooring the buildings are institutionalized now. The nearby *lycée* is used as additional teaching space for summer courses. It's a pretty outlook on to a little square and garden. Lots of space, very good video and film viewing room and ditto library.

Extremely thorough, highly structured and well-devised teaching. 'It's very hard work,' commented a German student, 'and you really can learn here.' Mornings (8.45 a.m.–12.15 p.m.) are for grammar, linguistics and written work. Afternoons are for oral work, conversation, history of art, architecture, history, business, etc. Twice-weekly excursions are put on during the summer sessions.

Students come from 50 different countries, especially Europe, the US and the Far East (Japan, South Korea, Thailand). This school has links with the universities of Bristol, St Andrew's and Lancaster who regularly send students there. Geographically an excellent springboard for anyone seriously interested in 'doing' the Loire châteaux, and Paris is near enough for frequent visits (money permitting). This could be a solution for students seriously wanting to learn French without the temptations, expense, pace and glamour of some other centres. Tours is a staid provincial town. Your over-sophisticated, dizzy London-y teenager may find it dull.

Accommodation: This is arranged with families (full or half board).

INSTITUT D'ETUDES FRANÇAISES POUR ETUDIANTS ETRANGERS

Université d'Aix Marseille III, 23 rue Gaston de Saporta, Aix-en-Provence, 13625 Cedex 01, tel: 01 33 42 23 28 43, fax: 00 33 42 23 02 64.

Vital statistics: Number of students: 1,500 pass through every year, but at any one time there are in the region of 450–500 from over 60 countries. Age: ranges from 17 (in which case parents must write a letter taking full responsibility) to 76 (retired priest at the time of writing), but the average age is around 20–23. Number of staff: 85 full time. Maximum teaching group size: 18 – but average size is usually 7 or 8.

Director: M Jean-Jacques Bousquet.

Languages

Administrator: Mme Cécile Globbe – a gem. A mother-hen figure, she sits at the top of the stairs behind a large desk keeping a watchful eye on all the comings and goings, and is bilingual in English and French, good-humoured, warm-hearted – and she doesn't miss a trick.

What it does: Specifically teaches French to foreigners at all levels – from *débutants*, through *faux débutants*, to preparation for entry to universities in France. There are three basic levels, and within those, twenty or so different ability groups.

Length of courses: one year (two semesters: October to the end of January; February to May), or one term only. Intensive courses are also offered of one (or two) months in June, July and September. The courses are 20 hours per week (consisting of oral work, grammar, written work, translation and understanding texts, journalism, etc.), plus a daily 'workshop' (one and a half to two hours) on a variety of subjects, e.g. contemporary French poetry, French political life, etc.

What it's like: Glorious place – a wonderful setting, ravishing and distinguished buildings, high standard of teaching and huge fun. There are 150,000 inhabitants in the capital of Provence, and 40,000 of them are students: there are three universities here, and the Institut is attached to one of them (engineering is a famously strong faculty), 'though not nearly as much mixing as we would like with the French students,' commented a young Scot. The atmosphere at the Institut is outstandingly *accueillant*, warm and friendly (not as common as all that among the French). Students drift into the office to get advice on all manner of things: staff *tutoient* them, relations are delightfully informal, a sense of family: this is not a huge daunting university where you would get lost.

A mini-United Nations, students hail from 60 + countries: there are Japanese, Eastern Europeans, South Americans, Americans including regular batches from universities in California; also Dutch, Swedes, Germans and Brits, though (good news) not in great numbers (occasionally some from UCL). 'We try to encourage students to stay for two terms; it is very little extra money, and then they can really learn.' As well as study of the French language,

French civilization is studied via a series of 'options'. Tests and exercises in all areas are fairly rigorous.

Short of space, battered and beloved, the rooms are magnificently proportioned. Originally built as a private house in the seventeenth century, the Institut stands right opposite the cathedral (bells clang sonorously), and all the main teaching rooms are around a charming courtyard. Classes are staggered (to get maximum use from the classrooms), and the director wrings his hands, longing for funds to repaint, etc.

Outings are organized for the weekends: Mont St Victoire, St Tropez, Avignon, etc. are all within striking distance. You have to get through the drearily built-up environs immediately surrounding Aix.

In July, the city is home to an international music festival, with lots of opera (the university's courtyard is sometimes used): it can be steamily hot and stuffy then, but there is the vibrant excitement of music in the making. In fact, the old central part of the city where students spend their time is altogether like an opera set. Loads of cafés, *bien entendu*, and food shops which are an education in themselves. This could be an excellent place for young *anglais/anglaises* to immerse themselves in French culture – and become frafrancophiles for life.

As the excellent Mme Cécile says, 'They can really learn here if they want to – provided they don't treat it as sex in Provence or holidays *en vacances.*'

Accommodation: Allow approx. 3,300fr. per month for staying *demi-pension en famille*.

Cost: Aix is the third most expensive town in France (after Paris and Cannes). Fees for the year: (two semesters) 8,700fr.; or one semester, 7,700fr. For the intensive course, per month, it's 4,600fr.

L'ECOLE FRANCE LANGUE

2 rue de Sfax, 75116 Paris, tel: 00 33 45 00 40 15, fax: 00 33 45 00 53 41.

Directors: M François Vouilloux and M Bertrand Piot

What it does: Offers year-round courses. Study is 15 and 30 hours per week for a minimum of one week, with a maximum of 15 students per class. There's a weekly lecture on French culture. Private tuition is also available (including a nine-hour-a-day non-stop option).

What it's like: Very professional, thorough, traditional, safe; also up-market, with mature student appeal, as befits this smart, very central staid *arrondissement*. Some afternoon activities are put on (one outing per week to a monument, or a walk, with a *professeur*) – but this school really works best for self-starters who want most afternoons free to do their own thing (but is this the best way to learn French?).

Accommodation: A good area for *bonnes familles* (aristos on their uppers) with whom to be a paying guest, or possibly with whom to be working as a family help while giving English lessons.

PARIS LANGUES

30 rue Cabanis, 75014 Paris, tel: 00 33 45 65 05 28, fax: 00 33 45 81 26 28.

Directors: Mme Brigitte Verpraet and Mme Isabelle Lande.

What it does: Offers intensive courses (20 hours per week), semi-intensive ($12\frac{1}{2}$ hours per week); conversation groups; private tuition. Courses are held throughout the year. Special two-week A-level revision Easter courses are also available.

What it's like: Young, fun, international, buzzing. Near Montparnasse (excellent metro links), the school is based in the FIAP (Foyer International d'Accueil de Paris) Jean Monet International Youth Hostel. Huge emphasis on communication, but grammatical structure is taken *very* seriously.

There are loads of activities and extremely busy afternoon programmes: lively, bright young teachers mix in all the time, notice-boards are fizzing with events going on in Paris: cultural, social, *sportif*, etc. It's relatively inexpensive. Up to 500 students from all over the world stay at FIAP – some of them are studying at the Sorbonne or the Alliance Française – there is unlikely to be a single dull moment. A leisure centre is on hand, and a self-service canteen (delicious).

Accommodation: This is at FIAP (b & b or half board) and is decent and simple, with double rooms. Alternatively, stay with a family.

THONON FRENCH LANGUAGE COURSE

Contact: G. A. Perry at Portsmouth Grammar School, High Street, Portsmouth, Hampshire PO1 2LN, tel: 01705 819125, fax: 01705 870184 (during day and term), and at 34 Marine Court, Southsea, Hampshire PO4 9QU, tel: 01705 734606 (evenings and holidays)

Leader: Mr Gareth Perry, head of Modern Languages at Portsmouth Grammar School, a remarkably enthusiastic old-fashioned (in the best sense) schoolmaster with over thirty years' experience of teaching to A-level. Mr Perry has run French courses for English students at Thonon for over twenty years, previously for a language school and now off his own bat. NB Early booking is advised (by October and Christmas respectively): these courses are deservedly popular.

What it does: Runs pre-A-level courses for lower and upper sixth students: 12 days during the Easter holidays, three weeks in the summer, with around 40 students per course.

What it's like: This is hard work and serious, and also fun. It's intensive work (virtually entirely in French), with a three-hour lesson each morning, homework every day. There is course project work (e.g. something on local food) to be researched and written in French; a book (one of your 'set texts' would do nicely) to be discussed at the conclusion of the course. 'It seriously improves the French,' say students. On the summer course there is more emphasis on literature, *civilisation française* (contemporary), etc., in other words a wider curriculum is covered. The (shorter) Easter course is exclusively exam-targeted, most especially not forgetting the grammar. Mr Perry, every inch the schoolmaster, is also very much the course leader: 'a brilliant teacher', 'one of life's enthusiasts', comment students. He is assisted by French tutors.

Initially meeting up at Heathrow airport, students are likely to be handed a copy of *Le Monde* and told to read it, especially the articles on x and y, for discussion later in the day. 'It makes the French teaching at school look pretty weedy,' commented one boy.

Thonon-les-Bains is a spa on the south side of Lake Geneva, pretty, unspoilt and relatively unsophisticated. A programme of excursions and leisure activities is laid on – and there is time for café life too, 'lots of fun and friends'. Students come by word-of-mouth recommendation, no advertising, and it's jam-packed and highly successful. Radley, Winchester, St Paul's Girls, Wycombe Abbey, etc. are regulars, and Mr Perry insists on a full report on each student from their school head. 'Our daughter was bolshie about going,' said a parent, 'but absolutely loved it and had a ball.'

Accommodation: All the students stay (full *pension*) with reliable and caring French families, carefully screened over the years.

Cost: This is kept reasonable, and includes the air fare, full board and teaching. The 1995 rate is £589 for 12 days at Easter, £799 for three weeks in the summer 'Which makes you reflect,' said a parent, 'on the huge profits some organizations are raking in.'

UNIVERSITÉ STENDHAL

BP25, Grenoble 390440 Cedex, tel: 00 33 76 42 48 37, fax: 00 33 76 82 59 46.

Vital statistics: Students of around 70 different nationalities study here. Age: minimum 18. Maximum teaching group size: 15 students. Three levels only (beginner, intermediate, advanced).

What it does: Offers courses of four, five, six or seven weeks or by the term (early October until the end of January; end of January until early June). The courses are intensive (20 hours per week) and semi-intensive (eight hours per week); there's also language plus literature and French civilization (between 16 and 20 hours per week). Tests on arrival place you in the right set (there are around six sets).

What it's like: The main bulk of the university (founded in 1896) is for French students, the Foreign faculty is just a small part. There are also foreign language schools here so there is a large international student population. University bureaucracy is fairly unwieldy: be persistent. Grenoble is not a lovely city but it's in a super setting.

French language courses might well include, as they did for one recent public school boy, the 29-year-old son of a Venezuelan ambassador, a Russian ballet dancer (male), a 55-year-old American divorcee as well as the inevitable batch of British students in their gap year. 'It is very odd to be the baby of the class after being at the top of the school.'

The language, literature and *civilisation française* course offers two hours of language skills per day, plus two hours of literature, civilization and translation – there is variety here, and the choice changes after a fortnight. This course is a good bet for students whose basic French is up to it. 'Well taught and very stimulating,' commented an English student. He confirmed that English tended to be the lingua franca outside classes, 'despite boys and girls from all over the world'.

It is dangerously easy to misuse this opportunity, and there are plenty of rich kids who spend a lot of time skiing, bunking classes, socializing with other non-French foreigners and living on expensive *croque-monsieur*. For sporty types, it is worth joining a team (mostly French students), and there may be some travel involved.

Skiing is the reason most students choose this university. 'You join the ski club,' explained one student, 'and get cut-price transport and *abonnement*.' Local slopes are less than an hour away, so you can ski briefly every day and do afternoon classes, but two or three times a week does nicely for those on a tight budget or putting French first. 'But the temptation to skip the after-lunch sessions when the snow is good is frankly over-whelming – and it's not expensive,' sighed an ex-student. Keen skiers head for higher areas like Les Trois Vallées, and Deux Alpes at weekends. We hear parental worries about sons and daughters 'having bags of fun, but not really getting to grips with the French language'.

Accommodation: Living options include sharing a flat (inevit-ably with other foreigners), staying with a family who are out at work all day and you have a room in the attic, or staying *en famille*.

GERMAN

German is a structured and disciplined language – at some stage you need to sit down and *learn* it. Don't expect to get by by the seat of your pants. 'It isn't that it's ultra-difficult,' says an experienced German teacher, 'but it comes at you in a different way.' A basis of grammar is essential, however, and this does not come easily to the British, where the teaching of grammar has been out of favour (to put it mildly) in recent years. Expect to work hard – this is a German characteristic and some courses may seem heavy-going to easy-going Brits.

Where you do the course doesn't so much matter from the point of view of accent. Berlin is currently where the action is, and where students want to be. However this is heady city life, and sporting enthusiasts would be better off in the Black Forest. Munich, for example, the capital of Bavaria, is surrounded by glorious castles, lakes and mountains and is not too far from good skiing and every sport under the sun.

Germany is *expensive* (and proud of it). A Munich teacher reckoned 25DM a day would be in order for lunch and extras – subsistence, in other words. And, by the way, they don't like credit cards. Don't expect the easy charm of the Mediterraneans. It is not that Germans are unfriendly – on the contrary – but it comes wrapped in a different package and it so happens, for example, that smiling isn't on the instant menu. However they are wonderfully efficient, dedicated and a pleasure to do business with. Also – reassuring for nervous mothers – their laws concerning minors are comfortingly protective and strictly adhered to.

Contact

German Embassy of the Federal Republic: 23 Belgrave Square, London SW1X 8PZ, tel: 0171 235 5033, fax: 0171 235 0609.

German Travel Bureau: 18 Conduit Street, London W1R 9TD, tel: 0171 408 0111, fax: 0171 629 7442 for rail timetable and general information. There's also a *pension* booking service that will recommend good, cheap places to stay – not an easy matter if you're not familiar with the country.

Goethe Institute: 50 Princes Gate, London SW7 2PH. Language Department number: 0171 411 3451 (caveat – hours are restricted), fax: 0171 581 0974.

This is your first port of call. It is the state-subsidized establishment which exists to promote German language and culture throughout the world. There are branches everywhere and they are wonderfully helpful on all matters German. The Institute runs a network of language schools which by and large are good and reliable (don't expect them to recommend anyone else's language school). And don't expect Institute courses to be any cheaper.

German Language Schools

DIALOGE SPRACHINSTITUT

Burstergasse 5, D 88131 Lindau, tel: 00 49 8382 26626, fax: 00 49 8382 6596.

NB: Dialoge is a common name – this school has nothing to do with other Dialoge companies

Vital statistics: Number of students: maximum 150 in summer, far fewer in winter. Ages: all ages are accepted, from teens on. Number of staff: 5–6 full-time, 5–6 part time plus 'new' staff in summer. Maximum teaching group size: around 15.

Languages

Principal (managing and school director): Herr Frank Gebhard and his wife, who were in South Africa when we visited in the middle of the autumn term. 'Education and Pedagogics, Teaching Methods and Material' are the province of Judith Kleiner-Gebhard; and Accommodation, Accountancy, etc.: Sabine Kleiner (Frau Gebhard's sister), i.e., it's a family production.

We were initiated into the ways of the school by Rafael Boos – a young, enthusiastic and friendly teacher.

What it does: Basic courses are taught in the morning, plus bolt-on extras, e.g. one-to-one teaching, in the afternoon. Courses are two+ weeks in winter, three or four weeks in summer. Preparation for state-approved exams is also offered. The school closes at the end of August for two weeks' holiday – 'We need it,' says Rafael.

What it's like: Dear little school in the most glorious part of Germany – on an island in Lake Constanz. Dreamy. There are seagulls, an ancient lighthouse, boats bobbing (sailing is arranged in summer); cobbled streets, tall old houses, hidden courtyards; it's packed with tourists in summer and this makes the actual island noisy with revellers at night, though wonderfully peaceful in winter. You reach it by road and rail – a bit of a hike.

Everything you need here is within walking or bicycling distance (bicycles to rent). Only 5,000 or so people live on the actual island, which is a bit of a ghetto – Herr Gebhard knows *everybody* and thus finds it very easy to keep tabs on the students. Even the 12-year-olds are allowed out on their own, such is the confidence in the island's safety. 'We believe in the importance of atmosphere in learning,' says Rafael; 'Lindau provides this. We hope to provide the rest.'

The school has a passionate belief that learning 'should be fun' and many techniques are used to help you learn including, for example, translation word by word, to demonstrate how different the structure of the German language is; also the engaging of all the senses in order to learn. There are five 'levels' and much shuffling about, though the smallness of the school can make this an impossible job.

The school itself is a purpose-built, small centre tucked away in a backstreet. It's v. posh, with a room for videos – lots of thought has been given to design. In summer, the students spill over into the local Hospiz, which is rented from the church, with large rooms and high ceilings. The average age of students through the year is 20–25. Lots of Swedes, Italians and Swiss – who come over to study for their state-approved exams in order to work in German-speaking Switzerland (the exam is taken in a government-approved building in the nearby town of Friedrichshafen, into which the Gebhards are expanding in '95). *No* Brits at time of writing.

A terrific extra offered by the school almost as a by-the-way is *work experience*. At the end of the course, Dialoge will arrange for you to go and work in e.g. the local bank; they have in the past arranged for a student to work in a nearby Austrian ski resort. This will look invaluable on your c.v., and they 'may even pay a little salary'.

It's a safe, small place to be, fun and cosy; it almost feels like a holiday. There were some signs of teaching staff not being totally on their toes when we visited.

Accommodation: This is arranged mostly off the island (linked by a causeway). The school 'matches' the student with the family, so there's no chance of insisting on being on the island (a mixed blessing anyway in summer). The place has a slightly split feel to it, though, on the island, and off the island. There's no cafeteria in the centre (drinks only) – students take two meals every day with their family.

EF INTERNATIONALE SPRACHSCHULE

Herzogstrasse 36, 8000 München 40, tel: 00 49 89 33 60 81, fax: 00 49 89 33 29 89.

See p. 76 for the London office (EF International Language Schools), which you are asked to contact.

Vital statistics: Number of students: the school fluctuates between 40–50 and 160. Age: minimum 16. Maximum teaching group size: 15.

Principal: Herr Dr Jurgen Oehler. A most interesting and experienced head, who rules with an open door, doing at least half a dozen things at once. Multilingual, Herr Dr Oehler studied English, German and History at Cologne University, with one year at an American university, and spent time also at Sussex. He makes a point of visiting other EF schools to see what they are doing and 'to see how it is from the student's point of view'. Good news.

What it does: Runs a minimum two-week course of 24 hours' teaching that starts every two weeks; also intensive courses of 30 x 40-minute lessons; a three-month course; a nine-month course from mid-September to May (NB this is a bargain); also specialized language courses, e.g. business and German culture and tailor-made courses for e.g. Volvo workers needing to do a presentation in German.

What it's like: Lively teaching here – young, on-the-ball staff. There's a jolly, busy, businesslike atmosphere. Students are from all over – Italians proliferate, also some French, some Russians on grants. The school is in a nice big house on lease in the back of a courtyard in Schwabing – a leafier, less thrusting area than some in this pushy, grasping city. There are good big, light rooms called 'Wien', 'Köln', etc., and a language lab used in formal class teaching (much loved by the Japanese, says one of the teachers; 'they believe in technology') and particularly useful for tailor-made courses. The library is rudimentary (they use the public one across the road).

Speaking German starts at the first lesson – there's a 10-pfennig fine per foreign word used. Methods are a mix of grammar teaching and spoken-language work, plus projects, and use of 'flip charts' for e.g. the use of *ein*. Every Friday morning there is a 'revision' test to check on progress and move students up and down the various ability levels; on Friday afternoons there is a lecture on some topical subject, e.g. elections. Formal classes take place in the morning and 'activities' in the afternoon. Two to three hours of homework is expected (they *cannot* be serious). A register is taken every morning. There are lots of trips to Salzburg, the Black Forest, Venice, Paris even (they sleep on the coach) – students confirm these trips really do happen, and often.

There is a rudimentary cafeteria in the *keller* selling some food and drinks, run by the nine-month students. Students also use the university cafeteria where a reasonable lunch costs a few marks.

An excellent institution for those who want to learn seriously but also make friends. '*Alles gut*,' volunteered a student, flashing his new language skills. They're very patient with plodders.

Accommodation: This is with families, mostly in twin rooms with one other student of a different nationality (there is a supplement for a single room). The school has families all over Munich – they must be a maximum of 40 minutes away from the school.

GLS SPRACHENZENTRUM

Kolonnenstrasse 26, 10829 Berlin-Schoneberg (62), tel: 00 49 30 787 41 23, fax: 00 49 30 787 41 91.

Vital statistics: Number of students: July and August are the busiest months, with 200 pupils in the school (around 650 in any one year). Age: minimum 16. Maximum teaching group size: usually between 6 and 8.

Director of studies: Frau Christine Gehrmann, who welcomes students every morning. 'She's a very together, hands-on lady, very observant,' commented an ex-student, 'she knows us well, and cares.'

What it does: Courses are for two weeks minimum. A standard course consists of four 45-minute lessons per day. There are 'intensive' courses (i.e. standard plus two mini-group lessons per day, maximum five students per group). The crash course is a standard course plus one-to-one teaching. Eight-week and 12-week courses are also available, and courses for German teachers, tailor-made business courses, etc.)

What it's like: Fun, lively, international. This school recently moved out from the centre to the edge of Berlin. 'It's a hassle to find at first, and there's no underground station near by.' However these appear to be the only complaints from the young, who have a good time here and learn. Ultra-modern building, with snazzy lift, terrace for students to sit out on, coffee-making (free) area, café and canteen. The atmosphere is buzzing with energy, activity, excitement.

Morning classes are more formal – there's grammar, written work, etc.; afternoon classes split students into small groups of three, four or five for oral work, with emphasis on communication and discussion – topics may vary from the rise of neo-fascism to issues of the environment, relationships, what's going on in Europe, etc.

Staff are young, bouncy, enormously hard-working, and all are university graduates. 'Constantly communicating with us,' comments a student. 'You couldn't help but learn,' said another, 'it was German, German, German all the time.' A counsellor is on hand to iron out any problems. There's a very strong programme of extracurricular activities: visits to theatres, concerts, museums, etc. in the afternoons and evenings, which link in with class work, and are 'going on all the time'. These are not obligatory, but prices are included in the overall fee. German tends to be spoken on outings by students who sign on from different classes within the school for what takes their fancy; 'Good, because you meet more people that way.' 'A staff member leads all outings.

Berlin has something of a thirties feel about it now, with cabarets, theatres and a hectic night-life. Students go to pubs, beer gardens, visit the old Jewish quarter, corners of erstwhile East Berlin, etc. Young, international students are the norm (North American, Japanese, French, Scandinavian and some Brits). It's a young people's city, with sculptures being erected in gaps where the Wall used to be, galleries sprouting up everywhere, a sense of history in the making – with 'all the drawbacks of a big city too,' warns a student; 'It's big, people are fairly unfriendly, getting around is difficult.' Unlike other German cities, which are plush and organized, Berlin has plenty of scruffy, poor areas; it's a melting-pot. The school, according to one parent, 'is a safe haven, and well structured'.

Accommodation: The school recommends host families where students can stay. There's a shortage of good ones, alas, and there have been one or two complaints about lodgings in unsuitable areas.

GOETHE INSTITUT (Düsseldorf)

Box 10 26 03, 40017 Düsseldorf, tel: 00 49 21 19 929 90, fax: 00 49 21 17 710 84.

Vital statistics: Age: minimum 18 ('to 83'); average age: 25–30. Maximum teaching group size: 15; maximum for business courses: 18.

Director: Herr Alois Ilg. A truly inspiring, thoughtful teacher: 'I could have listened to him for hours,' reports our contributor. Nice, friendly, five-star communicator. Ilg says he 'treats the students as customers', and has a business contract with them.

What it does: Runs various short 'intensive' courses (of different lengths – two weeks, six weeks, eight weeks). It's a modular system at 'up to seven levels'. The school majors in business German for e.g. the tourism industry. It prepares candidates for the Prufung Wirtschaftsdeutsch International which is run in association with the Association of German Chambers of Commerce.

What it's like: Absolutely top-class language school for serious students. Düsseldorf is a big, rich, busy industrial city and it is not the place to come for a little learning plus a holiday. All teachers have an arts degree or diploma and are trained for one year in GFL at the Institut. The director is concerned about the quality of teaching (not a sentiment we often heard on our travels). Most of his staff are full-time teachers, though they do employ some part time in summer.

Valuable time is saved by students filling out a questionnaire and doing a proficiency test before they arrive, followed by a second, more in-depth test when they arrive. The Institut is in a huge, not too inspiring building in the centre of town on the Willi Becker-Allee – you can sit outside in summer. There is a small cafeteria inside the centre for coffee, etc., otherwise it's down the elevator and into another building to an outside canteen.

Main courses are in the morning – five hours, German-style – then 'mediatheque', then it's your choice: self-learning, videos, computers, etc. or you can choose to sightsee, visit factories, visit Bonn or generally go out into the outside world to put into practice what has been learnt in the morning. It is hard work. The courses concentrate on communication rather than grammar, 'so the teachers need to be very creative'. There are students from everywhere under the sun. 'Fabulous place,' comments a teacher. 'Yes it is,' volunteers an Israeli student.

Accommodation: double or single rooms in families. Host families are very carefully selected and if there are complaints, they are scratched off the list. One of the criteria of being a host family is that it 'has to love people': a nice, simple, novel idea . . .

GOETHE INSTITUT (Munich)

Sonnenstrasse 25, 80331 Munich, tel: 00 89 55 19 03 30, fax: 00 89 55 19 03 35.

Vital statistics: Age: minimum 18; the Institut has recently started a 'junior programme' for young people, but it's still 18 minimum, age 20 maximum (to avoid too many oldies spoiling the junior fun). Maximum teaching group size: depends on the course – there's a maximum of 12 for some, 14–18 for others.

Director: Herr Tilmann Waldroff.

Head of individual tuition and small groups: Frau Barbara Thoma.

What it does: The Institut runs morning courses of eight weeks, 24 lessons a week of 45 minutes each; afternoon courses of four weeks, 24 lessons a week; also super-intensive courses, evening classes, and courses for individuals and small groups; special courses for e.g. the hotel business; weekend courses, pronunciation courses, etc. It offers a comprehensive set of state-recognized exams from the 'Grundstufe' to the 'Sprachdiplom'.

What it's like: The HQ of the famous state-sponsored institution, something like our British Council. Thorough, traditional (in its best sense) and rigorous teaching, with a firm emphasis on grammar. 'No videos, no films, not much role play,' said an ex-student, disappointed to find it was all a bit like the old school. That said, this school is good, with friendly and experienced staff (from young and lively to older, staider), and some of the criticism you may hear could be from the competition (which finds it impossible to compete with the strength of the Institut) and the pupils looking for a more *gemütlich* atmosphere.

The Centre is upstairs in a large street two stones' throw from the main station. The entrance hall is decorated with posters showing colours: 'Gelb – Sie sprechen Deutsch', neatly demonstrating the use of different senses, which other institutions we noted pay lip-service to. There is a drinks-vending machine but no meals on site. Smoking is relegated to the small balcony at the back of the building – there is a lack of green space and places to sit.

English students tend to go in the summertime during the beer festival. Italians, French and Eastern Europeans proliferate. Munich feels provincial and 'not really a young people's city,' said a recent student who found the burghers 'rich and staid', and added despondently that it cost more than £15 to get into a club.

HEIDELBERGER SPRACHINSTITUT

Postfach 102766, D 69017 Heidelberg, tel: 00 49 62 21 16 60 07/48 07 38, fax: 00 49 62 21 16 08 99.

Vital statistics: A smallish school. Age: usually 18 +, occasional 17-year-old. Minimum teaching group size for GFL: 10, maximum 16, average 12.

Director: Herr Marschale and Frau C. Marschale. We couldn't see him – he was too busy even for five minutes, which could mean disorganization or it could simply be he thought we were touching him for money (a common tale in language guides).

What it does: Runs non-stop classes – 25 lessons a week in total, 45 minutes each lesson, four or eight weeks, also a 10-month course. If few students turn up, then fewer lessons are offered as it's more intensive. Both GFL courses and specialized language courses for advanced students are on offer, plus one-to-one teaching. Five courses are offered throughout the year for complete beginners. The school follows the Goethe Institut system. It prepares for the Zertificat Deutsch als Fremdsprache (i.e. GFL) exams.

What it's like: Cosy, in the central, old part of Heidelberg, in a two- to three-storey building which has been renovated. Everything is within walking distance: beautiful old cafés, lots of tourism, big old famous university. It's a young population, not to mention the American airbase near by. This is one of the most beautiful towns in Germany, and there's a more easy, laid-back atmosphere than in most. Language students here tend to be in their 20s. There's lots of culture and café society. It's not as high-powered as some of the courses we visited, but perfectly competent.

Accommodation: The school offers a 'dormitory' for students, and also farms out in private families. Breakfast is taken in the HFS centre.

INTERNATIONAL HOUSE LGS SPRACHKURSE
Werderring 18, D-79098 Freiburg, tel: 00 49 76 13 47 51, fax: 00 49 76 13 824 76.

Vital statistics: Number of students: fluctuates from a couple of handfuls of students in winter to 500 in summer. Age: 10 upwards. Maximum teaching group size: 10 for short summer courses; maximum 12 in a group for longer courses; maximum 7 in a class for adults.

Principal: Herr Dieter Loffner. A graduate of the University of Freiburg, Herr Loffner taught for five years at American universities before coming back to Freiburg to teach IBM employees. He expanded and went solo in '72, and moved into teaching young people.

Herr Loffner has a most sympathetic right-hand woman who showed us round – Frau Esther Muschelknautz. You will probably be dealing with the latter on a day-to-day basis – she's the one who rushes round tucking up the tinies, etc. – it's like talking to a good young housemistress at an English boarding school.

What it does: Runs summer holiday courses for 10- to 12-year-olds – maybe in groups, in *'residenz'* (i.e., boarding); three- and six-week summer holiday courses for 13- to 15-year-olds, also in *residenz*, ditto 16- to 19-year-olds. Fifteen- to 19-year-olds can also be housed in families. Twelve-month courses for 18 + university students are also offered, as well as courses for adults and companies.

Prepares for *and examines* (very unusual, this, for a private school) the language exam which is a prerequisite for studying in Germany. There are four different starting dates for the course preparing for this exam.

What it's like: Enormously useful to know about because of the courses offered for younger children. Alas, they have just (at time of writing) lost their pretty chalet for tinies in the sports centre just outside Freiburg, but are frantically looking round for another suitable building. Meanwhile, the little ones are to be taught in part of the Jugendherberge (it's a super position with light, open eating areas), but it's not ideal for young children. However it could still be your best bet. Children are programmed and tended 'non-stop' – it's more expensive therefore than courses for older children (and more exhausting). NB Frau Muschelknautz is of the opinion that two weeks is enough for a 12- to 13-year-old to be away from home in a strange environment.

Main lessons take place in the Werderring Street building which is open all year – a large old house right next door to the university (handy for students to nip in and use the cafeteria). This is the hub of the school. It has a lovely big terrace and some parking space.

There's no language lab; the school started to develop video material but it has a distinctly forlorn look. A maximum of one hour of homework is expected. Classes are split into grammar, project-type work and oral. Games are used to increase 'oral capacity', e.g. students pick a victim and grill him or her on family life.

One full-day excursion a week is put on, plus one half-day one. There's one free afternoon a week for older children. Sport is 'arranged' twice a week – this is flexible, though, and 'student-led'. There's a minibus on tap for the constant scurrying to and fro picking up students from airports, stations, etc. (this costs extra, however). Students in families eat lunch with their course 'leader', but spend one day a week *with* the family (apply early to get a family near the school). Students are mainly Italian, French, Spanish – there are a few Brits, which of course is a plus for those who do find their way here. Lots of Scandinavians to be found among the older students.

Freiburg is the quintessential Small Town in Germany. It's safe – around 200,000 people – in a perfect position on the edge of the Black Forest; pretty backstreets; wide pavements; it's dominated by the university – lots of students, lots of bikes. It's the perfect place for younger children to flap their wings a bit. Older pupils might find it a bit stifling. There's bags of scope for outdoor activities: cross-country skiing, swimming in the sports centre, etc.

All in all, here is excellent pastoral care allied to serious language teaching. Calm and laid-back – perhaps almost too laid-back at times.

Accommodation: Young children are housed in the Jugendher-berge, where they are taught (there are cosy bunk rooms). Older students are housed both in the youth hostel (up to six beds in a room; *'Beatraum'* for discos; complaints about the food) and in a *residenz* belonging to the 'technical centre' which the school rents during the summer. This has a very functional, redbrick university feel – good clean accommodation (two to a room), quiet; dining hall on site, plus an arrangement with a local restaurant. There's a games pitch in the front, vines growing up the hillside at the back, in the centre of town. Older students living out (i.e. in families) will also have their own day centre to congregate in, by the time you read this.

ITALIAN

Learning Italian should be pure joy. It is a wonderful sound, just listening to it is music; the people are warm-hearted, generous, laid-back and friendly and interested in you. (The other side of the coin is that some Italians are hopelessly unbusinesslike.) Expect to come back with a thousand different hand gestures: there is great use of body language. If you've studied Latin it will help, particularly with reading. The language is relatively easy to start with – hence the one-year A-level courses offered, and: 'All they seem to need for an A in Italian at GCSE is a return ticket to Italy,' said a bemused (English) headmaster. The finer points of the language are as difficult as any other, however, so don't get despondent if you reach a plateau and appear to get stuck.

Parts of Italy are very hot in summer and not conducive to learning. Also many areas are *stuffed* with tourists. The top tourist spots are expensive (remember tourism is a huge earner). Many of the seaside places are very disappointing – overdeveloped and overcrowded.

Florence is of course wonderful for culture, but it is also full of Americans looking for the European experience; mosquitoes; and there is hardly an Italian in sight. The Florentine accent is not good – it's guttural.

Sex note: your blonde prettiness will be much appreciated here – but don't take the flattery too seriously and do expect to get your bottom pinched. Sadly, English girls have a sullied reputation in Italy. Err on the modest side in dressing – you certainly won't get into many churches and some galleries unless 'properly' dressed.

Currency note: as we write, the lira is about 2,460 to the pound, i.e. you're a millionaire. Be careful – it is so easy to muddle the *mille* with the *milione*. Your pocket money will largely be spent on the best ice-creams in the world, and on café life out there on the pavement.

Contact

The Italian Cultural Institute: 39 Belgrave Square, London SW1X 8NX, tel: 0171 235 1461, fax: 0171 235 4618.

Well worth knowing about. Will recommend courses for you. They have a wonderful library, and lots of information pamphlets. Lots of lectures if you become a member. Altogether it is your first port of call for things Italian.

The Italian State Tourist Office: 1 Princes Street, London W1R 7RA, tel: 0171 408 1254, fax: 0171 493 6695.

Understaffed, but extremely helpful when it is your turn.

Italian Language Schools

ABC CENTRO DI LINGUA & CULTURA ITALIANA

57036 Porto Azzuro (LI), Isola d'Elba, tel: 00 39 565 92 01 55, fax: 00 39 565 92 01 66.

Vital statistics: Number of students: never more than 40. Age: any age officially from 16+, but exceptions can be made. Maximum teaching group size: 10 students.

Director: Sr Massimo Pasquinelli, an entrepreneurial figure of considerable charm. In his early fifties, married, with children, Sr Pasquinelli is convinced that teaching *al fresco* is a winning idea. 'Who wants to go to sunny Italy and sit inside a classroom all morning?' He stresses the 'interactive' approach adopted by his enthusiastic staff. Having hit on this highly successful formula, he is hoping to set up similar schools in Chianti and up in the hills behind Florence.

What it does: The centre caters for six different levels, from beginners to very advanced. Two-week courses are offered (some choose to stay longer), group courses (maximum of 8–10 per class) with four 45-minute daily lessons (not at weekends); two of grammar, two of conversation. The primary aim is oral practice in the use of grammar. Very intensive courses are also offered, plus individual and business Italian courses. Courses are run from May to September (book early).

What it's like: Brilliant – and it works. 'Serious study in a holiday atmosphere,' commented one student. A lovely informal family feel pervades, with students of all ages (14 to 65 at the time of our visit). The school (which opened here in 1984) is in a ravishing location, close to the celebrated mountain of Montserrat, one km from the sea. Classes are held in the open air under pines, olives and vine pergolas in the 60 acres of Mediterranean *macchia* that surround the villa.

After classes, everyone, including the teachers, piles into cars and heads for the beach. Or they go off on an expedition to one of the hill towns, for instance, or to Napoleon's villa, etc. The whole group often dines together in the evening. The teachers are all university graduates, young and fun.

Whole families come here (some members holidaying only), as well as singles and pairs, and it's particularly popular with Germans and Scandinavians (who recommend it to their friends). 'Teachers and class members all become friends,' said a German student, 'it's not like a school at all. The teachers don't just concentrate on the best in the class.' 'We did lots of activities together, and on the last day we all played a hilarious game of Trivial Pursuit in Italian,' reported a Swedish girl. Not surprisingly, people often opt to come the following year. In free time, there is heaps to do (swimming apart) on this stunningly beautiful island, with sports of all kinds (windsurfing, golf, tennis, riding, etc.). You can hire bicycles.

Accommodation: This is not a live-in school, but prices include accommodation. Options are: renting rooms in a house or flat, staying in a *pensione* or hotel, or renting a flat. The school will book accommodation for members of the family who are not actually here to do an Italian language course.

ARS GRAMMATICA
Via del Corso 12, 1-50122 Florence, tel: 00 39 55 28 31 02, fax: 00 39 55 21 79 85.

Vital statistics: Number of students: 24–30ish. Age: 16+. Maximum teaching group size: 10 ('often it's six').

Principal: Dr Elisabetta Spagnoli. Dr Spagnoli is a graduate of the University of Florence, and is married with two young children. She is very Italian, with all the wonderful things that that implies: warm, full of life and enthusiasm and fun. She is also well-organized, efficient and rigorous in her approach to teaching and monitoring students' progress.

Dr Spagnoli has recently taken on a partner, Dr Gaia Pieraccioni, to be in charge of the teaching.

What it does: Concentrates absolutely on the Italian language – there are six levels, like a ski school – G1, G2, G3, etc. (where 'G' = 'General'), plus specialized, more high-powered courses. Private lessons are also offered, as well as conversation-only courses, tailor-made courses – everything to do with the language. Also available are some 'culture' courses, including History of Italian Opera and History of Art, all taken in Italian, an excellent way to build on a good base of the language.

In the summer there is also 'full immersion in a Tuscan villa' – small groups are given six hours' tuition a day, and when that's over, you chat to the teacher and go swimming, riding, etc.

What it's like: The school is near the centre of Florence, up a hundred stairs, and currently occupies three rooms – one with a stunning view of the Duomo (worth signing on just for this). Dr Spagnoli is hoping to take up another floor of the house to expand into (the rooms they have are bursting), which would include a cafeteria: when we visited there were only coffee and crisps on offer.

The school is tiny. There was a preponderance of Japanese in their twenties there when we visited. However, the student profile changes, according to Dr Spagnoli, depending on the time of year.

Never mind the unfortunate name – you would be hard put *not* to learn Italian here: the staff are ultra-determined that you should. *Everything* takes place in Italian, even tricky explanations. Students are clocked in every morning and non-attendance is noted and followed up. Diplomas are handed out at the end of the course. New courses start each month.

This is excellent for the serious student whose total priority is learning the language. English yoof might find themselves a bit short of like-minded classmates, but they would be in very safe, very kind hands.

Accommodation: Give the school your dates early and *specify* what you want, says Dr Spagnoli. A room and half board in a family is around 700,000–1 million lire at time of writing.

THE BRITISH INSTITUTE OF FLORENCE

Lungarno Guicciardini 9, 50125 Florence, tel: 00 39 55 28 40 31, fax: 00 39 55 28 95 57.

Vital statistics: Number of students: approx. 150 students of Italian at the Institute's busiest month of September (and 1,000 +

students of English during the academic year). Number of staff: 28 full time; 6 part time. Maximum teaching group size for language courses: generally 10; maximum class size for cultural classes: generally no limit, but 10 for cooking.

Director: Dr Frank Woodhouse B.Com., MA, Ph.D., who read Italian at Cambridge and has held this wonderful post since 1988. He previously taught Italian at Cambridge, and came here 'to be romantic, but I'm not now'. Runs the place with a gentle rein and occasionally helps out with teaching.

What it does: The Institute offers Italian for foreigners, English for Italians, at different levels – non-beginners are tested. There are cooking courses in Italian in the kitchen of a restaurant (which looked good fun); business Italian; the ubiquitous History of Art, including A-level courses in this; and 'mini-breaks' in e.g. Siena; also one-year A-level Italian; plus drawing courses (see Hands-on Art chapter, p. 238); short courses in exotic subjects such as Language in Opera (Italian opera, that is . . .) are also available, and even, sometimes, Etruscan Studies. Summer courses change yearly: check them first. Wonderful evening lectures.

What it's like: The Institute feels like a corner of old England, although Italian is spoken everywhere. It's lively, bustling, teeming with Italians coming to learn English, which is a good thing, as it makes for opportunities for joint outings ('especially to the pizzeria') and two-way conversation practice (fostered by the Institute). This is one of the very few places in Florence where you have some hope of getting to speak with the natives, but there are lots of English employees. The Institute is praised with faint damns and reservations by educationalists. Detailed results of Italian and History of Art A-level courses are not given, but 'typically', says Dr Woodhouse, there are '20+ students for A-level Italian each year (average grade C) and 10+ for History of Art (average grade B)'. All Italian classes are taken by Italian nationals.

Its strength is that it is Establishment, has powerful benefactors including the Prince of Wales and, until his death, Sir Harold Acton, who bequeathed the building in which the library is housed. The library is now sadly strapped for funds and could do with more modern reference books, but there is a wonderful, 'olde worlde' atmosphere on three floors with a good collection of nineteenth-century English and Italian literature and it's perfect for historians seeking out of print reference books.

The Institute formerly had some funding from the British Council, but is now self-sufficient. It was in the process of switching the textbooks used when we visited. Italian is taught directly in Italian, with occasional recourse to English 'if it absolutely saves time'. Some outstanding teaching, from a team headed by Dr Alessandro Gentili who has translated Seamus Heaney and other Irish poets into Italian (a teaching pearl before student swine, perhaps).

There are two sites, wonderfully positioned on either side of the Ponte Santa Trinità – an easy walk from one to the other. Language classes are mainly in the Palazzo Feroni, above Ferragamo's (Signora Ferragamo owns the *palazzo* and is a governor of the Institute). The teaching rooms are a bit institutional, but have names like 'Byron', 'Dickens', etc. to encourage the students of English especially. Language classes are usually in the mornings, and cultural ones in the afternoons, and: 'e poi la sera, dopo un po' di grammatica, si puo fare la pratica', as it says in the clear, comprehensive brochure under a drawing of a trattoria.

Students are of 'every age': some old, most in their twenties, mostly English and mostly with English as their first language, 'but increasingly international', points out Dr Woodhouse. A popular choice for students doing a gap year. The pastoral side is benevolent but laid-back – don't expect spoonfeeding – it's fine if you've left school and are used to being independent.

Accommodation: Allow 'a good three months' for 'something particular': you *may* enrol 'yesterday', but 'don't expect the greatest lodgings'. Dr Woodhouse acknowledges that there is a tendency for A-level students to move out of families and into apartments to economize. There have been one or two complaints from students that some of the accommodation is 'miles away, you have to take buses everywhere'.

CENTRO LINGUISTICO ITALIANO DANTE ALIGHIERI

Via dei Bardi 12, Florence, tel: 00 39 55 23 429 84, fax: 00 39 55 23 427 66.

Vital statistics: Number of students: 1,660+ a year, from 28 different countries. Age: 25 on average. Average teaching group size: 10–12.

Principal: Sr Alberto Materassi, who was in Greece when we visited. We were shown round by Stefano Barbi, il Barone de Marzzano del Vallo.

What it does: Runs largely language courses, many at university level. Minimum course length: four weeks (the school reckons nine months are needed to bring you up to a reasonable standard). Also does Culture, History of Art, 'socio-political' courses and Cooking.

What it's like: This is the big one in Florence. It has its detractors, who say it's too big, too impersonal and doesn't answer faxes, but it still plays a central role in Florentine language courses for foreigners. It is in a fifteenth-century *palazzo* with some airy views, but lots of little passages and grotty undecorated rooms – a bit spartan. However, students restore the soul in the canteen in the vaults, which is decorated with montages of past students, and wine is on tap in vast vats – take as much as you want and be legless in the afternoon.

Many of the staff have been there 15–20 years (and more). There's lots of homework and some of the sessions are quite gruelling. Grammar and conversation can be taught at different paces. A couple of trips a month are arranged to e.g. Urbino. Socialization takes place via Friday-night dinners, gallery visits and other expeditions on Saturdays.

The Centro has links with several universities, e.g. McGill in Canada, Exeter in the UK, and the place was stuffed with Americans doing the European year option when we visited.

Accommodation: At least eight weeks' notice is needed. B & b with a family is from 700,000 lire for a single room for the month; studios are from around 1 million lire for a month at time of writing.

Languages

ITALIAIDEA

Piazza della Cancelleria 85, 00186 Rome, tel: 00 39 66 83 076 20, fax: 00 39 66 89 29 97.

Vital statistics: Ages: all ages are accepted, including young children. Maximum teaching group size: 10 students.

Directors: Signora Carolina Ciampaglia and her two co-founders (all in their early thirties) were at university together in Rome, and subsequently studied abroad (in London, Edinburgh and Dublin respectively), before settling down to teach Italian. 'We saw a need for a new approach to teaching our language to foreigners in Rome, so we started the school' (in 1984). All three are full of energy, imagination, and 'mind like mad about quality', said an ex-student. They're also v. stylish.

What it does: Offers a wide variety of courses (including, for instance, classes for children from 6 to 15): one-to-one survival in Italian; culture courses on various themes; a four-week intensive course. Short-, medium- and long-term courses are on the menu, and new courses are continually added. All courses are tailor-made and flexible. Special courses are organized for American and British universities.

What it's like: A seriously impressive and professional small school, well thought of by a good number of institutional clients, foreign academics, journalists and advertising agencies working in Rome. 'You learn a lot quickly here,' reported a Canadian student, who found herself in a class with the son of an ambassador, a German au pair, a nun, and an American whose husband is in the oil business. There's lots of homework. Very much *not* a sausage factory.

The teachers are young and enthusiastic, 'who care about you – and who really know how to teach', according to an English student.

Afternoons are left free (the directors find their students prefer to organize themselves). Students here tend to be self-starters – and often pretty sophisticated to boot. There's a good library with magazines, books and videos. Masses of brochures, posters and information on museums, galleries, exhibitions, churches, etc., so you know exactly what's going on in Rome.

The school is in a neoclassical *palazzo* set in the midst of Rome's markets (between the Piazza Navona, the Piazza Farnese and the Campo dei Fiori), so much sightseeing can be done on foot. The café downstairs lets students pay 'stand-up' prices at the bar (i.e. cheaper) and sit at the tables outside where they can watch the hub of Rome's daily life.

Accommodation: The school has a list of carefully vetted families where students can stay, mostly living on the outskirts of Rome (it may take up to one hour on public transport to get to the school).

LORENZO DE' MEDICI (LANGUAGE SCHOOL AND ART INSTITUTE)

Via Faenza 43, 50123 Florence, tel: 00 39 55 28 31 42, fax: 00 39 55 239 89 20.

See main entry, Hands-on Art chapter, p. 241.

Vital statistics: Number of students: at its busiest, around 400 (including language students). Maximum language teaching group size: 12.

Dean of academic affairs and programme director: Dott. Arch. Gabriella Ganugi.

What it does: There are 120 different classes, including language courses, ranging in length from one week to six months. Intensive one-to-one teaching is an option.

What it's like: The language centre is a brisk few minutes' walk from the Ponte Vecchio, in a light, large building attached to an ex-church (which is used sometimes for lectures). Language classes are dominated by American university students (a common fate in Florence) and the language building has a slight campus-y feel. V. few Brits.

MONDO ITALIANO

Via Firenze 32, 00184 Rome, tel: 00 39 64 74 69 16, fax: 00 39 64 74 13 57.

Vital statistics: Number of students: around 300 a year (of which 70 per cent take more than one course and stay more than one month). Age: minimum for group lessons: 16, but see below. Average age of students is variable: anything from 16 to 70. Maximum teaching group size: 12 (average 6–7).

Principal: Signora Teresa Civitelli. Kind and 'so helpful,' say students. Speaks perfect English.

What it does: Runs 'standard', 'intensive', 'extensive' courses, also specialist courses, e.g. Italian for Commerce, and super private lessons for around 40,000 lire. Students younger than 16 can be taught on a private group basis (e.g. from a school) – there are special tailor-made courses for this.

What it's like: A much recommended, dynamic school in the centre of Rome which, says an ex-student, 'will go to *endless* trouble to help'. Lots of outings and speaking Italian on them. There's also riding, and archaeological courses, and special summer programmes by the sea and in the countryside.

Accommodation: All the accommodation provided is within walking distance of the school. If you need to fund yourself a bit, the school will help you find an au pair job. A super school in a glorious city.

SPANISH

Spanish hours have powerful teenage appeal: you get up late, go to bed late. Supper at 11.30 p.m. or midnight is not uncommon – and takes some getting used to. 'It can be *awful* starting lessons at nine in the morning,' said one English student. This is a country geared to young people, given the sun, the great outdoors, sport, cafés, and street life even in the smallest village, plus the Spanish love of children. The Spanish tend to be gregarious and non-stop talkers; youths band together in (friendly) gangs. Staying with a family works particularly well in Spain – it is instant total immersion. Family life is not as we know it; they tend to be close-knit, often numerous, sometimes extended (live-in grannies, heaps of cousins), and guests get passed around within their peer group.

Expect huge lunches, and think siestas. Easter is a particularly good time to go: almost everywhere there are *Semana Santa* (Holy Week) celebrations. In the heat of summer, many of the big cities are deserted by the natives. Madrid, in particular, is a no-go zone mid-summer: it's burningly hot and expensive (though not compared to the rest of Europe). Even some seaside spots are unbearably hot at midday. 'It was so hot in August,' said an English 16-year-old, 'that the family didn't really leave the house till about five in the afternoon.'

There is a huge variation in the quality of teaching of the Spanish language in Spain itself, and some of it does not compare well with much else in Europe. This may be because Spaniards themselves are (usually) rotten linguists. What you want to learn is Castilian (not e.g. Catalan). Salamanca is the place to go – it's overloaded with language schools and overflowing with students. This is the Oxford of Spain, and it claims the purest spoken Spanish.

Beware of unstructured classes, *laissez-faire* attitudes, vagueness about timetables, an easy-going lack of precision and pressure in Spanish language schools. Choose with care. Make absolutely sure you know what you are getting, and do not take *mañana* for an answer. And, by the way, we found the Spanish Tourist Office not really very helpful.

Contact

The Instituto Cervantes: 22–3 Manchester Square, London W1M 5AP, tel: 0171 935 1518, fax: 0171 935 6167.

This was formerly the Spanish Institute, and is now one of about 29 similar institutes (all bearing the same name) throughout the world which exist to promote everything to do with the Spanish language and culture.

The Instituto holds much information on every aspect of Spanish culture and runs language courses (five mornings a week for four weeks, throughout the year, to four different levels; there are also longer, less intensive courses). The Instituto also arranges cultural activities: a very useful place for English students of Spanish.

Instituto Cervantes: 169 Woodhouse Lane, Leeds LS2 3AR, tel: 01532 461741, fax: 01532 461023. Does a similar job to the sister branch.

The Spanish Embassy: 24 Belgrave Square, London SW1X 8QA, tel: 0171 235 5555, fax: 0171 259 5392.

Spanish Language Schools

CENTRO DE CULTURA Y ESTUDIOS

Carmen de las Cuevas, Cuesta de los Chinos, 15 Albayzin, Granada 18010, tel: 00 34 58 22 10 62, fax: 00 34 58 22 04 76.

Vital statistics: Number of students: 45 maximum. Age: minimum 18. Number of staff: six; more (university graduates only) are taken on at the busiest times (July and August). Maximum teaching group size: 8.

Directors: Sr Nacho Martin and Sra Carmen Dinares (30s), both natives of Granada and university graduates.

What it does: The Centro teaches to five different levels. There's an 'intensive' course, with 15 hours of language lessons each week (i.e. three lots of five hours; all lessons last one hour) plus five hours of culture: history, art, literature, music, visits. There is a two-week minimum length for the intensive course and a maximum of four months, and many shades in between. Specialized literature courses are also available, and courses for teachers of Spanish. Students are prepared for Spanish language (DELE) certificates and diplomas, and can take the exams here. The Centro is closed from mid-December until mid-February.

What it's like: 'Fun, fun, fun,' said one English pre-A-level student, 'and I learnt a lot out of the classroom.' The school is in a fine old house, on five floors, with terraces and splendid views. There is a library and a video library, also a music library – all these are well used. Students are all given a key to the place, and can come and go at all hours, and also at weekends. Nacho Martin reckons that 'if students have self-confidence, they learn much quicker', and he and his staff make a point of boosting students' confidence.

The cultural aspect is part and parcel of the deal for all language students, and you're quite likely to be studying against a background of guitar music and rhythm in another classroom. The school also runs flamenco courses for Spaniards: professionals come (as students), beginners do a week, and there is an introductory course (with emphasis on rhythm and background history), which some language students choose to do as well as their language classes.

An unusual school in several respects, and with Spanish students coming here for music and dance, there is good opportunity for you to practise your Spanish.

Easter and September are the best times to be here. Tourist-ridden and steamily hot in the height of summer – but a fascinating city at all times.

Accommodation: This is arranged with local families, or in shared apartments.

Cost: Two weeks from around 30,600 pesetas.

ESCUELA HISPANA
Calle Granada 59-2, 29015 Malaga, tel and fax: 00 34 52 21 26 89.

Vital statistics: Number of students: 50–60 per month for the summer courses; 25 students per month at other times. Age: summer students: 16–17 on average. Number of staff: four permanent teachers, plus two or three more in the summer. Maximum teaching group size: 8.

Director: Sr Adolfo Barrientos, who studied at the Sorbonne, and specializes in Hispano-American Literature and Spanish and Hispano-American civilization.

Languages

What it does: Offers summer courses for young students in particular: course lengths are two, three, or four weeks. Other courses lasting two to sixteen weeks run throughout the year, taught at five different levels. All courses are intensive, with four hours of formal class work every morning; extracurricular activities are put on at least three or four afternoons per week. Commercial Spanish is also on offer.

What it's like: An extremely well-run school, with good, structured courses and plenty of extracurricular activities. Daily lessons consist of two hours on 'language structure', one hour for oral and visual comprehension and one hour for conversation. There are visits, walks in the old part of the city – where the school is situated, near the Cathedral – excursions (to Granada, Cordoba, Seville, etc.), sports, a weekly flamenco lesson; even the odd cooking lesson is thrown in. 'You are kept very busy,' said one post-GCSE student, 'you have to join in – and everyone does: it's fun.' She particularly enjoyed the debates and discussions about international affairs ('Fascinating to hear the Japanese view and what the Germans think'). Students come from all over Europe, especially Austria, Germany and Norway, and increasingly now from Japan, Australia, Canada and the USA. Shared flats are a possibility, but recommended families are on tap.

The school is run by a cooperative of university teachers ('friendly and funny, but quite firm too,' said an English student) from both Spain and South America, all of whom have at least 10 years' experience of teaching Spanish to foreigners.

Accommodation: This can be arranged with a Spanish family recommended by the school (double room and full board is the norm).

Malaga is costa-lotta territory (train-robbers, chips, casinos spring to mind) – but this school is wonderful.

ESTUDIO INTERNACIONAL SAMPERE (EIS)

Cielo 40, 11500 Puerto de Santa Maria, Cadiz, tel: 00 34 56 87 20 21, fax: 00 34 56 87 41 09.

Vital statistics: Number of students: 80 maximum. Maximum teaching group size: 9 ('but we prefer 6 or 7'). Open through the year.

Director: Srta Cristina Sampere (30s), daughter of the founders, and a graduate of Madrid University with many years of teaching experience.

What it does: The school teaches to seven levels (i.e. more than most). The lessons are 45 minutes, and there are four per day on the intensive course, six per day on the super-intensive. Short courses last two, three or four weeks. Long courses are organized per semester; they are 15, 16 or 20 weeks in length. Special courses are held four weeks before the DELE exams for teachers of the Spanish language. One-to-one teaching is also available. Minimum age: 16+.

What it's like: This is the sister branch to the school in Madrid, which was founded in the late fifties (a third branch is in Salamanca). It is still a family-run business: Cristina is one of three sisters and two brothers, all of whom are involved, 'and of course my parents are teaching and visit regularly'. The accent is on individual attention in small groups. All the teachers are women, 'because I believe women are better teachers,' says Cristina; 'But my brothers don't agree!' Student involvement is very much encouraged. 'They get at you if you don't join in,' said one English girl. Very practical all the way through; there is particular emphasis on everyday situations. There's daily homework, which varies between written work, reading and preparing material to discuss in class the next day. EIS have developed all their own teaching materials – books, tapes, etc. It's a popular school with Germans.

There are nine classrooms (air-conditioned – this is important), with a lemon-tree-filled patio where students meet up. Free coffee and tea are available on tap, and there is a café over the road. Activities are thrown in – you can take them or leave them. The school is in the centre of the town, which is in the Bay of Cadiz. Wonderfully untouristy, Puerto de Santa Maria is where Sevillians migrate for the summer, and is full of exuberant young Spaniards. Fabulous boat life, water skiing (if you can afford it). 'And brilliant *tapas* bars,' said an English boy. In summer, this is a bronze-and-learn Spanish course. The sea breeze keeps the temperature from being unbearable.

Accommodation: This is arranged in families that have been vetted by the school.

Cost: Two weeks' tuition and accommodation: 85,000 pesetas.

HISPANIA CENTER

Calle Pozo Hilera 5, 37002 Salamanca, tel: 00 34 23 26 48 32, fax: 00 34 23 26 48 32.

Vital statistics: Number of students: per year, variable: 'depending on grants in universities, and the worldwide economic situation'. Number of staff: three full time plus peripheral teachers. Age: 16+ minimum. Maximum teaching group size: 7.

Director: Srta Maria-Cruz Barbero (with her co-director, Srta Maria Auxiliadora Vicente – another live wire); small, dynamic, enormously energetic and enthusiastic: both directors are natives of Salamanca, and graduates of the university.

What it does: Runs courses in general Spanish. Students are mainly over 18, but you'll also find mature businessmen/women. It's four hours per day (two hours of grammar, two hours of conversation, reading and comprehension). Length of courses: two to 12 weeks. Courses are organized on beginner, elementary, intermediate and advanced levels. Language, culture and civilization are also covered at all four levels. Certificates and diplomas are awarded as applicable. The Center also teaches commercial Spanish, and is open all year.

What it's like: A teeny school up on the first floor off a main shopping street not far from the Plaza Mayor (the 'psychological centre of the city', as one tutor put it). Don't be put off by the lack of elbow-space – you will probably learn more Spanish here that elsewhere in Salamanca. 'They really gee you up,' said an educationalist. The rooms are small, though partitions can be opened up to enlarge or enclose space, a screen can be pulled down for videos; there are lots of games, lots of books on hand. Quite exceptionally personal, lively and friendly, with the lessons often going on well after official times as students are scooped up and taken to bars, parties, etc. 'It's great,' commented an ex-student, 'because they really want you to have a good time, they want you to learn Spanish, they are amazingly enthusiastic and jabber away all the time.' Staff like to organize 'intercambios' of conversation with Spanish students who are learning English and want to practise – giving foreign students the chance to meet more 'natives', plus their friends and families.

Day One consists of a test at 9 a.m. to diagnose your level, and then you're in at the deep end: speaking your own language is seriously frowned on. Excursions, films, debates, parties, outings and visits are pretty non-stop (NB Bristol Polytechnic, now West of England University, have regularly sent students here with great success). 'At first I felt thwarted at not being part of the massive university student lot,' confessed one 18-year-old. 'Then it hit me that I was getting *really* personal teaching.' Students are mainly from Japan, Germany and Britain.

Accommodation: Families for students to stay in are chosen with the utmost care (the family plus one of the directors meet new students off their bus). Full board is roughly £10 per day (less for a double room), plus clothes-washing.

Cost: Two weeks at the school cost approximately 35,000 pesetas (12 weeks for 160,000 pesetas).

INTERNATIONAL HOUSE

Calle Zurbano 8, 28010 Madrid, tel: 00 34 13 10 13 14, fax: 00 34 13 08 53 21.

Vital statistics: Age: minimum 18, though younger pupils are sometimes accepted (especially school groups: see below). Maximum teaching group size: 10, but often there are fewer. Students come from all over the world.

Director: Sra Helena Mazo, a graduate of Madrid University, who has lived in England and is in charge of the Spanish courses for foreigners. Young, attractive and very helpful.

What it does: You do four hours of Spanish language classes per day ('*intensivos*'), for a minimum of two weeks. Courses run throughout the year (they start every fortnight). Length of courses:

from two to 12 weeks. Special tailor-made courses can be arranged for groups of schoolchildren through their own teachers; one-to-one lessons are also on offer. Executive courses are available for businessmen/women; also courses for students learning to teach both Spanish and English.

What it's like: Bang in the centre of Madrid, and therefore a good choice for anyone seriously interested in spending time in the Prado, etc. Highly efficient and well organized, and very structured. Notice-boards everywhere, plenty of *va y viene* of students who are indeed international, the majority of them training to teach, so the average age of students is 22+. An extremely high standard of teaching here, as you would expect from a school with branches around the world (including London), famous for its TEFL courses. The teachers are young, jolly and sparky, all university graduates and, obviously, all have been thoroughly trained in the school's own teaching methods.

During the half-hour morning coffee break students and staff mingle and everyone talks Spanish. This café area is also cleared for regular parties. Homework (written) is set every day, and there are heaps of activities available, e.g. cultural outings and lectures, walks around old Madrid; a day trip to, for instance, Segovia, and always with a tutor. The school has a good library with periodicals, newspapers, books, etc. for students to browse through and borrow, also a video library (v. popular). There is decent space to study, read, meet. Students are given a useful manual on arrival which explains how everything works – in and out of the school (metro, buses, where the nearest bookshop is to be found, and even cartoons of some of the professors–*¿quién es quien?*).

The school is thoroughly competent and professional on all fronts. Remember that Spaniards avoid Madrid in the summer; Easter or autumn courses are your best bet.

Accommodation: The school has a residence, though they recommend staying with a family, and have masses on their books. Full board staying with a family for a fortnight is approximately £120.

Cost: Two weeks cost around 50,000 pesetas.

SALAMANCA UNIVERSITY

Cursos Internacionales, Patio de Escuelas Menores s/n, 37008 Salamanca, tel: 00 23 29 44 18, fax: 00 23 29 45 04.

Vital statistics: Number of students: 5,400 pass through each year; around 2,100 on the month-long summer courses. Age: minimum 16. Staff–student ratio:1–10. Maximum teaching group size: 8 for 'guided conversation'; between 12 and 15 for other classes. Book in by Easter for the summer sessions (but try later also).

Director: Sr Jose J. Gomez Asencio

Contact: Sra Carmen Mota, who is charming, young, vivacious, a graduate of the university here and speaks English (if you're desperate).

What it does: A vast number of options are possible. Summer courses (July, August, September) last four weeks (with a choice of three, five or six hours of classes per day); also available are six-week courses (on offer in July and August). Cultural options such as Contemporary Spanish Literature or the History of Contemporary Spain supplement the staple diet (two hours minimum per day) of language and grammar.

Other courses of variable lengths (from one to 10 weeks, or three terms) are run throughout the academic year. These include Spanish for specific purposes (e.g. business, translation); advanced courses on Spanish language and literature. Exams are held and certificates and diplomas awarded as appropriate.

The prospectus gives a summary in English (but be warned, it is complicated).

What it's like: *The* place for young foreign students to go for a fun and interesting time. It's wonderfully beautiful, with ancient buildings, courtyards, colleges, stupendous domes in honey-coloured stone, and right in the heart of the city. In fact the university, one of the oldest in Spain, *is* the heart of Salamanca (Law and Languages are its specialities). Many modern languages are taught here (including, of course, English), and students come from all over the world, especially North America, with plenty of Europeans and some Japanese, but remarkably few British.

Languages

Salamanca claims the purest Spanish is spoken here. All the teaching is in Spanish.

The place buzzes with young people and high spirits, everyone carrying books and folders, going back home for the long lunch break and trailing back again for afternoon classes (4 till 7 p.m.). 'I was horrified,' said one English parent, 'Justin's classes didn't begin until four o'clock; it seemed to be playing into his lie-abed habits.' Much time is spent in cafés on the Plaza Mayor and in little bars in the streets near the university – not always speaking Spanish, you may be sure. 'Huge fun and it's an inspiring setting,' comment students, who often make friends with Spaniards learning English, and chat away in both languages far into the night.

Lots of extracurricular activities are offered, with group excursions (very regular buses to and from Madrid, a two-hour ride away). University staff are young and dedicated: though teaching is formal, relations between staff and students are definitely informal. Homework is set daily, with considerable emphasis on the practical, for example, 'Go to the market and see what is different there from markets at home and talk about it in class tomorrow.' The university produces its own extremely good work books; it also prints literary books with guidelines and question-naires at the back (extremely useful for GCSE and A-level students), and runs its own newspaper – daily in the summer, weekly at other times – to which students are encouraged to contribute, mistakes and all. 'That was *really* good fun,' said a journalistically minded sixth-former. Students are allowed to work in the huge, many-floored library, a clever modern conversion within ancient walls.

Huge numbers of locals go away for the summer. It is not intolerably hot (35°C maximum), but it does get crowded (overcrowded, some think) in the summer, with Spaniards as well as foreigners of all sorts moving to the city for English language courses, as well as the Spanish language courses at the university. International friendships spring up.

Accommodation: Some 700 families are registered with the university to take in paying guests – make sure to ask for a real mother-father-children family. It's approx. 2,100 pesetas per day for a single room, full board, with a family (all within walking distance, the furthest afield is twenty minutes away). Rooms in halls of residence are also available.

Cost: A four-week course costs 67,500 pesetas for the basic three hours a day (sliding costs for other options).

OTHER COURSES RUN BY UNIVERSITIES

Barcelona: Universidad de Barcelona, Secreteria de los Cursos para Extranjeros, Plaza Universidad, 08007 Barcelona, tel: 00 34 918 42 66, fax: 00 34 302 59 47.

Barcelona is now *the* place for the young in Spain. It's not just youth culture – there is heaps of historically rooted culture on hand, and the contemporary art scene is lively. It's a huge, commercial city, and Barcelona works best for those whose Castilian is fairly well established already, otherwise there will be a right old muddle with Catalan, which is, of course, the local language. If you are choosing a family, make absolutely sure that they only speak Castilian at home.

There is a huge number of language schools, and the university runs courses for foreign students, and is well regarded.

Madrid: Cursos de Lengua y Cultura Españolas para Extranjeros, Universidad de Alcalà, Plaza de San Diego, s/n, 28801 Alcalà de Henares, tel: 00 34 1 885 40 89, fax: 00 34 1 885 41 26/40 69. Course director: Sr Francisco Moreno Fernandez.

One of Madrid's three universities, but outside the city (about half an hour away), where the temperature is tolerable even in midsummer. Alcalà is the birthplace of Cervantes. This is an ancient and famous university (its history spans seven centuries). The director of the Spanish language courses is generally reckoned to be dynamic and a brilliant organizer. The prospectus for the courses he runs is a model of clarity.

Many varieties of Spanish language courses are on offer, all geared to four basic different levels (elementary, medium, advanced, superior). Maximum group size is twenty, but they are often broken down into smaller sections within that. Minimum age: 18 years. In July and August (for three weeks) the intensive course teaches five or six hours a day. Language is taught, plus general history of Spain, contemporary Spanish literature, geography and history of art of Spain. 'Excellent courses,' comments an educationalist, 'hard work and worth while.' Similar courses are also run on a termly (one, two, or three) basis, but with only three hours' teaching per day. Also available are business and commercial Spanish courses.

Santiago de Compostela: Universidad de Santiago de Compostela, Facultad de Periodismo, Emilio Montero Cartelle/Jose Maria Folgar de la Calle, Pza. de Mazarelos, 15071 Santiago de Compostela, La Coruña, tel: 00 34 81 58 69 77, fax: 00 34 81 57 46 46.

There are two summer sessions, one in July and one in August, both for four weeks, with four hours of classes each day, with a maximum of 15 students in each group (minimum age: 16), and a total of 150 places on each course. In other words, this is not an overwhelmingly large set-up – and takes place in one of the most splendid and beloved places in Spain. There's still a tremendous pilgrimage attraction, and, alas, it's something of a tourist trap (though not the Ambre Solaire and chips variety).

6

Gap Expeditions, Working Abroad, Saving the Planet

The gap year is your big opportunity to travel. Depending on whether you are embarking this year or next year on the next stage of your life, you will have either four or sixteen months at your disposal when you leave school in June. It requires careful planning: start early (i.e. the first year of sixth form).

Seeing the world and broadening your outlook are probably your main reasons for setting off. For parents who fear their offspring may fall by the wayside (months of bumming on Bondi Beach), then organized expeditions and projects are a boon. Most aim to combine the challenge of 'doing something useful and worth while', with character building. Teaching English or working on community projects in Third World countries is one very good way to start your travels: it roots you in another culture and gives you time to take stock before setting out on your own journey.

But ask yourself first: Is it best to go straight from school to the next structured set-up? Would it be better to make your own decisions and plans? It is likely to be cheaper and just as worth while to organize your own 'project work' through contacts – godparents, local charities, your church, missionary societies, friends who have done similar charity work in Third World countries.

To keep pace with increasing numbers of 'gappers' (the recession notwithstanding) and their perceived needs, large numbers of agencies have sprung up and are running expeditions of all kinds – 'volunteer' projects, 'fieldwork', community work. All these elements may be included in an 'expedition'. Beware: much of what is on offer is exceedingly expensive, and you may just be buying an adventure holiday. Watch out for the Mickey Mouse scientific expeditions. In principle, the longer the project or expedition, the better. Inquire where the money you have to raise goes: how much is used to help the upkeep of expensive (possibly far-flung) offices and staff? How much actually goes to the needy Third World country of destination?

Some of these projects are slick commercial enterprises run by men in suits; others (this is the character-building industry, remember) are all brawn, run by ex-army chaps, hell-bent on developing courage and taking calculated risks, with emphasis on team leadership and physical skills in the great outdoors. You will need to ask yourself: What do I want to get out of all this? What can I give?

'Recruitment' may simply be on a pay-up-and-turn-up basis; or you may be put through hoops and hurdles of interviews and testing weekends. Beware of organizations which sell their expeditions to schools – do you really want to be stuck on the other side of the world with a school group, at great expense, with no interaction with others?

Shop around. Telephone. Get brochures (don't be put off if they're not on glossy paper). Look carefully at the aims of the organization. Ask questions: it is perfectly reasonable to ask the qualifications of the leaders (bearing in mind that the outdoorsy chaps won't necessarily have academic qualifications). Think about value for money.

Your key points:

* What am I going to be doing? The answer may be anything from woolly to officious, and will tell you much.
* What kind of pastoral care is there? This is relevant at HQ too: how much information and help are you given? What kind of pastoral care will there be once you arrive at your destination (important for parents, this)?
* Can they put you in touch with students who did this work last year?
* Are there offices abroad on the spot? Or project managers out there?
* Are reports made? By students, by overseeing project managers?
* Look carefully at the size of the group you will be part of – avoid anything too large.

* Go for professional, experienced leaders, particularly on adventurous expeditions.
* Don't be put off by the large sums of money involved: it will get you motivated, and it can be done. See Money chapter, p. 252.
* Closing dates for application will be given, but ring up: with the recession, there are drop-outs and fewer demands.

Here we write about some of the gap expedition organizations which we have found to be reliable.

EXPEDITIONS

BRITISH SCHOOLS EXPLORING SOCIETY

c/o Royal Geographical Society, 1 Kensington Gore, London SW7 2AR, tel: 0171 584 0710, fax: 0171 581 7995.

Director: Col. John Flemming. He explains the thinking behind the expeditions: 'Scientific research is the medium, if you like, and the excuse, and some very important research is undertaken, but the real object is the development of young people.'

What it does: Sends young people (16–20) on expeditions – all of them scientifically based – to such places as Iceland, Greenland, Alaska, Papua New Guinea, the bush of Zimbabwe, and the Himalayas. Work is frequently in cooperation with overseas research organizations, monitoring the ice-cap, wildlife, etc. Gap year expeditions take approximately 36 people for three or four months, leaving in March. Applications must be in by the February of the previous year. (Larger numbers of school students, minimum age 16½, go on shorter summer expeditions.)

What it's like: BSES is an excellent organization, very much the real McCoy, run from its (fairly chaotic) offices in the RGS building. It was founded in 1932 by Surgeon Commander G. Murray Levick, a member of Scott's 1910 Antarctic expedition, who initially put an advertisement in the personal column of *The Times*, inviting 'a small number of public school boys to join him on an adventure in Arctic Finland'. Lord Lewin, Lord Inchcape, Campbell Adamson,

Roald Dahl, etc. all took part in expeditions in their teens. These days about four-fifths of the participants are state-educated. Applicants *must* be able to get on with others in all kinds of conditions.

Expect impressively high levels of expertise and professionalism: fieldwork is led by experts drawn from the UK and host universities, the teaching and medical professions, and expedition leaders are all extremely experienced. Each expedition is divided into 'Fires', a group of about 12 people (as many as the founder could comfortably get around a camp-fire). Conditions are always challenging, sometimes hostile.

A student comments: 'The best thing was the feeling of having no cares in the world – living totally in the present, with no newspapers, no telephone.' Another admitted to being 'initially stunned by the silence and the space' in Arctic Norway.

Cost: Young explorers (YEs) need to raise approximately £2,800 for a three- to four-month trip (£2,200 for summer six-week trips).

GAP ACTIVITY PROJECTS (GAP) LTD

44 Queen's Road, Reading, Berkshire RG1 4BB, tel: 01734 594914, fax: 01734 576634.

Director: Brigadier John Cornell CBE, short, voluble, astonishingly energetic, ceaselessly enthusiastic. He works closely with the Foreign Office. He comments: 'The only skill all eighteen-year-olds have in this country is that they speak English.'

What it does: Offers voluntary work overseas to over 1,000 school-leavers, in 32 different countries at last count; anything from teaching to restoration and conservation work, to looking after the elderly (and there are some jobs in industry too). Placements are likely to be between 6 and 9 months, and a few for 4 months, starting in autumn or spring.

What it's like: GAP was originally founded in the early seventies by a group of schoolmasters, whose prime mover was at Wellington College, keen to help the enterprising young find challenging but not-too-risky jobs which would be of service to others, as well as interesting in themselves, and which could combine well with travel.

GAP's aims remain essentially the same. Critics complain at the placement fee of £395, 'Equivalent to seven days' average fees at public school,' retorts Brigadier Cornell. Others claim there's either too much or too little work: 'It took a while to realize that it was up to me; there was no one to tell me what to do,' said an ex-Gapper who taught in Malaysia; 'I had to work out the timetable – and I wasn't used to taking the initiative after all those years of being spoonfed at school!' Loneliness can be a problem: people are placed in pairs, but never in pairs of friends, because of the emphasis on getting to know yourself. (GAP is currently carrying out a survey on culture shock . . .)

Overseas agents, both local and expats, are on hand to liaise – and sometimes come in for criticism. 'I never saw the agent or heard from them,' moaned one boy. 'I stayed with my agent's family most weekends, and they were utterly wonderful,' said a girl. Project managers, based in the UK – typically retired senior teachers and ex-heads – are responsible for a particular geographical area, which they visit each year to meet with the local agents, check up on placements, and sometimes to see the Gappers on site.

At interview, expect beady questions: serious attention is paid to the letter from the candidate's headteacher, and also to the application form.

The recession notwithstanding, GAP is oversubscribed, so apply before the end of the March before you leave school, or better, before the end of the previous October; interviews are held between the following October and April. Placements are given on a first-come, first-served basis – and do not expect to get your first choice. The African countries offered, plus Malaysia, South America, Canada and Australasia, are currently the most sought-after spots.

On acceptance, Gappers are sent a fat and detailed 'bumpf' packet, put in touch with their 'pair', and then called in to a briefing – to which parents are encouraged to go (not all do so).

Cost: There's a £20 registration fee, plus a £395 payment to GAP for a job placement, plus your air fare, immunization, insurance, and, if applicable, a one- or two-week TEFL course (specially run in

London for GAP students, and costing around £120–£200). Payment to students varies from board and lodging full stop, to board and lodging plus pocket money.

PROJECT TRUST

The Hebridean Centre, Ballyhough, Isle of Coll, Argyll PA78 6TE, tel: 018793 444, fax: 018793 357.

Directors: Major Nicholas and Mrs Lavinia MacLean-Bristol, who are splendidly outgoing, enthusiastic and fun.

What it does: Sends around 200 young people (aged between $17\frac{1}{2}$ and 19) to one of 17 countries – Brazil, Cuba, Thailand, Indonesia, China, South Africa, Namibia and Japan among them – for 12 months. Work includes teaching in schools, especially English language, also science and maths. Then there are social projects, e.g. in children's homes; also outdoor work (mainly for boys), for instance jackarooing in Australia, and at Outward Bound centres.

What it's like: This has been described by one headmaster as 'the most grown-up and certainly the most dedicated of the agencies that send young people to work abroad – and certainly the one that demands the most commitment'. However, critics claim that Project Trust's selection methods are outmoded and often unrelated to what is really required in the Third World. Others consider this to be an expensively run outfit. The MacLean-Bristols are adamant that volunteers put time and not money into a local community: 'We want them to be valued for the contribution they make, we don't want hosts who require them because of money they bring in.'

Volunteers usually set off in August (often before they know their A-level results). Why the full year? 'Because it takes a while to get to know the dynamics of a country, and it's the only way to be effective,' explains Major Nicholas MacLean-Bristol, under whom Project Trust has evolved since 1968 when he initially sent three youths to Ethiopia.

Recruitment involves around 2,000 initial inquiries which are eventually reduced to just under 300 hopefuls who go to the Isle of

Coll for the selection process (October, or late January of the A-level year). This is tough, Outward Boundish and testing on many fronts. 'It's hard to give a profile of what we are looking for,' says Mrs MacLean-Bristol, 'but awareness, ability to communicate, a lively, outgoing personality and good health are all important ingredients.' Language ability is also essential – you will need to pick up some of the local lingo.

The induction course usually takes place after volunteers have been working 'in the field' for six weeks, when all the volunteers working in the same country (usually around thirty) get together. There is good care locally, often in the shape of expat wives. 'We have a posse of high-powered ladies who don't need a job as such,' says Mrs M-B, 'and who have access to their husbands' contacts, fax, etc.' Usually mothers themselves, they are often experienced hands with teenagers.

'My son went away a teenage rebel,' commented one mother; 'he had just about scraped through his exams, and the one thing he wanted was to be far away for a year: he came back far more thoughtful, more motivated, not just thinking of himself.' Mrs MacLean-Bristol comments that Project Trust is increasingly spending time counselling parents: 'We seem to have a generation who are less independent.'

Cost: Students have to raise £2,950 – and the maximum time they have to do so is ten and a half months post-selection and before setting off. This sum includes air fares and insurance. They receive bed and board plus pocket money in the field. Project Trust is good on fund-raising advice (there's a London office – 0171 490 8764, but NB Coll is the HQ – recently set up to advise on this, complete with backup kit and videos with which to excite potential donors).

RALEIGH INTERNATIONAL
27 Parson's Green Lane, London SW6 4HZ, tel: 0171 371 8585, fax: 0171 371 5116.

Chief executive: Mr Jaimie Robertson-Macleod, a smooth operator, ex-Royal Green Jackets, then ADC to Princess Grace of

Monaco for three years; next, he turned account director first at a marketing consultancy, subsequently for a PR firm, and started out at Raleigh as Commercial Director, before taking over the hot seat (in '92) from Colonel Blashford-Snell (who now runs similar but shorter leadership training programmes for adults).

What it does: Sends 1,000 'venturers' each year on expeditions lasting 10 weeks to remote parts of the globe (e.g. Chile, Zimbabwe, Malaysia, Belize). Volunteers (aged between 17 and 25) come from all over the world, but three-quarters are from Britain, mainly school- and university-leavers, also young executives and some young people at risk, referred through social services.

Community projects (e.g. building a clinic), environmental work (e.g. research at a game park) and adventure programmes (e.g. trekking, canoeing expeditions) are all built into each session.

What it's like: The organization has been criticized for being large and commercial (though strictly speaking this is an educational charity). It also comes under fire for the superficiality of the experience, owing to the short time allocated to each section of the programme. Which said, this does give an opportunity to get a taste of something completely different.

Raleigh evolved out of a programme for youth in tall ships (called Operation Drake under the aegis of the Prince of Wales); then it took to 'yomping through the jungle' (to quote an ex-staff member), and now, since 1984, emphasizes green issues plus adventure.

Expeditions leave this country in January, March, June and October, usually in groups of 100, which are subsequently subdivided into smaller groups of about ten. On arrival, everyone undergoes an induction programme, which includes such vital ingredients as basic first aid, how to mend your mosquito net, keeping kit dry, lighting fires, etc. Generous supplies of staff members, often with military backgrounds, go on each expedition.

The venturers are then subdivided into smaller groups and set off to their different project sites (accompanied by a medical officer); here they are usually in 'pretty remote' areas, and often work alongside locals, sometimes with professionals and experts (local or British: for instance, a palaeontologist from the Natural History Museum). When they have done their stint on the 'project' (community, environment or adventure), everybody goes back to base, to be regrouped again to tackle the next project.

Application is in writing first (at any time), followed by assessment weekends (cost: £20): these are ongoing and are held at numerous outposts in the UK. 'Testing,' said one girl; 'we had to be up all night, it was Outward Boundish.' But you don't need to be super-fit or super-bright. 'How you cope is all that counts.' Eighty per cent + of those that try to get on an expedition are successful. Humour and compatibility are both important. 'Enthusiasm, commitment and getting on with people matter most', according to the Raleigh HQ.

Cost: Hefty. You need to raise up to £3,000 (NB The drop-out rate by candidates has increased considerably during the recession). And you need your kit: sleeping-bag, mat, walking-boots, compass, etc., etc.

SCHOOLS PARTNERSHIP WORLDWIDE
17 Dean's Yard, London SW1P 3PB, tel: 0171 976 8070, fax: 0171 963 1006.

Founder and director: Mr James Cogan (50s), a charming idealist, who teaches English at Westminster School (he was deputy head, and was a boarding housemaster for 16 years). He was previously in the army, lived in Nigeria, and worked for a British company in South America and the Caribbean. Mr Cogan set up SPW in 1987 as a result of three Westminster boys asking him about what to do before going to university. He is totally convinced and convincing about the importance of informal learning during the link year, working 'outside institutional structures and hierarchies, and to no set syllabus, with highly educable, open-minded young adults'.

What it does: SPW is a charity, which organizes programmes of educational cooperation in Nepal, Tanzania, Zimbabwe, Namibia and India. Forty member schools in the UK pay an annual sponsorship subscription and put forward a candidate each year to teach at 'their' Third World school for a minimum of four months, usually six or nine months. Places are also available to individual students whose schools are not members: they must raise £600 (see below). English is the main subject taught, also maths and sciences, in community or government schools. There is work in children's homes and communities, and environmental programmes undertaken with local students.

What it's like: The organization is run from a small London office, with an answering machine and fax. Good health, robustness, tenacity, adaptability, willingness to be involved, natural curiosity and initiative are all needed 'in fairly large doses' by candidates. SPW is currently tightening up its methods of screening candidates from non-member schools.

Initially, volunteers meet with counterparts who have been out in the field the previous year, and briefings (minimal) are held at Westminster School. Parents are kept at bay: this is part of SPW's formula for school-leavers to practise independence and responsibility. However, parents are positively encouraged to visit their offspring during their time abroad. SPW's philosophy is that being involved at grass-roots level allows the students to become sensitive to the world's developmental and environmental problems; and that by having responsibility to move money, they can explore the real needs of a community. Most of the £600 goes towards what the *volunteers* deem to be most needed at the host school or community, whether it is dormitory windows at a school high in the mountains, buying cows which will generate cash, or purchasing necessary books.

Students are posted in pairs for mutual support (a boon for friends), and are part of a larger group (more mutual support), usually 50 to 60, but fewer in India. There are two full-time SPW representatives in each country: a local (male) indigenous director, and a field officer (white female), probably an expat. Students go out together (departures are in January, February, October and November), and start with an induction course (this includes learning the local language). Fixed dates for returning to base camp (not compulsory) are useful for coherence, feedback, problem-sorting – and fun.

Work may not be structured: 'You need to use your initiative,' said one boy who worked in Nepal, now at university. He and his partner found that the daily three hours of teaching left too much time to lie by the river and play the guitar, and so took to walking (one hour) to the nearest town, to teach in the university as well. 'The students there really wanted to learn, and tied us in knots asking tricky questions.'

There have been some reports from returning students of 'lack of organization' in the field, and also lack of liaison between SPW's London HQ and some overseas projects.

Cost: £600 (paid by member schools, transferred to the overseas school or project; less minimal administrative charges, approximately £70). The total bill at the time of writing for travel, insurance and training and including the £600, for a student from a non-member school going to work in India, was £1,297. Very good value compared with some other organizations.

SHORT SERVICE LIMITED COMMISSION

Contact: The Schools Liaison Officer, Brigadier I. W. McLaughlan OBE, or Lt.-Col. T. A. Barnard, Parsons House, Ordnance Road, Aldershot, Hampshire GU11 2AE, tel: 01252 347473, fax: 01252 347396.

An absolutely brilliant idea for gap adventure, travel, etc. *with pay*, and no need to sign your soul away, is to apply for a short-term service commission with the army. The competition is very stiff, not surprisingly, and only top-class chaps (and chapesses) are chosen. You don't have to be startlingly bright, but do need to show leadership qualities, e.g. head of the school, first eleven, etc. You spend 3 weeks at Sandhurst (normally it takes a year for longer commissions), and can choose to spend from four to eighteen months altogether.

Apart from the opportunity to travel (you might even get to the Arctic, for example), there is physical training and exercise. Some do not have responsibility but others may be commanding a a platoon. You will not be asked to go where there is active service. The majority taking this commission do not go on to join the army; the idea is to go on to be good ambassadors for the army. Many go on to be captains of industry, etc. – an example of early networking.

To get in, you have to be over 18 and under 20, recommended by the head of your school, have a UK university place (any uni), be unmarried, and pass the medical and the selection board (you are commissioned as an officer). There is only a 25 per cent acceptance rate, even with all the pre-weeding. Money: you get the lowest rate of pay for a lieutenant – £9,742 for the year at time of writing, rising to £10,406, plus allowances e.g. for uniform.

TREK FORCE EXPEDITIONS
134 Buckingham Palace Road, London SW1W 9SA, tel: 0171 824 8890, fax: 0171 824 8892.

Director and co-founder: Mr Wandy Swales, ex-Royal Marines, who was also in a parachute regiment, and formerly an expedition leader on Raleigh International (see p. 134) and Operation Drake. Mr Swales is an old and experienced hand in the expedition business, hale, hearty, talkative, relaxed. He describes himself as 'almost resident in Indonesia these days'.

What it does: Trek Force Expeditions sends between 150 and 200 young (gap and university students, occasionally older bodies fed up with everyday life) in groups of 15 and 50 for six-week expeditions, working on scientific or conservation projects in Indonesia, leaving Gatwick between March and October.

What it's like: The style here is purposely not too regimental, but very friendly and relaxed, with a serious conservation element – which can be very hard work. 'Tough, fun and incredibly fascinating,' summed up one student. Selection takes place at Scout camp in north London over various weekends; it's a useful two-way process of seeing if potential trekkers will fit in and vice versa. At the first briefing: 'I say, hello, I'm Wandy, I'll be in the rain forest with you, chopping, clearing, sweating and getting bitten like the rest of you – then I give a geography lesson.'

Near the time of departure, trekkers spend a day together, with more briefings and kit inspection. Parents may come, 'But essentially our attitude is that they're eighteen and on their own now – and we give them quite a bit of responsibility.'

The entire team dances the first night away at a disco in Jakarta, thereafter follows jungle training. Young leaders *in situ* are mostly British with some Indonesians, as are the conservationists. 'But on reflection,' said a thoughtful ex-trekker, 'I wish I had gone with a set-up where there were less Brits, more real involvement with the native peoples.' As one English boy reported: 'They couldn't understand why all these white people were over there to work for nothing, so we told them we were trying to help the environment.'

Some senior university staff have been heard to make approving noises (hardly surprising, since such experts may well head the scientific work on site, e.g. locating the long-nosed bandicoot and collecting data on local deer). Most of the work is undertaken at the request of the Indonesian Department of Forestry. The official name of this organization is the International Scientific Support Trust; it is currently looking to expand, by working in and recruiting from other countries – which may or may not be a good thing.

Cost: £2,650; includes air fare, etc. but not the kit.

Joining an Expedition is published by the Expedition Advisory Centre (£5, cheques made payable to the Royal Geographical Society (1 Kensington Gore, London SW7 2AR). This lists well over thirty organizations which offer expedition experience to individuals, and has a sensible foreword by Nigel Winser, the expedition officer at the RGS.

University students wanting to set up their own expedition should head straight for the **Advisory Centre at the Royal Geographical Society** (they deal with between 10,000 and 15,000 queries each year): here you will get brilliant and professional advice from Mrs Shane Winser.

WORKING ABROAD

This sounds like fun and may sound easy – you contact the cousins in Hong Kong, make a mint and press on around the other half of the world. In reality, jobs abroad are hard to come by and work permits are often necessary. It pays to set up contacts and placements in advance. Working abroad is a useful experience *per se*, whether it involves immersing yourself in a foreign language, learning to live with people from another culture and other backgrounds, or acts as a steady-up period mid-travels. Observe the golden rule: in Third World countries never attempt work (e.g. picking coffee beans) which can be done by the indigenous population.

Agencies and organizations which are well worth contacting:

BUNAC

16 Bowling Green Lane, London EC1R 0BD, tel: 0171 251 3472, fax: 0171 251 0215.

BUNAC stands for British Universities North American Club. This club helps students to organize working holidays in America, Canada and Australia. Information sessions are laid on both in the UK and on arrival. The organization gets you a working visa which allows you to work legally in these countries as a student for a limited period. Registration fee and membership fee is around £75.

BUNAC exists chiefly for students already on degree courses, but there are possibilities open to gap-year students who have the offer of a firm university place to work in Canada, the USA and Australia.

CAMP AMERICA

37a Queen's Gate, London SW7 5HR, tel: 0171 581 7373, fax: 0171 581 7377.

This organization sends large numbers of students to work in summer camps in the USA. Well known and well regarded, the scheme was set up (twenty-plus years ago) by the American Institute for Foreign Study, and continues to be funded by this privately run company. 'Hard work and fun,' summed up one student now at Bristol University; 'It was an instant plunge into life in the US – a stepping-stone for travelling around.'

There are different possibilities: you can use your skills and know-how (arts, crafts, sports, pony club, etc.), or work in the day-to-day running of the camps (kitchen work is especially popular, washing dishes, helping with young children, etc.). There are more than 600 camps spread all over the United States, and they vary considerably (they may specialize in sports, or be run for the handicapped, for instance). Alternatively, you could join the family companion scheme (you may be with the elderly or with children at home – a driving licence comes in handy here).

Recruitment takes place between October and April, via a wide network of interviewers all over the UK and also on the Continent. Maturity, responsibility and a real liking for American kids are essential. Graduates and teachers are also encouraged to work with Camp America, which sends around 7,000 people worldwide each year. All the placements are for nine weeks, but you can stay on (at your own expense: the air ticket is open for four months). British students are mixed in to work with students from all over the world.

Cost: It's £25 to register at the interview, plus around £140 for a placement. Travel to the destination is laid on (visas are also arranged); camp workers get board and lodging, and pocket money – between $150 and $450 – at the end of their stint.

CENTRAL BUREAU FOR EDUCATIONAL VISITS AND EXCHANGES

Seymour Mews House, Seymour Mews, London W14 9PE, tel: 0171 486 5101, fax: 0171 935 1017.

Government-run, long-established and well-known for its publications, the Central Bureau takes linguists as junior assistants in schools in France, Germany and Spain, for one, two or three ants in schools in France, Germany and Spain, for one, two or three terms. You find your own way out; board and lodging and some pocket money are offered. You need an A-level in the language of the country you will be working in, and to be deemed suitable via an interview. This is a brilliant way to learn how to teach on the hoof, to see how schools abroad work, and improve your language skills.

Also sixth-formers, gap students and teachers can apply to teach in

English language camps in Poland, Turkey and Hungary for three or four weeks in the summer. These camps are attended by children between the ages of 10 and 18. Board and lodging are provided; you pay your own way out.

'JOBS IN THE ALPS'

PO box 388, London SW1 8LX, telephone number not given.

This is well known in its field, and has been so for over twenty years, under the fierce ex-military eye of Mr Rob Tillard, who has now retired. The organization has been bought (in April '95), and is now run, by Mr Alan Mullins.

The agency sends the young in summer and winter to work in first-class hotels in famous mountain resorts (good salaries). Languages are essential (German-speakers are much sought-after, French less so). Jobs include working as night/day porters, kitchen helpers, chambermaids, dishwashers, waiters, etc. Expect nine-hour days, with two days off a week. 'I was surprised to find it was very hard work – suddenly I was in the adult professional world of work,' comments a recently returned student, adding: 'There was a firm line between ski-bums and us . . . My French and my skiing both improved a good deal.'

Emphatically, this is *not* a free holiday, but a job with skiing opportunities. British boarding-school products have run up grisly reputations in the past, as being 'arrogant, lazy, unreliable', according to one top hotelier. All this means: don't bother to apply unless you *really* mean to work: there are now heaps of young from former Eastern bloc countries 'who know how to work'. Placements are from mid-December until April, and at summer resorts from mid-June until the end of September.

PROJECT 67

10 Hatton Garden, London EC1N 8AH, tel: 0171 831 7626, fax: 0171 404 5588.

Project 67 organizes working holidays in Israel. This is the official UK representative of the kibbutz movement, and open to anyone aged between 18 and 32 (there are no interviews and you don't have to be Jewish), so long as you are fit and healthy (a doctor's certificate is essential). Eight weeks' work is guaranteed (but you don't know what or where until you arrive): 'That's the problem, because you may never get to where you want to be,' wailed one student. Work will be on a six-days-a-week, eight-hours-a-day basis, and might be indoors (cooking, etc.) or agricultural work. Free accommodation and meals and laundry are provided, plus some pocket money (up to £20 per month).

There are also placements on moshavim (cooperatives similar to the kibbutzim, but there's less emphasis on communal living). This offers outdoor work, and it's *far* harder work, with higher pay (though food is not included).

Departures are scheduled throughout the year (January and the summer being the most popular times), and the open-return ticket (plus placement fee) costs around £289. Famous for camaraderie.

For accomplished cooks, jobs might be found through cooking agencies (see Traditional Alternatives – Indoors chapter, p. 149).

Au-pair work abroad is well worth thinking about, especially if you are considering careers in nursery work or child care, or wish to learn a foreign language at grass roots. Length of stay is variable: anything from a few weeks in the summer to a year. There are a large number of agencies, and a tendency for these to mushroom up and die a sudden death: go for the long-established ones. Get a copy of *The Au Pair and Nanny's Guide to Working Abroad* (£8·95 plus £1·50 for p&p) published by Vacation Work, 9 Park End Street, Oxford OX1 1HJ, tel: 01865 241978.

Summer Jobs Abroad (£7·95) and *Work Your Way Around the World* (£9·95), plus £1·50 p&p, are available as above (they're also in good public libraries): both provide ideas for student travellers, and are regularly updated.

A most useful little booklet is *Opportunities in the Gap Year*, published by the Independent Schools Careers Organization (ISCO), 12a–18a Princess Way, Camberley, Surrey GU15 3SP, tel: 01276 21188. It costs £3·50.

Go For It by Martyn Lewis (published by Lennard Publishing, produced in association with the Prince's Trust, Drive for Youth and the Institute for Citizenship Studies, price £7·99) lists a vast number of organizations, activities, training opportunities, etc. all over the country, and is well indexed and cross-referenced.

SAVING THE PLANET

BARCLAYS YOUTH ACTION AWARDS
(in association with Youth Clubs UK)
11 St Bride Street, London EC4A 4AS, tel: 0171 353 2366, fax: 0171 353 2369.

These awards are only available to groups of people up to the age of 25 for projects which benefit the local community in any of the following categories: health and fitness; fostering creativity; community participation; international awareness; coping with change; helping young people in trouble or at risk; integrating people with a disability; environmental youth work – a wide scope. The closing date for applications is 31 March.

EARTHWATCH
Belsyre Court, 57 Woodstock Road, Oxford OX2 6HU, tel: 08165 311600, fax: 01865 311383.

Earthwatch is a charity which exists to 'improve human understanding of the planet, the diversity of its inhabitants and the processes that affect the quality of life on Earth'. Scientists of every discipline come to Earthwatch with projects, for which they need funds and volunteers. Earthwatch then matches them up with funding and paying volunteers (this means you). They directly fund up to £200 of the volunteer's costs, and give fund-raising information, which obviously works: two volunteers recently raised £1,000 in two weeks.

There are well over one hundred projects on the go at any time, from dinosaur excavations in Montana, to radio-tracking elephants in the Etosha National Game Park, and studying maternal health in

Africa. For anyone interested in science and travelling this is sheer joy
– and good value too.

THE MERLIN TRUST
The Dower House, Boughton House, Kettering, Northamptonshire
NN14 1BJ, tel: 01536 82279.

Founded in 1991, the Merlin Trust has helped people go to
Cameroon, Darjeeling, Madagascar, Nepal, Moscow, Ireland:
anywhere where they can study hardy plants, trees and shrubs that
will survive in, and enhance, British gardens. Study can be anything
from painting and photography to seed-collecting and helping on
conservation projects, but there must be a British angle: the study of
purely tropical plants, such as Malaysian orchids, won't be funded,
nor, normally, will postgraduate or highly technical laboratory
research. There are grants available at the time of writing
of up to £500 (or more) to successful young horticulturists,
whose travelling and other expenses will be paid by the
Trust. Candidates need to be at least 18 years old. 'We want
more Gertrude Jekylls, Beth Chattos and Marjory Fishes,'
explains Valerie Finnis, the honorary secretary. If this is the
clarion call you've been waiting for, send a large SAE to the above
address.

SHELL BETTER BRITAIN CAMPAIGN
Red House, Hill Lane, Great Barr, Birmingham B43 6LZ, tel: 0121
358 0744, fax: 0121 358 5250.

Grants of up to £2,000 at time of writing are awarded for any
practical project that will tangibly improve the local environment –
but only if it is undertaken by a local voluntary group (e.g., you and
your friends). Projects funded (hundreds of them) include heritage
trails, recycling schemes, the restoration of ponds, gardens, caves.

Have a look at the *Guide to a Better Britain* published by Shell. It
is an invaluable source of information on helpful organizations
from the British Hedgehog Preservation Society to Rural Action for
the Environment, plus information on how to run environmental
projects.

SHEPLEY-SHEPLEY TRUST
12 Manor Place, Edinburgh EH3 7DD, tel: 0131 226 6051, fax: 0131 225 9833.

A Scottish number: grants for 16- to 25-year-olds living in Scotland for arts projects to be undertaken in Scotland. Anything from rap, video and film to drama, literature and all the visual arts.

THE VOLUNTEER CENTRE
Carriage Road, 183 Eversholt Street, London NW1 1BU, tel: 0171 388 9888, fax: 0171 383 0448.

This is a charity organization. Ask for the department called 'Signposts'. It has a database with details of organizations in need of help up and down the country, grouped under different interests (e.g. children, outdoor work).

Alternatively, go to your local **Volunteer Bureau** (there are hundreds all over the UK). Look in the telephone directory, or ask at your local Citizens' Advice Bureau. You could be doing 'anything from pushing trolleys in hospitals to reading to the blind, and drivers (with cars) are always welcome'.

ARCHAEOLOGY

Information on archaeological digs, and how to become a volunteer, is available from the Council for British Archaeology, Bowes Morrell House, 111 Walmgate, York YO1 2UA, tel: 01904 671417, fax: 01904 671384. They publish *British Archaeology*, which not only lists projects and opportunities, as well as short courses on training excavations, but also gives updates on current issues in archaeology.

Post-excavation work is often easier to find than excavation work itself. Contact the Museum of London Archaeology Service, tel: 0171 972 9111, or the Newham Museum Service, tel: 0181 472 4785, for further information.

7

Traditional Alternatives
— Indoors

BUTLING

THE IVOR SPENCER SCHOOL OF BUTLERS
12 Little Bornes, Alleyn Park, Dulwich, London SE21 8SE, tel: 0181
670 8424, fax: 0181 670 0055.

Head: Mr Ivor Spencer (70s), *the* toastmaster. Quietly unassuming (as all true butlers should be), Mr Spencer is very proud of his course and occasionally teaches himself, but most of the teaching is done by his assistant, Donald Weedon.

What it does: There are two five-week courses held each year, starting in October and March (private courses are held in the USA). The courses take place at the Queen's Hotel, Church Road, Crystal Palace, London.

What it's like: The courses provide training in all forms of butling and how to organize a private household, how to organize large and small parties. Much of the teaching is geared towards work in the hotel trade. The good, useful basic training includes first aid, hiring staff, and buying food and wine – lots of hints and short cuts.

This is a training for life, useful to exercise during holidays, and all over the world. Ivor Spencer runs an employment register for his own students.

Courses are held in the conference room of the hotel; students are expected to wear dark suits, shirt, collar and tie, and girls to wear a dress, or a skirt and blouse. Fluent English is essential. Minimum age: 17. Mr Spencer takes up to 27 students on each course.

Cost: A course costs over £3,000.

COOKING

Cooking courses tend to be hugely expensive. This is partly, of course, because of the cost of the food and equipment. Regard this as an investment: you can make your money back faster than you would believe possible. What's more, you can do this during your holidays, or as a career, particularly if you work through agencies. Yachts, chalets, lodges in Scotland, directors' lunches and dinner parties are all possibilities. You can cook your way around the world: it is a portable skill, and it is well worth getting a qualification which will be widely recognized.

Live-in courses often cover more ground than daily courses, because they should involve you in menu-planning, and balancing a whole day's and a whole week's menus rather than just an expensive one-off. However, career chefs would probably be better opting for specialist courses.

Look for courses that will teach you to cook from a wide variety of books; you don't want too much demonstration; you do want to learn about ingredients, and a bit of theory (the chemistry of cooking) is essential if you're serious. A perk of the job is that you eat well: you may well need to go on a slimming diet after you've finished your course.

Contact

Book-A-Cook: Throop House, Throop, Dorchester, Dorset DT2 7JD, tel: 01929 471 505, fax: 01929 472 398.

Lucie Morton: 16 Star Street, London W2 1QD, tel: 0171 402 7339.

Lumley's: 85 Charlwood Street, London SW1V 4PB, tel: 0171 630 0545, fax: 0171 976 6000.

BALLYMALOE COOKERY SCHOOL
Kinoith, Shanagarry, Co. Cork, Eire, tel: 00 353 21 646785, fax: 00 353 21 646909.

The Good Gap and Sixth Form Guide

Principals: Mr Tim and Mrs Darina Allen (both 40s) who started the Cookery School in 1983. Darina, the moving light behind the cooking, came to Ballymaloe House, the hotel run by her mother-in-law, Mrs Myrtle Allen, in 1968, married Tim (who had trained as a horticulturist), and the rest, as they say – four children later – is history.

As gassy and charming an Irish couple as you would meet anywhere. Darina is currently restoring and adding to the original Victorian garden, and short gardening courses feature greatly in their summer programme, when they are not writing cookery books or dreaming up new cookery courses.

What it does: By far the most popular are the twelve-week certificate courses, starting in January and September, but there are lots of mini-courses including a cookery course for clergy (Gardening and Oriental Carpets courses are on offer as well). Book early.

What it's like: Forty-five minutes' drive from Cork, set in fabulous deep countryside, with sea views (just). There are some local students, the rest come from all over the world and from the UK (quite a lot). Most students either bring cars or bikes. The pub in the village is the only entertainment, 'but students are usually so exhausted that they only go there occasionally'. Cooking is in the converted stables; there are three kitchens and a demonstration area which will seat eighty at most, 'but we try to stick to around sixty-five,' says Tim. Regular visits are arranged to fish smokeries and oyster farms.

'One of the best-equipped cooking schools in Europe', according to foodie-king Paul Levy. Up to 44 students are taken on at a time (minimum age is 18). There's a ratio of six students to one member of staff, most of whom are home-trained, but external teachers are welcomed; 'it adds breadth'. Regular visiting lecturers teach on Wednesday afternoons, with wine-tasting in the evenings. Students work in pairs, swapping partners each week; they cook and eat their own lunch (rather a festive affair, this), and have tastings in the evening of the afternoon's demonstrations; 'they are not really that hungry thereafter', but any food left over is given to the students for supper. Students wear white hats and chef's overalls.

It's very practical, very hands-on, and: 'If the brown bread doesn't work, then throw it away, go and see one of the staff, and start again'.

Accommodation: There's self-catering for 40 in cottages (twin or single rooms).

Cost: The twelve-week certificate course costs I£3,575, plus accommodation.

BONNE BOUCHE

Lower Beers, Brithem Bottom, Cullompton, Devon EX15 1NB, tel and fax: 01884 32257.

Director: Mrs Anne Nicholls, a most engaging person, a foodie with tremendous knowledge, contagious excitement and interest in her subject, and totally professional.

What it does: Runs a four-week Professional Foundation Course four times a year (March, May, September and October). An optional extra: Business for Cooks. Short specialist courses are available too.

What it's like: A small and outstandingly good cooking school run by Mrs Nicholls and her husband (he is an ex-accountant, and does the business and the wine sides). It takes just six students at a time – and there can be personality clashes. It's extremely personal: Mrs Nicholls teaches all the way (continuity a great plus).

Most suitable for gap year students (who must be at least 18 years old) is the four-week Professional Foundation Course. This is not a doddle. Anne Nicholls makes her students work incredibly hard. She believes in seasonal foods, and in top quality. She claims truthfully that her foundation students 'tackle at least three times the amount of work covered in the same period of time under less intensive regimes'. It does not matter how much, or how little you know: this is suitable for beginners, and the more experienced may have to un-learn.

The foundation course concentrates on essential skills and techniques, menu-planning and use of leftovers, starting with basics and proceeding quickly to more complex techniques. Mrs Nicholls has devised a brilliant menu scheme, which concentrates on different meats week by week: lamb, beef, chicken, followed by the pig. Potatoes are *never* cooked the same way twice. Lunch is simple; dinner a three-course affair; then there are cakes, jams, chutneys, herb vinegars, etc., according to season, and always home-made bread.

Students work on a rota system: one is the tweeny, two cook the dinner with one assistant, one lays the table and prepares wines, etc. The following morning there is a review of the previous night's dinner: 'It reinforces what they've done the day before.' A weekly written test is set. If a student gets something wrong in the kitchen they do it again and again, until he/she gets it (e.g. mayonnaise) absolutely right.

There's a pretty garden and a herb garden right outside the kitchen, and this is a glorious part of Devon. Students are not all young (visit first with a friend to get the feel of the school for yourself) – this is a good place for career-changing men and women. Some will go straight off to cook in chalets, on yachts, in directors' dining rooms. 'Huge fun, and *really* hard work – I wasn't expecting that,' said one 18-year-old, 'but, golly, I learnt a lot.' For those wanting to go into cookery as a career, Mr Nicholls adds a Business for Cooks course which covers costing, etc. (and ends with a diploma).

Accommodation: Students live in the old, beamy whitewashed house (with Mind the Step notices everywhere, and all the rooms have private bathrooms), with high standards of creature comforts.

Cost: The four-week course (including residence and VAT) is approx. £1,450.

LE CORDON BLEU CULINARY INSTITUTE

L'Art Culinaire, 114 Marylebone Lane, London W1M 6HH, tel: 0171 935 3503, fax: 0171 935 7621.

Principal: Since 1968, Miss Lesley Grey, herself a graduate of the (old) Cordon Bleu, assisted by Mrs Susan Eckstein (who calls herself 'Sales', and knows the students well) who has been here 27 years, and was previously a teacher here.

What it does: A myriad of courses, from single demos for anyone, to three- and five-day courses; also 10-week courses starting in October, January, March and June. Each 10-week module offers six half-week courses, i.e. cuisine or patisserie to three standards. (NB Each course is complete in its own right, though students must complete the Basic course before graduating to Intermediate, and Intermediate before Superior.)

What it's like: The school is very, very professional (and very expensive with it). There are two demonstration rooms with video monitors, four brilliantly equipped kitchens with marble worktops and super stainless steel Therma cookers and fridges (refrigerated cupboards) for each student ('Not like any kitchen I'll be working in,' sighed a student). Lots of electric gadgets: pasta makers, mixers, etc. There are specially equipped pastry and *boulangerie* kitchens (where marble worktops have chilled water running through them).

Each day is divided into four parts, beginning at 9.00 a.m., 1.30, 4.30 and 7.30 p.m. (they also put on Saturday classes for children, 'Le Petit Cordon Bleu', and other short courses). Each week students get two demonstrations and two practicals on the pastry courses, and three demonstrations and three practicals on the cuisine courses. 'There are too many demonstrations', is a complaint sometimes heard.

Lots of chaps do the courses (about half the students), learning to be proper chefs. Practicals are v. gassy, with lots of chat, *and* a washer-upper. There are lots of guest lectures and guest chefs' demos on Thursdays between 5 and 7 p.m. The London Cordon Bleu was reacquired in 1990 by M André Cointreau of the Paris Cordon Bleu, and 26 master chefs migrate between the two schools (there is also an outstation in Japan). Quite a lot of foreigners come here (help given with accommodation), students of all ages and backgrounds. Students wear natty check trousers, jackets with pinnies, and buy their own kitchen sets. Chefs wear hats and clogs. All cooking terms are in French (French classes are on offer) and students can opt to do a term in Paris. Chefs in Paris, and French chefs in England, have translators.

This is a serious option: lots go off to manage chalets, yachts, etc., after the original ten-week basic cuisine. Outstanding students can become working students after the Cuisine de Base and finish the course on a scholarship as chef's assistant; and there's lots of networking for jobs.

Cost: Expensive.

THE EASTBOURNE COLLEGE OF FOOD AND FASHION

1 Silverdale Road, Eastbourne, East Sussex BN20 7AA, tel: 01323 730851, fax: 01323 416924.

Vital statistics: Number of students: 100 maximum. Age: 16+. Maximum teaching group size: 12 or 14.

Principal: Since 1986, Mrs J. E. Jenion B.Ed., MIHEC (40s), educated at Bradford Grammar School, followed by Keele University and a cordon bleu school in Paris. Came here via the British Council in the Netherlands. Mrs Jenion is fun, energetic and friendly; the girls and staff like her enormously (she was eight months pregnant when we met her). Mrs Jenion has upgraded and revamped the college, and is keen to expand.

What it does: Offers a one-term intensive cordon bleu certificate or advanced diploma. The course starts in September, January and April. There's also a three-term diploma course, with two terms spent following a foundation course (in basic cooking plus options) and the third specializing in Cookery, Catering, Sugar Craft, Fashion or Child Care. Or you can do the three-term Career Cooks or Fashion and Design courses: all courses include weekly flower arranging and word processing; there's also a Wine certificate course. There will be a two-year NNEB course from September 1995. The college can arrange for GCSE or A-level retakes, plus speech therapy (elocution) and remedial help for dyslexia, etc.

What it's like: This is not a finishing school, more a halfway house, and brilliant for the less confident. It's also popular with pre- and post-degree wannabe cooks. Good atmosphere. Classes are distinguished by colour of necktie (all girls wear uniform).

The college is housed in a row of seven Victorian houses close to the sea front, with a tiny garden at the back with barbecue. All the cooking courses are very much hands-on, there are no lectures. Homework might consist of making a soufflé. 'It doesn't feel like work, after school,' said a 17-year-old.

Lots of evening and weekend activities are put on: beauty care, first aid, sport at the David Lloyd Centre, plus sailing, windsurfing, also language and music lessons. There's a smoking room but it's miserable. The college can handle mild disabilities. A number of foreigners are on the diploma course (extra English tuition is on offer).

Getting in and on: No entrance qualifications are necessary (but a good understanding of English is essential for foreigners). They have good links with employment agencies, who find these girls 'very employable'.

Accommodation: All girls live in jolly double and single dorms. The atmosphere is traditional boarding schoolish (with a resident matron), and weekend arrangements are strictly supervised: girls have been sacked for lying about 'arrangements', and Mrs Jenion will check with parents. All meals are taken in the dining room (the food, as you might expect, is delicious), with a signing-in and -out book by the girls' door.

Cost: Fees are on a par with private boarding schools.

THE EDINBURGH COOKERY SCHOOL

Newliston, Kirkliston, Edinburgh EH29 9EB, tel: 0131 667 3960, fax: 0131 662 9320.

Principal and Owner: Mrs Jill Davidson (50s), a qualified teacher who holds a diploma in Home Economics and Business Studies (her husband is a professor of medicine).

What it does: Offers a multitude of courses including one or four weeks in the summer, and three one-term courses which can be taken either separately, or at Foundation, Intermediate, or Advanced levels; plus an Intensive Certificate which starts with a one-week refresher in January, followed immediately with two terms as for the Advanced Certificate. Longer courses include business set-up classes.

What it's like: Founded in 1987, this claims to be Scotland's only private cooking school, and is exciting and fun. Based in the converted stables of the Robert Adam-designed Newliston house (and he probably did the stables too), it is only 20 minutes from Edinburgh's Princes Street. A lovely, light conversion, with an Aga downstairs and two kitchens plus prep area above.

The school takes a maximum of 24 pupils (from 17-year-olds upwards); there's a hotchpotch of up-market gap year boys and girls and really serious students. Quite a few chaps. 'The greatest fun,' said a current student, 'I think I'll stay for the rest of the year.'

There's lots of hands-on experience, very few demonstrations, lots of practical approaches. Courses cover Fish (a whole salmon), Vegetarian and Game Cooking (and pheasant-plucking). Some flower arranging is included, and there's a wine course (including a Wine and Spirits Education Trust Certificate on longer courses). Four-week courses are said to be enough for 'cooking in shooting lodges', and that kind of thing, and are a splendid preparation for the university life. Students eat what they've cooked at lunch or take it home (cooked breakfast is very popular). Silver service waiting and pocket money opportunities are available if students help with the school's own outside catering department (Anders Drew, paying £3·50 per hour).

Students wear smart check trousers, chef's jackets, hats and clogs (there's a reduction if these are bought from Alexander's at Shandwick Place, Edinburgh). Students must also buy their own knives. Daily hours are: 9.00/9.30 a.m. to 3.30/4.00 p.m. The courses are oversubscribed, but there are waiting lists.

Cost: The four-week course costs £700 plus VAT; one term costs £1,650 plus VAT.

THE GRANGE

Whatley Vineyard, Frome, Somerset BA11 3LA, tel and fax: 01373 836579.

Director: Mr Robin Witt (30s), helped by his wife and partner, Pippa. They also run the family vineyard here.

What it does: They run an intensive four-week course, 'Basic to Béarnaise': there are seven courses held throughout the year. A wide variety of other courses is also available (specialist weekends, four days, six weeks, etc. at very different levels).

What it's like: Brilliant – fun, lively and very hands-on. The intensive four-week course covers a great deal of culinary ground and is extremely practical, with experts passing on proven short cuts, as well as e.g. the intelligent use of leftovers. There are some demonstrations. It leaves students confident, able to tackle any recipe, and with a very good knowledge of what the Grange's directors call 'everyday French', but what most of us would consider way beyond everyday. 'Terrific – and hard work,' enthuse students.

Students work in groups of about 14, and are taught by two main cooks, plus two part-timers: Rosie and Moira are everyone's favourites. A team of helpers wash up. 'Samantha learnt to cook quite wonderfully,' commented one mother, 'but she hasn't got the knack of clearing up yet.' There's lots of personal instruction and encouragement all down the line. Fat folders of recipes are to be found here, culled from all over the place.

The kitchen could be straight out of *Country Living* (gas and electricity, but the Grange does not approve of microwave). Hand-beating is done as well as using electric mixers 'because you may be cooking in a lodge in Scotland which does not have all the mod cons'. This is a live-in course; coffee and tea breaks mean that bread, cakes, pastries, jams and biscuits are made and consumed. Lunch is light, the three-course candlelit dinner is the highlight of the day, planned and prepared by the students, whose tasks are all on a rota system.

By the end, students emerge with ambitious menus suitable for directors' dining rooms, dinner parties, chalets, etc. NB Highly thought of by cooking agencies, e.g. Lumley's, p. 149.

The Basic to Béarnaise course is particularly popular with school-leavers, and in August the cooking school resounds with shrieks as the A-level results come through. (On other courses, ages are mixed, and students are mainly female.)

Accommodation: Some students live in the house, which is old grey stone and full of charm, with its own vineyard and a marvellous herb garden. Others stay locally. The whole house is prettily decorated, with flowery prints, wicker chairs and piles of glossies: 'You feel you could be staying with your godmother', as an 18-year-old put it.

Cost: The four-week course costs from around £1,440 (this includes accommodation from Mondays to Fridays).

LEITH'S SCHOOL OF FOOD AND WINE

21 St Alban's Grove, London W8 5BP, tel: 0171 229 0177, fax: 0171 937 5257.

Principal: The Hon. Mrs William Waldegrave – positive, popular and a brilliant cook. Prue Leith's partner since the early days (the school was founded in 1976) and in 1994 Mrs Waldegrave, together with Sir Christopher Bland, bought the school.

What it does: The school has a huge menu of courses, including the one-year diploma, one-term certificate, ten-week beginner's certificate, and two- or four-week courses. Particularly popular with gap year students is the three-month October to Christmas course. There are 96 full-time students, though several hundred pass through every year, by the time you include those who come for the one-off lecture or demonstration. The student–teacher ratio is eight to one.

What it's like: This is definitely a school – marks are deducted if you arrive late, the uniform consists of the traditional hat and checked trousers (boys *and* girls, though not always necessary on short courses). It's terrifically efficient, there are exceedingly high standards and courses are well taught, though they are not necessarily conducive to a lot of individual attention, with several courses running in a number of different kitchens at the same time. 'I think it feels more like being in the kitchens of a big hotel or restaurant – not at all like being in a private house,' observed one school-leaver. The kitchens are functional, and gas is used throughout.

Lots of handy hints are given for the embryo restaurateurs, with emphasis on hygiene and fire regulations, etc. You may wonder whether the demonstrations are really that useful. Is there enough hands-on experience? On the short courses, there is not much possibility of menu-planning or choice of ingredients, but you will learn to cook, albeit in what appears to be an odd order, e.g. cottage pie in week two. Sauces will take up one whole day; 'Not exactly like learning to cook for home,' wailed a girl who 'enjoyed all the blokes being here', but confessed to finding the atmosphere 'uncosy and impersonal'.

The short courses (9.45 a.m. till 4.30 p.m. five days a week) are fun and full of young students, and you will emerge a competent user of *Leith's Cookery Bible*. This is *the* fashionable name, and it's big business, internationally known and with a designer label.

For those seeking a serious career in the cookery field, this is probably where to learn your trade. Employers (cooking agencies, restaurants, catering firms, etc.) are constantly in touch with the school. For girls and boys in their gap year, or keen to learn the ropes before that, choose the four-week beginner's course held in July, or the four-week advanced course, if you're up to it, starting at the end of August.

Cost: A lot – e.g. the four-week intensive course costs from £1,174 (plus around £34 for compulsory extras, i.e. aprons, hat, *Leith's Cookery Bible*).

THE MANOR SCHOOL OF FINE CUISINE

Old Melton Road, Widmerpool, Nottinghamshire NG12 5QL, tel: 010949 81371.

Principal and owner: Miss Claire Gentinetta (30s) holds a cordon bleu diploma, and worked at The Grange (p. 156) before converting the Manor in 1987.

What it does: The school runs a variety of four- and five-day courses, and evening demonstrations, etc., plus five highly popular residential four-week courses. Eight people are taken on at any one time, as well as day students.

What it's like: A gentle, nurturing place; very much hands-on cooking, with occasional demonstrations. There are lots of good practical tips, and basic menu planning, shopping, dinner parties, freezing, jam making, etc. Flower demonstrations are given for table decoration. There is an Aga demonstration kitchen, plus a second student-oriented kitchen with all mod cons (and study chairs that adapt for left-handers!). Good practical cookery is taught, including game and offal cookery. Microwave ovens, the Aga, gas and electricity are all used.

The school is housed in a charming converted seventeenth-century manor house, known locally as Dick Turpin's house, about twenty minutes from Nottingham, surrounded by its own grounds (a couple of acres), with duck pond and stables with real horses (this is Quorn Monday country – students can bring their own horse). The day starts with a home-cooked breakfast (croissants and *pains au chocolat*) at 8.30 a.m., classes start at 9.30 a.m. There are regular candlelit supper parties, and working lunches on the lawn in summer.

A wide cross-section of students come here, from 16+ upwards. There's lots to do at weekends, with bicycles on site, excellent nearby leisure centres at Keyworth and water sports at Holmepier Point. There's also riding, walks, etc. It's a safe package, and pretty up-market. The bull terrier called Blaze is a permanent gourmand.

The school has no agency, but can place students on three months' work experience. Lots of students end up cooking on yachts, in chalets or lodges, or doing directors' lunches (particularly locally).

Accommodation: Students live in cosy, pretty bedrooms and share a sitting room and video, telly, etc., Monday to Friday. Foreign students or those from farther afield can b & b over weekends (£12·50 per night).

Cost: Good value at £989 + VAT for four weeks (including accommodation).

TANTE MARIE SCHOOL OF COOKERY
Woodham House, Carlton Road, Woking, Surrey GU21 4HF, tel: 01483 726957, fax: 01483 724173.

Principals and owners: Mr and Mrs John Childs. An ex-student, awarded the 'top cook' accolade in 1980, Beryl Childs is in charge of the teaching and student welfare, and John Childs FCA does the accounts and was playing porter with a trolley of raw ingredients when we visited (a practical man, he also 'does the drains').

What it does: Offers a one-term cordon bleu certificate course (starting in September, January and April); and a two-term intensive cordon bleu diploma (starting in September, January and April); or a three-term cordon bleu diploma (starting in September). Some cooking experience comes in handy for diploma courses. Longer courses include Practical Business Skills from John Childs.

What it's like: A much loved school which has withstood the test of time, even through a change of ownership.

There are over twenty staff, lots of hands-on experience (over 70 per cent of the time is spent cooking) and demonstrations. Maximum 12 students to a class, 24 for demonstrations: 'sleepy-making,' said one ex-student. Students graduate from manual to labour-saving devices and progress from basic cookery (plus tips and professional finishing touches), to Christmas cakes and canapés. Students are taught budget cookery (including shopping) and have a seminar on wine (a four-day Wine and Spirit Education Trust certificate course is taught for diploma students). There's also basic flower arranging.

The school is in a natty Victorian house (with fabulous stained-glass windows) on the edge of Woking, down an unmade road with cars parked everywhere. Most students drive, and either live near by or commute daily from London (the train service is good). There's a herb-filled veggie garden 'for relaxation'. Smoking is permitted outside only. Food is either eaten at lunch-time, or taken home. Basic hours are 9.30 a.m. until 4.30 p.m.

Job vacancies are advertised on the pin-board in the hall, but the principal keeps the special list of goodie jobs (e.g. cooking at Highgrove). Agencies come to the school and interview prospective cooks. Many go on to chalet or lodge cooking. 'I worked all over the world,' said an ex-student. A thoroughly good grounding is what you get here.

The one-term courses are attended almost exclusively by gap year students (the winter term is the most popular); although ages range from 16+ to 40s/50s. Overall you'll find more girls than chaps, and some of those are quite senior citizens. Some foreign students are on the courses (fluent English is needed). The maximum number of students here at any one time is 84.

Cost: From £2,200 to £2,500 per term.

DRESSMAKING

LONDON ACADEMY OF DRESSMAKING & DESIGNING
3rd Floor, 27–9 Westbourne Grove, London W2 4UA, tel: 0171 727 0221/2850.

Principal (and part owner): Mrs Pamela Parkinson, a naturalized South African-born Indian. Charming, chatty and full of enthusiasm.

What it does: Offers full-, part-time or evening classes (Tuesdays and Thursdays) and correspondence courses. The school awards its own diplomas and certificates to successful students (at extra cost). The prospectus is muddling, but basically Mrs Parkinson will teach you everything from draping to beadcraft via cushions, millinery and swimsuit-making, but no office skills ('tips' only). Courses are strong on pattern-making and adjusting.

What it's like: The school was founded in 1969. It is housed in a converted flat on the third floor between an Indian restaurant and a grocer's. The tuition is skilful and professional. There is a maximum of 25 students at any one time, and lots of individual attention. 'Full time' equals five lessons a week, 'part-time' equals three.

Students are accepted from the age of 16, there are some chaps, some schoolgirls in the holidays and for evening classes. This is not a Sloanes' haunt; a fair number of foreigners attend, and quite a lot of bored housewives, but for sheer instant experience this place is good news. You could learn basic dressmaking, pattern-cutting and designing in three weeks, flat out – and make three dresses and a skirt in the process.

Cost: Five lessons in basic dressmaking, pattern-cutting and the like costs around £120; a three-year full-time course (four and a half years for part-time students) is £5,900 at time of writing.

THE LONDON CENTRE FOR FASHION STUDIES

Bradley Close, 78 White Lion Street, London N1 9PF, tel: 0171 713 1991, fax: 0171 713 1997.

Principal: Mr Martin Shoben MA, FCI (50s), who has a string of publications on pattern-cutting and grading to his name. Mr Shoben was previously Senior Lecturer in Pattern Technology at the London College of Fashion for 21 years, and left there to start this in 1991. He is a superb teacher and really interested in people. Bearded and knowledgeable, Mr Shoben is totally immersed in fashion and all its implications, and still does serious international consultancy and lecture tours, and has lots of 'hands-on' contacts within the British fashion industry.

Mr Shoben's wife, Jenny, runs a one-year Apparel Marketing and Merchandising diploma course for aspiring fashion merchandisers, which includes 'clothing technology', i.e. pattern-making and garment manufacture as well as the more cerebral side.

What it does: An enormously adaptable two-year course is on offer, but this is less popular than the ubiquitous 'modules'. There are Saturday morning and evening courses, either for experienced designers, or for beginners. Special Friday programmes are available for 12 weeks for a kick-start into the trade, plus a 'free professional four-day start-your-own-business programme'. Courses can be mixed, added to, and students can start at any time (providing space is available).

What it's like: A brilliant, inspiring course: if you want professional stuff, this is where to come. The centre is situated opposite the Angel tube station. It is equipped with lots of professional kit, cutting-tables, sewing-machines, heavy irons and steamers. There is a feeling of purposefulness about the place. About 50 per cent of the students are British. Courses can even be tailored to allow for paid work experience (Jeff Banks is a very popular placement). Career-change people are normal here. There's no history or book-keeping on the courses, but there is lots of involvement in projects for industry. This is a serious course, 'not for dilettantes', but they could learn better here than a lot of places. Capacity for 60 students.

FLOWERS

MARY ADAMS
4 Kinnerton Place South, London SW1X 8EH, tel: 0171 235 7117.

Principal and owner: Mrs Mary Adams, qualified teacher and graduate of Constance Spry and the Inchbald School of Interior Design, with many, many years of experience from Ceylon to Suffolk. Mrs Adams taught freelance in the basement of Pulbrook & Gould for 17 years, before opening her own shop and school in '83. She is charming, gentle and in great demand internationally for her demonstrations and lecture tours; her architect son, Diccon (*sic*), does the books and holds the fort when she is away.

What it does: Mary Adams runs a variety of courses, including one-to-one teaching if need be. Four-week certificate courses in flower arranging and floristry are held in January, February, August and November for three days a week; the diploma course includes business administration, marketing, etc. Trips to Covent Garden are extra. There are lots of day classes and demonstrations from half-day sessions to three consecutive days. Children from age eight can have a taster lesson including flowers and container.

What it's like: Lovely, and not the least bit schooly. Courses take place in a tiny green-painted oasis smelling strongly of essential oils – pepperminty when we visited. Dried flowers are hanging everywhere, and there are fold-away oilcloth-covered tables to work at. Seats 36 for demonstrations. Many of the flowers she uses are 'grown privately for her'.

Five part-time teachers are on hand, otherwise Mary Adams *is* the flower school. Classes are no bigger than six for certificate courses, which means lots of individual attention. Students keep a record book of their work. Hours are 10 a.m. to noon, 1 p.m. to 3 p.m.

Students vary from 'teenagers to grannies', with the occasional chap; there's always a smattering of foreigners, and the odd estate agent learning the trade to tart up houses. Mary is madly helpful at finding successful students jobs in the trade.

Cost: The four-week certificate courses cost £1,692, the diploma course is £2,000 and the children's taster lessons are £17·50 each.

JANE PACKER

3 Lanark Road, Maida Vale, London W9 1DD, tel: 0171 286 5835, fax: 0171 266 4533.

Principal: Mrs Jane Packer, who opened her school in 1982, and is assisted by Mark Upton (30s) who trained at the Welsh College of Horticulture. Charming, talented and enormous fun, he enthuses his students with skill and expertise, helped by Packer-trained Donna.

What it does: Offers a combination, ranging from one-day Christmas, Valentine's, Easter, summer flower courses, through three-day flower-arranging or dried-flower courses, to two-week bridal and four-week Career courses.

What it's like: Courses are taught in a light airy basement with a huge raised table in the middle and flowers everywhere. Students wearing various aprons (Jane Packer ones for the qualified) stand stuffing an assortment of unlikely-looking foliage into the most marvellous shapes.

Students are taught everything, from the buying (Dutch flowers are most expensive, but last longer), through wiring, theme management; how to arrange flowers for a wedding, with matching boutonnières, bouquets and head-dresses as well as the church flowers (which they were doing for an actual wedding with *Brides* magazine in attendance when we visited), and the reception.

Costings, and how to run a shop or a business, are also on the curriculum.

No more than 10 students are taken on at any time; their ages and nationalities vary widely (this is popular with the Japanese), but there are also some school-leavers and enthusiasts who want to start a new and interesting career.

'Surprisingly tiring and very creative', was the general comment. The course was friendly, chaotic and fun. Apply early, though occasional last-minute places may arise. The courses are held in the basement of Jane's house; go down the stairs and straight in: there is no bell.

Cost: Courses are not cheap; costs vary from £75 for the one-day courses (£125 for the Christmas course), to £1,850 for the longest course.

THE LADY PULBROOK FLOWER SCHOOL

Pulbrook & Gould, Liscartan House, 127 Sloane Street, London SW1X 9AS, tel: 0171 730 0030, fax: 0171 730 0722.

Principal: Lady Pulbrook, who started Pulbrook & Gould over thirty years ago with Rosamund Gould. The Flower School opened in 1993 in the new conservatory shop.

What it does: The school offers a series of day and two-day courses: students completing three full days qualify for a diploma. There are also evening courses.

What it's like: A maximum of eight students in green pinnies work round a high table to the right of the main shop, and are highly visible to the world at large. Classes are given by Spry-trained Mrs Susie Edwards who used to do the previous P & G evening classes. Masses of unusual foliage abound, as do herbs, flowers and dried flowers. Lots of brilliant ideas are passed on (some might be money spinners). No wire or guttering is used. Courses are primarily designed for 'our customers', and include arrangements for church – mega pedestals are taught. Lots of help is given on how to pick and treat flowers, and gardening hints as well. Students when we visited were in their late twenties and thirties. All ages are welcome.

Cost: £145 per day, which includes a light lunch, coffee and flowers.

SPARSHOLT COLLEGE
See main entry on Farming, p. 188.

Director of Horticulture: Mr J. R. Dennis MHort (RHS), Cert. Ed., MIHort.

What it does: Two one-year courses are offered: the BTEC First Diploma in Floristry is open to all: 12 months' practical experience is required for the National Certificate in Professional Floristry. Remarkably popular.

What it's like: The Floristry department is a Centre of Excellence for 1994–5 and is held in a charming complex to the north of the main college, surrounded by ornamental gardens with a fountain which formed part of a previous horticulture course. Students (up to 20) work in a light, airy shed, which looks just like a classroom, and write their names on the board when they want their work to be inspected and marked.

Lots of hands-on experience here, plus visits (including to Chelsea), and information on dried flowers and grasses. This is a complete course, with students from both home and abroad (though few of these latter when we visited). Students also work in the college shop, selling and giving advice on plant care, etc. Many of the flowers used are grown in the Horticulture department.

CONSTANCE SPRY
The Flower School, Moor Park House, Moor Park Lane, Farnham, Surrey GU10 1QP, tel: 01252 734477, fax: 01252 712011.

Principals: Mr Robert and Mrs Martine Frost, who bought Constance Spry in 1990, following the demise of Winkfield. They also run the Campana International College, and both schools are based at Moor Park House.

What it does: Here is everything from daily demonstrations with visiting lecturers, foundation courses, certificate courses, diplomas in Floristry Management (20 weeks, including day placements at the London shop).

What it's like: The great household name in flower arranging, which still has a worldwide reputation. The school is in a charming mid-seventeenth-century manor house set in 75 acres near Farnham, institutionally converted for student accommodation. Teaching is done by four full-time staff, most Constance Spry trained, and extras are on call.

There is a subsidiary branch in Tokyo.

Cost: Very expensive.

FURNITURE–MAKING AND RESTORATION

DAVID CHARLESWORTH
Harton Manor, Hartland, Bideford, Devon EX39 6BL, tel: 01237 441288.

Principal and owner: Since 1974, Mr David Charlesworth (40s), who trained under Edward Baly, a founder member of the Devon Guild of Craftsmen in 1973 (after attending Bristol University). A craftsman with a commendable portfolio of serious commissions to his name, long-haired and besandalled, Charlesworth is an inspired teacher and enormous fun.

A keen surfer, he lives, with a fine collection of cats and dogs, in Harton Manor which is, in reality, an incredibly complex cottage with staircases and superb examples of Charlesworth furniture everywhere. Surfboards everywhere, too.

What it does: Courses run from three months to a year, with occasional weekend or five-day week courses if space and time permit. All courses are personally tailored, with masses of individual tuition. Students regularly get firsts at national exhibitions.

What it's like: Perched on the North Devon coast, Hartland is a haven for surfers, and, although primarily a summer tourist resort, it is good all the year round. It also has an enviable selection of shops and pubs. There's a maximum of four students, who all work happily in the large converted barn with massive dust extractors. A former student, Geoff, has partitioned off one end, from which he produces and sells in profusion desk tidies and the like.

Students work at their own benches (which they make if they want – but you don't have to, there are school benches available) from 9 a.m., technically till 4.30 or 5 p.m., but often in practice far into the night and over the weekend. Having said that, there is no feeling of compulsion, and when we visited, two of the four were in Bideford for the day. This is a relaxed place of work.

It is also highly professional, and students start by designing and making a box for their whetstones and are taught how to work in their tools. They then move on either to making their own benches, or a table with a drawer, or, as in the case of Louise, who 'couldn't even put in a screw when she came', according to Charlesworth, producing the most delightful concave framed mirror. Joints and finishes are explained in detail and all aspects of wood are seriously discussed. Students keep their own work.

Students of all ages, and from all walks of life, with one or two from abroad. Potential students should bring 'some evidence of aptitude', something they have made themselves, though there is no problem as long as the student is keen (see Louise above). Students go on either to find an apprenticeship, or set up their own workshops, though caveat: cabinet-making is a lengthy business, and commissions are hard to find unless you have the reputation of a Linley.

Accommodation: Students either rent furnished cottages or take digs locally (someone is always around to keep an eye on them).

Cost: A five-day week course costs £200; 12 weeks, £2,400. A tool kit costs extra.

BRUCE LUCKHURST
Little Surrenden Workshops, Bethersden, Kent TN26 3BG, tel: 0123 3820589.

Principal and course director: Mr Bruce Luckhurst (50), a self-confessed slave-driver, 'but the students love me'. He worked commercially in London supervising restoration for a German company. He started his own workshop in '77, and the school in '83. With over twenty-five years' experience in restoration, he is the fifth generation to have 'wood in his blood'.

What it does: The furniture-making course is divided into three modules. The first term is basic woodwork, the second term 'hand-made furniture construction', which includes finishes, and the third term includes marquetry and inlays of all sorts. Also available is a three-term restoration course, complete with veneers, patching and marquetry. All courses qualify for the relevant City and Guilds exams. Entrance is by interview (held in the Easter holidays), plus two references.

What it's like: The machine-tool workshop (COSHH regulations apply here: there are massive dust extractors) and the twin workshops are purpose-built. The furniture-making courses are very tightly structured: 'Students may not touch a project for nearly half the course', and all work is regularly assessed – there are up to fifty assessments. Students work in small groups in adjacent workshops, each with their own workbench. The work is mainly practical and hands-on, and there's lots of to-ing and fro-ing between the courses. Also lots of lectures and visits (including to the Singleton Open Air Museum – wizard – furniture and houses back to the twelfth century), plus really good tuition and skill demonstrations, also furniture history and business studies.

On the restoration course, students have to make veneers, patches, marquetry, joints, etc. before graduating to actual furniture restoration. Great emphasis is laid on conservation and traditional glues and finishes. City and Guilds exams can be taken (some cramming is needed for ancillary skills) but basically this course teaches in three terms what you might expect to learn in three years at a tech. There are visits to stately homes, auctions, and regular cross-fertilization with the furniture-makers, and students from both courses sit in on all the lectures.

There are around fifteen on both the furniture-making and restoration courses, including a few foreigners (the Channel ports are close).

Accommodation: Help is given with finding accommodation locally.

Cost: £2,150 per term, plus the cost of the basic tool kits; the courses qualify for grant aid and career development loans.

THE MYRESIDE INTERNATIONAL SCHOOL OF FURNITURE

Myreside Grange, Gifford, East Lothian, Scotland EH41 4JA, tel: 01620 810 680.

Principal and owner: Mr Anselm Fraser (30s), married to a merchant banker, Antonia, with two small children. A cousin of the Frasers of Lovat fame, he has 'always wanted to restore furniture' and his time since leaving school (Ampleforth) has been spent doing a variety of things (meat and egg wholesaling in Canada) while building up the capital to start his own school.

He trained with Michael Haywill in Sussex in 1980–81, and started the school two years later. Fraser is one of that rare breed of enthusiasts who really can teach, though he has a somewhat Highland attitude to money, and definitely operates a Robin Hood system in his charges: 'We ought to bring the locals in, this is a living business, we should be able to accommodate a few floaters' (i.e. non-payers). Children are charged for their Saturday and holiday courses according to the state of their shoes!

What it does: Most students opt for the three-term Career course, which covers all aspects of restoration, brass work, tortoiseshell, buhl, you name it. But courses are individually tailored, and students can stay on and learn more. There are also short courses – primarily for women whose husbands are golfing locally; they can bring their own furniture to repair – plus evening classes if there is enough demand, as well as holiday courses.

What it's like: Myreside is still in a state of flux, and the school operates in the Victorian cart shed which is gradually being reclaimed and marvellously refurbished, with ancillary farm buildings and a derelict farmhouse. The office-cum-kitchen also doubles as the Frasers' bedroom, behind the glass-fronted cart shed, and early morning lectures take place round the Aga with a double bed in the background. Each day starts with a 45-minute lecture on some form of restoration or history or how to make estimates.

The workshop itself, totally dust-free, is in the covered farmyard, lovely and light with a perspex roof. All wood-cutting and planing is done in the machine shop (another barn). Students and worker/apprentices work on opposite sides of the huge shed, each with his or her own colour-coordinated workbench – with all the heavy machinery on castors, and lots of safety precautions, dust-masks and space helmets everywhere. Various bits of antique furniture in assorted states of distress wait to be assessed and repaired, each piece clearly marked with the estimate given: serious antiques vie for attention with bits of lesser importance.

There's a maximum of 10 students, plus about 4 employees, including secretarial help. Hours are officially 9 a.m.–4.30 p.m., students are supervised till noon, and after that can work on as late as they want. There are regular visits to furniture auctions, museums, etc.

These are serious professional courses, and students learn the whole range of restoration techniques. They buy their own tools: there is a vogue for the old-fashioned ones, which are already worked in, and are of much better quality than the modern equivalents. Students are from all different backgrounds, with the occasional foreigner and some people making a career change. Minimum age: 18. A keen desire to learn must be shown.

Accommodation: Students are found accommodation in furnished farm cottages or in nearby Gifford.

Cost: The Career course costs £6,750 plus VAT.

INTERIOR DESIGN

THE COUNTRY HOUSE COURSE
Holmstall, Mayfield, East Sussex TN20 6NJ, tel: 01435 872275.

Principal and owner: Mrs Moreen Biron FIDDA, trained in History of Art and Architecture at the Barclay School of Architecture in London, followed by a course at the Academia in Florence and a Cert. Ed. at Sussex University; she is Tutor of Architecture at Kent University. Masses of experience, including hands-on.

What it does: Everything from A-level Interior Design (London

Art and Design with an Interior Design option – which counts as a foundation year), through to a one-year advanced full-time diploma, plus masses in between, including a five-week gap year 'module', and one-week courses for locals. There's also a summer school from the end of July to mid-August: 'a bit of everything' (interior design, garden design, etc.; maximum 12 people).

What it's like: The course is based in a charming Sussex cottage attached to the house where Mr and Mrs Biron live, everything is on a mini-scale. Lots of TLC.

A caring, nourishing atmosphere pervades, which is good for self-confidence, though classes are small (maximum 16), and less sophisticated than the London courses: indeed, the place is almost used as a finishing school by some; small and furry. Students have to produce work boards and 'esquisses' (preliminary architect's drawings). The courses are run to a very high standard, but there are no computers. Very professional teaching with masses of hands-on experience, fabric handling, and students (both sexes attend) have to make curtain headings by hand 'to see how difficult and time-consuming they are'.

There is no secretarial service, so expect to hear the answerphone during the day. There are some foreign students, and EFL is on offer. Normal hours are 10 a.m. to 4 p.m.

Accommodation: Students are found accommodation in the village, usually with families whose children are 'away at boarding school', from £70 per week all-in.

Cost: A year's course is around £7,000. Some courses are NVQd.

THE INCHBALD SCHOOL OF DESIGN

32 Eccleston Square, London SW1V 1PB, tel: 0171 630 9011/2/3, fax: 0171 976 5979.

Admissions Office: 7 Eaton Gate, London SW1 9BA, tel: 0171 730 5508/6969, fax: 0171 730 4937.

Vital statistics: Number of students: around 140 a year all told. Ages: 18–60 + . Teacher–student ratio: exceptionally high.

Founder and principal: Mrs Jacqueline Duncan (in her 60s, formerly married to interior decorator Michael Inchbald), who set up the design school in 1960. A formidable lady (shades of Thatcher), with a forceful voice in the design field – RCA, ISID, you name it. She still lectures, writes and consults.

What it does: There are three divisions to the school: Interior Design, which takes place at Eaton Gate; the Design History faculty, and Garden Design: see p. 194.

There is an almost bewildering number of courses. The school can be all things to all people; however, the main courses are the one-year ones in each of the three divisions, which can be taken one after another to give you a Master's degree. The school is perhaps best known for its interior design courses, which is what it was originally set up to do. There are also innumerable short courses, e.g. the summer Design and Drawing foundation course – from three days to 10 weeks.

What it's like: The Eaton Gate site is a tall thin London house, converted for educational use. On the whole the plasterwork is still intact, but it smacks of fifties postwar make-do-and-mend (with the exception of the principal's own office). There is a lecture room, six design studios and a computer room. There were 42 students when we visited, from all over.

There is serious project work, and homework, plus lectures; not so much hands-on curtain-making, etc., more the ideas and the costings of fabrics than the intricacies of frills and piping. That said, it is strong on basics such as plumbing and floor coverings. There are lots of working visiting tutors plus resident staff. Continual course assessment is used to grade students: 'Not many failures, about one a year'; lots of tears – the staff are good at mopping up those.

A former student and current employee wishes that the design course had more office management: 'They're frightfully good at ideas, but dodgy on the office side when it comes to ordering fabrics and checking that they have arrived in time.'

The library is based in Eccleston Square, where the Garden Design courses are held. There are masses of periodicals and reference books: the school subscribes to at least fifty art and design magazines. Hours are short, alas: 10 a.m. to 12 p.m., 1 p.m. to 3 p.m. There is a canteen in the basement of both the Eccleston Square and Eaton Gate sites, with baked potatoes, soups and sandwiches, coffee and tea ad nauseam. About 75 per cent of students are foreigners – extra English is on hand if there are problems – including Japanese, Thais (courtesy of their government), plus Canadians, Americans, Europeans, etc. It has lots of contacts, but students have been known to grumble that they came thinking it was the way into a job, but it was not. Accredited to the BAC.

Cost: Very expensive: from £3,000 for a 10-week term; £14,000+ for the interior design diploma with advanced studies.

KLC SCHOOL OF INTERIOR DESIGN

KLC House, Springvale Terrace, London W14 0AE, tel: 0171 602 8592/3, fax: 0171 602 1964.

Principal: Mrs Jenny Gibbs (40s), who started KLC in 1960 and has gone from strength to strength. Elegant, fun and bubbly: KLC perfectly mirrors Mrs Gibbs's obvious efficiency.

What it does: Everything from one-day workshops on decorative finishes, china-mending and curtain-making, through for four-week certificate courses, and a year-long diploma course. The school also does two correspondence courses (good and popular).

What it's like: This is an outstanding place, with lots of star teachers, tucked behind Olympia (handy for the tube). KLC House is a marvellously light converted warehouse, with a double-opening studio on the ground floor; there are skylights and windows as well. There's a studio and lecture theatre above.

The library is full of glossies and books written by KLC tutors, as well as reference works, and there is a pretty entrance hall and kitchen area.

The school has masses of contact with magazines: it runs an advisory service for *Ideal Home*, and puts on competitions in association with *Homes and Gardens*, *World of Interiors*, etc. They are also invited every year to take an advisory stand at the Ideal Home Exhibition. Students keep a style notebook, and study history of style as well as the psychology of colour, etc. The school is a real winner, though again employers have been heard to mutter about 'more office training on courses being a good thing'.

The courses are a combination of lectures (including planning rules) and masses of projects and hands-on work. There is homework and research with visits (usually just after the end of a project when students are mentally whacked). There are in-house and visiting tutors for specialist subjects.

Getting in: Entry is obtained by interview. No minimum qualifications are needed for the certificate or foundation courses. Minimum age: 18. Two A-levels or the equivalent are needed for the diploma course, plus artwork.

Cost: The cost is not small (e.g. £10,222·50 for the diploma).

OFFICE SKILLS

BASIL PATERSON SCHOOL OF SECRETARIAL AND BUSINESS STUDIES

Dugdale McAdam House, 22–3 Abercromby Place, Edinburgh EH3 6QE, tel: 0131 556 7695, fax: 0131 557 8503.

See main entry, Crammers chapter, p. 39.

What it does: Offers a multitude of options, ranging through various secretarial and business administration courses, to combinations of secretarial and academic studies (one-year courses); there are also 12-week intensive secretarial courses with and without shorthand. Basic touch-typing and word processing courses start every Monday throughout the term. These can be taken as 20 lessons a week or 10 lessons a week, and customized courses can be designed to meet the specific requirements of individuals or companies.

What it's like: Computer and word processing rooms are scattered throughout the buildings. Shorthand and Business Studies share facilities with EFL and the crammer side of this establishment (i.e. non-office machine rooms). Not very schooly, but B.P.'s will chase up non-attenders. Students come from all over, some on a gap year. There is strong competition for the short courses and 12-week courses, particularly in September.

Cost: The courses are not cheap. Refresher courses (10 lessons) start at £65 per week; the short courses: two weeks £250, four weeks £460; the 12-week secretarial skills course costs from £1,232 per term; the intensive secretarial course, £1,706 per term plus £300 per term foreign language supplement (French only). RSA exams are extra.

BROOKSIDE SECRETARIAL COLLEGE

3 Brookside, Cambridge CB2 1JE, tel: 012233 64639, fax: 012233 66429.

Principal: Mrs Catriona Tuson (30s), who comments that 'there is something of a revival of shorthand, possibly because of the increasing use of mobile telephones'. She also observes that a lot of boys and girls are 'extremely hazy' about the IT they learned at school, and 'they often don't know whether it was Windows or something else'.

What it does: The college offers six- and nine-month personal assistant courses, three-month intensive secretarial, and one- and four-week keyboarding courses, word processing and IT for beginners or refreshers. Part-time courses are run in all individual subjects: shorthand (Pitman's or Teeline), typewriting, word processing, setting up a database, producing spreadsheets, business English, audio typewriting, secretarial practice, book-keeping and all modern languages (for written and oral business). RSA and Pitman's examinations are available at all levels. Individual tailor-made courses can be arranged.

What it's like: The college shares the premises (taking up the ground floor and some of the basement) with Mander Portman Woodward (see Crammers chapter, p. 46), who are its owners. The rooms are light and bright, there's a very pleasant atmosphere – positive, efficient, fun. The building is close to the botanic gardens. IT and word processing are taught to groups of 6–8, otherwise the classes number 16–18.

Popular among school-leavers (and graduates) is the three-month intensive secretarial course (beginners in shorthand can go from scratch up to 80–120 words a minute), typing up to 60 words a minute. Or, three hours' tuition per day (with machines available for private practice) can bring the beginner typist from zero to 40 words a minute within a fortnight. Obviously this is used by MPW students, but they are in a minority; there's lots of fraternizing anyway, especially in the canteen (shared with MPW).

Cost: Around £1,630 for the three-month intensive course.

THE OXFORD AND COUNTY BUSINESS COLLEGE
(The Ox and Cow)
34 St Giles, Oxford OX1 3LH, tel: 01865 310100, fax: 01865 310444.

Principal: Since 1988, Miss Joy Thompson, who did a degree in Eng. Lit. with the Open University. She is into 'running small companies'; previously worked in 'fashion, publishing and engineering'. A fellow of the British Institute of Management, she thinks it important to have contact 'with real people'. Very efficient.

What it does: The college offers one-term courses starting in September (oversubscribed) and in January, offering various degrees of secretarial excellence plus French business conversation lessons once a week. These courses can stretch to two terms. Three-term courses range from executive secretarial to private secretarial plus Euro-bilingual courses with work experience in the country concerned in French, Spanish or German. Spanish and German conversation classes can be made available on demand, in conjunction with Collingham Brown and Brown (p. 41). There are also joint courses with business schools, particularly in the Netherlands and Norway.

What it's like: It's very traditional Oxford: the college is housed in a slightly scruffy, narrow building with one or two classrooms on each floor and ancillary activities stuck out the back. Classrooms are crammed with machines ranging from the slightly old-fashioned to the latest computers and laser printers. There's lots of good hands-on experience. Good backup is given; the college can and will find jobs.

Students come mainly from the fee-paying sector; there are a few boys. Classes number no more than 22 students (generally around 12–15), with some non-UK students doing either joint courses or following standard secretarial courses (extra English is on offer). Maximum number of students: about 40 on each of the short courses. 'Socially it's very good, but you spend an absolute fortune.' Courses are very popular, both for school-leavers and new graduates. It's a good place for boosting self-confidence. Age: from 16+. A minimum of five GCSEs (or equivalent) is required.

The college is associated with Schiller International University (which specializes in business studies), with campuses in Florida, Paris, Strasbourg, Heidelberg, Berlin, Engelberg and Madrid. The year course equals 29 credits towards the 124 needed for a full four-year course in the States.

Accommodation: The college also provides its own accommodation in self-catering flats or catered hostels.

Cost: The fees are reasonable – and the courses are good value.

THE OXFORD BUSINESS COLLEGE

15 King Edward Street, Oxford OX1 4HT, tel: 01865 249484, fax: 01865 247393.

Principal: Mr Stanley Hunter MA, previously head of the Marlborough College which was bought up by the Oxford Business College in January 1994. **Principal of the secretarial discipline:** Mrs Marilyn Coles (40s).

What it does: The college offers one-, two- and three-term courses in basic secretarial, intensive and executive business administration (September and January are the only entry dates for the two-term course). Two- and three-term students now only do secretarial from 1 p.m. to 5.30 p.m., leaving mornings free to do additional courses such as Marketing and Business Studies. There's an optional term of study in Spain.

What it's like: The college is tucked into an alleyway off King Edward Street, in the middle of the High Street, surrounded by other colleges and cheerful undergraduates. The Marlborough College has taken on a new lease of life since its amalgamation with this one.

Lots of gap year students come here, particularly to do the one-term September course, though they find themselves under fairly heavy pressure to stay on for longer courses. Classrooms are spread over three floors, with a collection of word processors, and (when we visited) rather sad computers (with sticky paper over the function keys) which are IBM-compatible.

Commercial French, Spanish and Italian are available throughout, plus shorthand, IT, etc. A reception area and office are on hand for practice interviews, etc. Pitman and RSA qualifications are awarded. This is a good place for computer, keyboard and business management skills, and a useful excuse to be based in the middle of Oxford. Minimum age: 16. Class size: 15. There are lots of lectures, including one on hairdressing.

Accommodation: Can be found from approximately £50 per week plus food for hostels to £600–£800 per month for two-bedroom flats.

Cost: £1,644–£1,767 per term. Languages, etc. are extra.

QUEEN'S SECRETARIAL COLLEGE
24 Queensberry Place, London SW7 2DS, tel: 0171 589 8583/8331, fax: 0171 823 9915.

Principal: Mrs Marion Feibush BA (Hons.) (40s) was educated at Strathfield Girls' High School in Sydney, Australia, and read Philosophy at University College, London, and has oodles of business administration and secretarial certificates. Mrs Feibush is an assistant examiner in Management Appreciation for the London Chamber of Commerce and Industry, and previously managed the Ra-Ra Zoo, which is really a circus, as they globe-trotted!

What it does: Everything from four-week beginners' typewriting, via desktop publishing (one week), through six-week careers skills (i.e. separate modules) to one-term intensive and two- and three-term executive secretarial courses, as well as evening courses specifically for medical and legal secretaries. The college also offers three-term marketing and administration, business studies, or European business administration courses; the latter includes French, German, Spanish or Italian (business) language. There are shorthand courses in both French and German – graduate or bilingual students are preferred for these courses. Basic secretarial and English tuition is on hand for well-qualified non-English speakers.

What it's like: The college is situated in a terraced house opposite the French Lycée; there's apple-green paint all over inside ('we are a green school: recycled paper, no smoking anywhere'), and lots of dried flowers. Marilla the lunch lady calls with exotic sandwiches, and the college has its own café. Maximum number of students: 124 (including a few chaps in the summer). Maximum class size: usually 15. It's intellectually tough: not for slackers, 'training people to be the best', and is not an easy option. There's around one hour's homework each night. This is a popular choice for girls from fee-paying schools such as Benenden, Wycombe Abbey, Downe House. Jeans are almost a uniform.

There are six or seven part-time language staff. Teaching is traditional, always with a teacher in the room; the machines are modern and upgraded (keys not covered). On offer was Word Perfect, spreadsheets, desktop publishing and Teeline and Word for Windows. Two weeks' work experience is part and parcel of longer courses, and there's the opportunity of work experience abroad.

Pastoral care is good. Students are issued with green bags full of books on the first day of term. Most famous old girl: Fergie, a.k.a. the Duchess of York. The September and January intensive courses are heavily subscribed (not so in April). A-level standard is required entry for all courses, and hard work is expected (non-workers get chucked out). There's a lengthy initial interview. Minimum age: 17+, although you'll find some mature students (Shirley Conran was one such).

Queen's is a registered recruitment agency, and the Mount-batten internship (whereby successful students' names get put up for high-powered jobs in the USA, and their fares over are paid) is a feature. A careers fair is held regularly, and there are lots of contacts with other employment agencies and good networking on the job circuit. Students can use the office facilities for completing job applications.

Accommodation: This can be arranged (Queen Alexandra's (p. 184) is popular).

Cost: From £2,100 per term (plus extra for languages); books are extra.

ST ALDATES COLLEGE

Rose Place, Oxford OX1 1SB, tel: 01865 240963, fax: 01865 242783.

Principal: Since 1994, Mrs Pauline Martin.

What it does: There's a selection of one-, two- and three-term courses, the latter two starting in September or January. A myriad of options is available on the secretarial and business executive front, plus A-level retakes and career skills courses. The September one-term courses are particularly popular with gap year people. French shorthand is on offer; also business and commercial French, German or Spanish to students with a GCSE in the language.

What it's like: The college is in a marvellously light and airy revamped building, decorated inside in pinks and blues, at the end of Rose Place, with broad staircases and scenic views. There's masses of modern machinery, with photocopying machines, etc., as well as state-of-the-art computers, word processors and switchboards. The school has its own coffee shop on site.

Maximum number of students: around two hundred, with around fourteen in each class, and ten in the one-term groups. Large numbers apply for the September one-term course. St Aldate's has links with the Mountbatten internship programme, regularly sending young women to work for a year in the States, and also has a good record of placing students in the UK.

Accommodation: This can be arranged, and costs around £50–£60 per week on a self-catering basis.

Cost: Really quite expensive (around £2,000 per term).

THE ST JAMES'S SECRETARIAL COLLEGE

4 Wetherby Gardens, London SW5 0JN, tel: 0171 373 3852, fax: 0171 370 3303.

Principal: Since April 1993, Mr Nigel Knight (40s). Ex-army (Green Jackets till 1975), then worked for Grand Met., and came to

Traditional Alternatives – Indoors

St James's from Bosworth Tutors in Northampton. Charismatic, outgoing and straight-talking, Mr Knight brooks no nonsense and tries to instil 'discipline in work and learning', and sacks for persistent absence. Keen on punctuality, girls 'must dress as for an office' – jeans are not allowed.

What it does: Courses range from three months (usually graduates or gap year students), to a six-month certificate and nine-month diploma course. Also on offer is a three-month graduates-only course in July (oversubscribed).

French, German, Spanish and Italian (written and spoken, for commercial application) can be a part of the course for those with at least GCSE in a language. French shorthand is taught; EFL is available. Two weeks' work experience is undertaken on longer courses. The three-month courses start in September, November, January, February and April. Six- and nine-month courses start in September, January and April.

There are also 'modular' courses for individual keyboard, computing and shorthand skills (Teeline) of variable length, working with tutors and tapes (the same training is available as in the three-month course, but you clock into your own timetable). Other options available include journalism and public relations courses. Refresher courses are also offered (£7 per hour).

What it's like: Extremely professional in all respects. There's a happy, fun atmosphere. The college is in a converted terraced house leading on to shared private gardens. The machines are new, and the usual desktop publishing, spreadsheet production, etc. are taught, and Word Perfect and Word for Windows. Students are graded by ability, and there's much use of headphones so students can go at their own pace. All modular students are given a thorough interview and test before they sign up, to work out a suitable programme. Having an aim in view is considered important.

A canteen and smokers' corner are located in the basement. Maximum number of students at any time: 175. Maximum class size: 22. St James's is open till 8.00 p.m. (but the normal working day runs from 9.15 a.m. to 4.15 p.m.). An up-market place, 'not a

Sloane experience,' said one, though it's popular with Sloanes. One or two lads are to be found. Minimum age is 17, but the average age is somewhere in the late twenties, taking into account the graduates and modular students (who may include bankers, lawyers, etc.).

St James's is a registered recruitment agency (and is part of the Mountbatten internship programme in New York). Mrs Baskey is a hotshot at placing people in jobs, and Mr Knight is dead keen on not helping those who won't help themselves: 'If a student says they will let someone know on Tuesday, and they don't, and lose the job, then that's tough, they've bust it.'

Accommodation: Lists are available, but Queen Alexandra's House (Bremner Road, London SW7 2QT, tel: 0171 389 1120, fax: 0171 589 3177) is the most popular. This is much used by the Royal Academy of Music, and impromptu concerts tend to feature in the evenings.

Cost: From £2,100 per term.

WETHERBY PITMAN TRAINING COLLEGES

93 High Street, Edinburgh EH1 1SG, tel: 0131 225 8626, fax: 0131 556 2552.

Also at: 35a Union Street, Aberdeen AB1 2BN, tel: 01224 582514, and at 166 Buchanan Street, Glasgow G1 2LW, tel: 0141 332 6879.

Principal: Senior partner of these colleges is Mr Tom Maclean (30s), who trained as a civil engineer. Frances Maclean, his wife, runs the Edinburgh office.

What it does: Offers a full range of computer or secretarial courses which can be taken on a part-time or on an intensive basis. The courses range from 1 week to 30 weeks. The colleges also run Pitman update courses.

The Edinburgh branch is also a language school, and offers French, Spanish, Portuguese, Danish, Russian, Hebrew, Japanese, Korean, German, Italian, Dutch, Swedish, modern Greek, Arabic, Mandarin and also English.

What it's like: This is an international franchise operation, which offers a very high standard of training. The resources department is enormous: it goes in for national marketing and advertising. Utterly adaptable and consistently on the ball, these courses are winners.

The Edinburgh branch occupies a first-floor suite of rooms, and has a busy, purposeful atmosphere, with 19 typing, 17 computing, 6 shorthand and 3 book-keeping workstations – full almost to capacity at the time of our visit.

Several members of the Maclean family are involved with running the three colleges.

Cost: Very reasonable.

WESTGATE SECRETARIAL COLLEGE

Floor C, Milburn House, Dean Street, Newcastle-upon-Tyne NE1 1LF, tel: 0191 261 7959, fax: 0191 233 0037.

Principal: Since 1983, Mr E. Mmiro, an accountant by trade.

What it does: Operates on the Wetherby system, using a loose-leaf work book. Sixty-two different subjects are offered, e.g. producing spreadsheets, desktop publishing, Word for Windows, not to mention Word, Word Perfect etc. etc., and courses are from 4 to 80 hours' duration. Shorthand and basic business French are among the many other skills taught here. Courses are taken in two-hour modules with students working at their own pace. Teeline shorthand is more popular than Pitman 2000, which is also on offer. Lots of refresher courses.

What it's like: This college operates from three rooms in busy Milburn House under the shadow of Newcastle cathedral; even the loos are protected by entry codes. Work is done using tapes; there are 12 office machines, 7 typewriters and 3 computers, and everything is new and up to date. A busy and purposeful atmosphere pervades the place. A large percentage of students come from private schools. Successful students are awarded the Wetherby's diploma. The college has good links with local employment agencies.

Cost: Very reasonable.

8

Traditional Alternatives — Outdoors

FARMING

With the increase of mechanization in farming and the decrease in farm workers, it has become progressively more difficult either to get a mud-studenting job or even a toe-hold in the industry. For pure basic practical skills, it is worth doing a short agricultural course. Time was, agricultural colleges aimed almost entirely at budding farmers. Today the base of learning has broadened considerably, taking in everything you might need to know if suddenly dropped into the country – migrating yuppies and country weekenders would also find browsing through the county college prospectuses most profitable.

Take any opportunity between school and college to do the essential COSHH and other statutory courses stipulated by the government: using a chain-saw, operating a fork-lift, sheep shearing, and spraying, welding, etc. You will not be able to do any of these things even on your own farm without the requisite courses under your belt ('We have to take these things very seriously nowadays,' says a farmer).

Contact

The National Federation of Young Farmers' Clubs: YFC Centre, The National Agricultural Centre, Stoneleigh Park, Kenilworth, Warwickshire CV8 2LG, tel: 01203 696544, fax: 01203 696559.

The Scottish Federation of Young Farmers' Clubs: Ingliston, West Lothian, Scotland, tel: 0131 333 2445.

These offices put members in touch with member organizations all over the world, particularly in Europe and Australasia (not so hot on the Americas). Well worth joining for this alone – they're tried and tested.

AGRICULTURAL COURSES

ROYAL AGRICULTURAL COLLEGE

Cirencester, Gloucestershire GL7 6JS, tel: 01285 652531, fax: 01285 650219.

Principal: Professor Arthur S. Jones B.Sc. (Dunelm), Ph.D. (Aberdeen), etc.

What it does: Among other things, the college offers a one-year degree foundation programme which covers farming basics.

By far the most popular non-degree course here is the two-year diploma in agriculture and farm management (you can't really learn enough in a year for today's modern farming techniques).

The college also runs degree courses in agriculture and farm management, international agribusiness, etc., plus lots of short courses and the statutory add-ons.

What it's like: This famous college, founded in 1845, is the oldest agricultural college in the English-speaking world, with marvellous (but much adapted) Victorian Gothic buildings and superb facilities – the computer rooms are second to none. With the aid of satellite, the exact yield of a particular field can be predicted as the combine is working (i.e., if there is a heavy yield, send another trailer to the middle of that field, by the third tree on the right) – brilliant. Also has superb labs.

The college owns over two thousand acres of farmland in three blocks. There are three main departments: the School of Agriculture, the School of Business, and the School of Rural Economy and Land Management, plus the Centre for Agricultural and Rural Skills up the road, where the short courses take place. There is a huge library (hundreds of publications are on screen and in stacks, going back into the mists of time).

There's a seriously good social life, not forgetting the Colonial Ball, the May Ball, Freshers' Ball and Christmas Ball. Masses of clubs to join – rugger, sailing, music, choir, beagling (the college has its own pack), and the Andoversford point-to-point. The jailbreak rag is still v. popular (see how far you can get on a tenner – Rio de Janeiro is the one to beat). Masses of farm visits are arranged, both here and abroad.

Class sizes vary, depending on the course. There is a huge refectory, with staggered mealtimes, and a slightly public school atmosphere, but the japes are jollier, and you don't get sacked for going OTT (though you may have to dig the local pensioners' gardens). There's very strong tutorial back-up. There are six hundred and eighty students (about 35 per cent girls and 10 per cent foreigners). Smoking is allowed in the common-room or outside only.

The college is C of E, but there are three chaplains: C of E, RC and Methodist, and all are welcome. There is a chapel on site, with a lovely student-designed Piper-like window. There are EFL and other language classes in everything from English (special needs) to Spanish, French, German, and, if there is enough interest, other languages, held in the evenings. There is a conference centre, and the college is much used by the locals – the Ladies' Luncheon Club was in progress when we visited.

All in all, this is *the* place to be if you can afford it.

Cost: From around £4,000 per annum (not counting accommodation and extras).

Accommodation: Great living accommodation (with good security) on site. Some rooms have bathrooms *en suite*. There is usually enough accommodation on site for all the first-year students who want it: any overspill goes into cottages, etc. in the neighbourhood.

SPARSHOLT COLLEGE
Sparsholt, Winchester, Hampshire SO21 2NF, tel: 01962 776441, fax: 01962 776587.

Principal: Mr L. Norman B.Sc., Ph.D. (Reading), M.Sc. (Wales), F.R.Ag.Ss., F.I.Agr.M.

Director of Agriculture: Mr T. D. Jackson B.Tech. (Hons.), Cert. Ed.

What it does: You name it, you can do it. There's a rich mix of courses on offer, from gamekeeping to deer farming and land management, 'countryside skills', horticulture, and a one-year BTEC First Diploma and NEB certificate in Agriculture, along with lots of bolt-on extras and short courses. Three-day 'taster' sessions are available in the Easter holidays. Courses are roughly divided between hands-on practical and academic work.

What it's like: Sparsholt is considered to be one of the best county agricultural colleges in the country. It's seriously good news. It was originally founded in 1899 in Old Basing and moved to the present site in 1913. It is now a huge conglomerate of 1926 redbrick buildings, and still expanding, with a magnificent glass-roofed curved library completed in 1993.

The main estate consists of 281 hectares, including 334 acres at Abbots Ann near Andover; the college also farms a further 750 acres in partnership with the Lainston Estate near by. There is a commercial deer farm (sika, fallow and a herd of red deer) and venison is produced, and eaten in the dining hall, and butchery lessons are given (but not necessarily in that order). There's a huge modern dairy unit on site.

Sparsholt has around 1,100 students plus 600 part-timers. The complex is let to holidaymakers during the vacations. There are masses of computers and a conference suite, which is used for weddings, etc. There's a student bar, launderette, a rather worn gym, but good sports grounds, with Winchester only four miles away (good bus service).

This is a huge college, and many students come daily. There are a number of students from Ireland, and quite a number of foreigners. Wardens are on site, and students are sacked for drugs offences.

Accommodation: There are three hundred study-bedrooms (around £70 per week including 10 meals in the dining hall at time of writing) – if cash is tight, then students can share; the management will put in bunk-beds. One hundred and ninety-two rooms (the modern ones) have bathrooms *en suite*.

GAMEKEEPING

THE GAME CONSERVANCY LTD

Fordingbridge, Hampshire SP6 1EF, tel: 01425 652381, fax: 01425 655848.

Contact: Mrs Liz Scott

The Game Conservancy runs regular short courses, either on site at Fordingbridge, or at various places throughout the country. They are attended by people from all walks of life, from would-be gamekeepers to shoot managers and landowners.

Courses on offer include Game Conservation and Shoot Management Week (usually in the spring) which is a serious course, covering all aspects of gamekeeping, trapping, poaching and the law, deer, fisheries, birds of prey and what not to shoot, as well as rearing and land management for shooting, plus organizing the shoot itself.

The three-day part-time Gamekeeper's course is an encapsulated version of the above, and accommodation is organized in local pubs and guest-houses. Rooms are shared.

There is also a grouse and hill keepers' course held in Scotland, and various Advisory Service Game Management Days scattered throughout the country. (The minimum age for all the above courses is 18.)

The Game Conservancy also offers a 'Young Shots Course' which is brilliant and should be made compulsory for anyone (young) who carries a gun. Accommodation for this course is with members of the Game Conservancy staff in their private houses, and transport is arranged. It is just like an old-fashioned house party – except that the booking form comes complete with all the legal bumf about travelling with a gun. There are demonstrations, discussions, practical training and gun-dog work.

Cost: It varies, but the cost is invariably hefty. There are reductions for Game Conservancy and BASC members.

GARDENING

Gardening as a career is sadly overlooked by schools and as a result, serious students tend to come to it rather late in the day as they suddenly wake up and realize that this is what they really want to do. 'The image schools have of gardening,' says a professional, 'is that it's for thicks. This is no longer the case. It has become very high-tech, and the artistic side is big business.' Consequently there has been an explosion of short courses up and down the country – *Horticultural Weekly* does a round-up every year – and you need to apply individually. There is no clearing-house system and local authority grants are discretionary.

Contact

Royal Horticultural Society Garden: Wisley, Woking, Surrey GU23 6QB, tel: 01483 224234, fax: 01483 211750. A useful source of information on all things horticultural. A bookshop is on site.

GARDEN DESIGN

THE BATH SCHOOL OF HORTICULTURE & GARDEN DESIGN

The Barn, Pound Hill House, West Kington, near Chippenham, Wiltshire SN14 7JG, tel: 01249 782702, fax: 01249 782953.

Principal: Miss Lois Stuart-Black, who organizes short garden design and allied subject courses in the magnificent barn attached to Barbara Ellis's fifteenth-century Cotswold stone house. The

Ellises' garden and commercial garden centre are next door, and are open to visitors.

What it does: There's a popular fungi-identification course. Also a much praised garden design course, ranging over two to three days. This is an excellent taster course, with good flower identification, etc., and a good nucleus of young visiting lecturers, including Mrs Ellis's daughter, and there is a strong family feel.

What it's like: A charming place (if a slightly misleading title), and particularly good if you want to give the subject a try. A maximum of 10 people are accepted on the garden courses, which are cosy and friendly, with lessons taken either in the barn or on site. Students are of all ages, with lots of students coming back; there's lunch in the Ellises' house (round the kitchen table with a glass of wine when we visited). Bring a photographic survey showing every part of your garden 'preferably when it is at its worst'!

Accommodation: B & b lists are handed out with course information.

Cost: The garden design course is around £300.

INCHBALD SCHOOL OF DESIGN
32 Eccleston Square, London SW1 1PB, tel: 0171 630 9011/2/3, fax: 0171 976 5979.

See main entry under Interior Design, p. 173.

Head of Garden Design: Mr Andrew Wilson.

The school offers three 10-week 'modular' garden design courses leading to a diploma, with lots of projects and 'research-based holiday work'. Visits are also arranged, including to the house of the principal of the school. Maximum course size: 20.

SCHOOL OF GARDEN DESIGN AT CAPEL MANOR
Capel Manor, Bullsmoor Lane, Enfield, Middlesex EN1 4RQ, tel: 01992 763849/0181 366 4442, fax: 01992 717544.

Course director: Professor David Stevens FSGD, FIHort, Governor of Capel Manor and on the RHS Shows Committee, is a regular author and broadcaster; tutors include Miss Jill Billington of *Gardeners' World* fame, and Mr John Moreland.

What it does: Among other things, the school runs a five-week course spread throughout the year, plus lots of homework, leading to the school's Certificate of Garden Design.

(It is also possible to do a two-year National Diploma in Horticulture, with 10 core and 10 specialist modules, and a six-month placement in a garden of a member of the Historic House Association.)

Getting in: Entry is obtained by interview. There is a waiting list. There is no minimum age or qualification for the five-week course, but you need to be at a certain level: it's not for beginners. (Minimum entry qualification for the National Diploma: four GCSEs at C or above, including a science.)

What it's like: Capel Manor was rescued, derelict, in 1968. Lectures take place either in the manor itself (redbrick 1750s, very elegant) or the various outbuildings, with some work done out in the 30-acre gardens. Basic principles of garden design are taught, and there's practical work. Maximum people per course: 12–15. All ages are taken on, and there are some career-changers.

The courses are good and helpful. Ideas abound in the garden itself, which includes several 'sponsored' displays, as well as scented walks, water gardens, etc., and the gardens are open to the public.

There is a busy refectory, serving rather good coffee and masses of mega sandwiches – and all-day breakfast.

Cost: Around £1,500 for the five-week course.

GARDEN PRACTICE

LACKHAM COLLEGE
Lacock, Chippenham, Wiltshire SN15 2NY, tel: 01249 443111, fax: 01249 444474.

Principal: Mr Peter Morris F.R.Ag.Ss.

Head of Horticultural Department: Mr Oliver Menhinick: a star.

What it does: Among other things, it offers a National Certificate in Horticulture, in professional gardening, or organic gardening, or turf husbandry. There's a part-time course in garden design. 'Taster' courses begin in April for the coming year.

There are also lots of add-on evening options, such as car maintenance, the Royal Yachting Association Diesel School (funnily enough), plus a host of fishing courses, pet maintenance, quilt-making, stencilling, languages, flower arranging, etc. etc.

What it's like: Lackham started as an agricultural college but has now blossomed (some would say spread like a weed) into other areas, with particularly good, imaginative teaching in the Horticultural department.

When we visited, the entire horticultural unit – all sixteen of them – were removing the plants from the bed which was about to become part of the new refectory. We then saw the same plants being stripped, pruned and put away for future use in the huge heated potting shed. This is a practical, hands-on department; students tend the ornamental gardens which surround the college, and learn the basics of fruit-growing in the 1·6-hectare orchard (there is an apple-naming day in September, when locals can bring their fruit for identification), as well as working in the glasshouses producing pot plants and flowers commercially, with polythene tunnels and the like. No minimum qualifications are needed (minimum age: 16), but keen interest is a must, and some practical experience may be necessary.

The college was founded in 1946 round an elegant Palladian building with traditional institutional add-ons (the dining hall was recently extended). There's a bar, and the usual sports facilities. There's a regular bus service from Chippenham (three miles away), and daily buses from round about. There is a mile-long drive with hideous bumps, and the college itself has spread round a motley collection of sheds and farm buildings (immaculate farm workshop as always), in the midst of a 500-acre estate.

There is a library and resource centre, a computer centre, and a bee-keeping unit; a rose garden as well as a walled garden and all that farming. All courses have learning support on offer throughout, with a strong tutorial system and backup.

The gardens are superb, with magical 'Country Attractions'

(open to the public) including rare breeds, an adventure playground and a fab agricultural museum (barns on saddle stones, a huge collection of antique farming implements, and old-fashioned traditional cheese-making), not to mention the statutory shop and glasshouses the public can make purchases in.

Accommodation: There are 220 study-bedrooms, otherwise students stay locally in digs or farm cottages.

PERSHORE COLLEGE OF HORTICULTURE

Pershore, Worcestershire WR10 3JP, tel: 01386 552443, fax: 01386 556528.

Principal: Dr David Hall

Head of Horticulture: Dr Mark Simpkin

What it does: Courses are on offer for all levels, starting with BTECs for 16-year-olds, and Higher National Diplomas, right up to B.Sc.s

What it's like: Magical. Acres of serious garden, more acres of greenhouses, organic gardens, landscape gardens, woodland gardens, and a nursery unit: 72 hectares in total, surrounding 1810 Avonbank House. Lots of jolly outings and student-inspired entertainment are organized, such as trips to the local ice rink and dry ski-slope as well as cultural visits. The college itself is about one mile west of Pershore.

The output of the commercial nursery is sold in the college garden centre, or to local garden centres or landscape contractors. There's a specialist veggie unit, as well as an organic department, and computer-controlled greenhouses. A huge library, computer rooms, and IT.

Students need to have their own knife and secateurs, goggles, safety caps and a hard lens.

Accommodation: There are three hundred study-bedrooms, plus accommodation in bedsits.

Cost: Very changeable, but the cost is reasonable compared with some courses we visited.

HORSES

CATHERSTON STUD AND EQUESTRIAN CENTRE

Hurstbourne Priors, Whitchurch, Hampshire RG28 75E, tel: 01256 892045, fax: 01256 896225.

Principal and owner: Mrs Jennie Loriston-Clarke MBE, FHS (50s), international dressage rider who represented Britain in the '72, '78, and '88 Olympics. Bubbly, enthusiastic and incredibly hard-working, she is assisted by husband Anthony and her grown-up daughters Lizzie and Ann.

What it does: The Centre teaches riding skills and horse management to AI standard and beyond. Three-, 6- and 12-month courses are run, covering BHS stages I, II, III and the Preliminary Teaching Test, plus NPS Stud Assistant Exams parts I, II and III. Working students can bring their own horses. There's lots of serious stud work. Short, intensive courses are also available.

Minimum age: 16 and a half. Entry requirements: there's an interview. It's very selective: talent, ability, willingness, a decent riding standard and general attitude are all important.

What it's like: Here are 350 acres of paddocks, plus 200 acres of water-meadows leading down to the River Test; lots of riding round the stud – there's a proper gallop – and masses of hacking round the local bridle-ways.

This is a serious working stud, with 15 stallions kept in an American barn – all of them in the same barn! The stud also has mares and foals, plus dressage horses and horses for breaking, selling, etc., with a basic nucleus of 150 horses at any one time, rising to 300–400 in the stud season.

There are two indoor riding schools, one with seating for 500 and the Dutch Courage function suite where a hot lunch is provided for everyone daily. Evening meals are on a serve-yourself basis in the main kitchen. The RDA (Riding for the Disabled) use the school once a week with their own animals.

Up to 15 working students do the 12-month course, and more come in during the stud season. Hours are long, starting at 7 a.m. and ending with evening stable duties – usually on a rota – at 9 p.m., with one day off a week and a long weekend every six weeks. Students attend regular lectures and demonstrations on all aspects of horse and stud management. These are often given by internationalists, feed merchants, etc., and demonstrations are open to the general public, who must pay. Students accompany Mrs Loriston-Clarke to shows in rotation, e.g. Germany this week, Basingstoke the next.

It's good fun, and very hard work. This is a very professional yard and you can get no better training in this field. All in all, it is highly regarded, and very good value.

Accommodation: Boys live up by the house, girls in the newly converted former calf pens, with double and single bedrooms plus showers and a laundry room.

Cost: Tuition, lectures and demonstrations are free; board and lodging costs £75 per week; livery for a working student's own horse is around £60 per week.

THE TALLAND SCHOOL OF EQUITATION

Church Farm, Siddington, Cirencester, Gloucestershire GL7 6EZ, tel: 01285 652318, fax: 01285 659409.

Co-principals and owners: Mrs Molly Sivewright (very highly qualified) and Mrs Pammy Hutton FBHS (née Sivewright). Pammy Hutton was formerly a member of the British International Eventing and Dressage squads.

What it does: Training courses are offered of four months plus, leading ultimately to BHSI level. There are intensive pre-exam, competition and short weekly refresher courses throughout the year, and also teaching practice.

What it's like: It's a brilliant place – you'd kill to come here. It is a proper working yard, stables in every nook and cranny, with an indoor school as well as a huge outdoor ménage and lots of fun horse activities, in addition to the standard eventing and dressage – side-saddle, hunting with the Vale of White Horse, and most do the local pony club. Very practical hands-on experience is what you get here, with minimal classroom activity. This is a competition-based yard, and students can compete on their own animals if they're up to standard. The school is set in 135 acres of land; there are eight instructors plus around 30–40 students. There are over eighty horses, and a breeding programme.

The hours are long (up at 7 a.m. and evening stables at 8.30 p.m.), students get every other Sunday and every Tuesday afternoon off (the RDA use the indoor school with their own horses), plus a long weekend every six weeks, and there's two weeks' holiday for the year students.

Accommodation: There is accommodation in Church Farmhouse (Pammy lives on the top floor), a delightful Grade I traditional cottage with a resident cook/housekeeper (male), or with local families. Working students are really well cared for. Up to thirty students live in, aged between 16 and 21.

SKI TEACHING

If skiing is your thing, this is the moment to take a ski instructors' course, which in theory will allow you to teach. However do not think this is the instant route to paradise in the job stakes abroad: Continental rules are very tight, and quite rightly designed to protect local jobs. Your best bet is networking, to get yourself attached to a private group. Very occasionally Brits build up enough friendship and trust to be accredited to a ski school. Alternatively, look for employment in this country, either in Scotland or on a dry ski-slope, or by applying to a British tour operator.

Contact

The British Association of Ski Instructors (BASI): Grampian Road, Aviemore, Inverness-shire PH22 1RL, tel: 01479 810407, fax: 01479 811222.

Ski instructing courses are run by BASI throughout the winter months (including the Christmas and Easter holidays, so it might be worth thinking about it early). Training courses are held on the Continent and in the Cairngorms throughout the season. NB It's not cheap. Expect more or less dormitory accommodation in Italy, and at Glenmore Lodge in Scotland (cheap and popular).

In order to take part, you need to be at least 16, and to have passed your BASI grade 3 and a preselection clinic, either on a dry slope or on snow. (If you don't pass, then you will be told to go away and practise and come back again.)

After the course, you then have to do a minimum of 60 hours' teaching practice either on dry (in which case you will become a dry ski-slope instructor only) or on 50 per cent snow, 50 per cent dry ski-slope. You will then be assessed within two years, at which point you will qualify for a ski instructors' licence, which is then renewed annually.

The Ski Club of Great Britain: 118 Eaton Square, London SW1W 9AF, tel: 0171 245 1033, fax: 0171 245 1258. Runs courses for its reps, but for the real thing contact:

9

Art Appreciation

Do you want a career in the art world? Or do you want to grab the opportunity, before you disappear to the City or to university, to absorb some understanding of our culture and history of art? There are some outstanding courses, mainly London-based, which could be a springboard for your future. At the very least, this period of immersion might be the beginning of a passion which will feed your leisure hours all your life. Some courses are ferociously expensive, but you are often being taught by experts of world renown.

Most courses are attended by the well-heeled over-25s and often by the over-40s (expect to sit next to ladies in fur coats). The John Hall course excepted, 18- and 19-year-olds are very definitely in the minority, and a high level of commitment is expected. The pace is fast. For those with a real 'feel', this can be the start of vital art-world networking. It is well worth discovering in advance what specific skills and extras might make you more desirable to prospective employers in the field afterwards, e.g. foreign languages, office skills, and brawn for boys who might start portering behind the scenes.

Accommodation note: most of the establishments running art appreciation courses keep lists of families in central London where students can live as paying guests, and occasionally know of flats to share.

Free daytime lectures are given daily throughout the year – usually during lunch-time – at the National Gallery, the British Museum, the Victoria & Albert Museum and the Tate Gallery. Lecturers are generally in-house experts, and lectures are given in the gallery with the objects under discussion, not gazing at slides.

Ring the education or information departments of the museums and galleries for details.

Before you embark on a course:

* be honest with yourself about why you are doing it
* do you want essays and reading-lists or do you want a more relaxed approach?
* discover the level of experience at which the course is pitched
* ask what past students go on to do afterwards
* check that the practical and academic aspects are in the right proportion for your needs

COURSES

CHRISTIE'S EDUCATION

63 Old Brompton Road, London SW7 3JS, tel: 0171 581 3933, fax: 0171 589 0383.

Vital statistics: Approximately 800 students annually (200 on year-long courses, 600 on short courses). Open to all ages. Minimum age in theory is 19, but committed, enthusiastic, etc., 18-year-olds are accepted.

Course director: Mr Robert Cumming, who read Law at Cambridge, practised briefly, returned to Cambridge to do History of Art, joined Christie's and set up these courses 'because it's what I would have liked'. Mr Cumming has an eyes-on, hands-on approach, 'almost in the old Berenson style'. Utterly convincing about London being the centre of the art world: 'Even the very best French furniture is within 40 miles of Hyde Park Corner – which makes the French pretty cross.'

Mr Cumming is keen on keeping students busy on all courses. 'If they're not gasping for breath, then there's something wrong.'

What it does: Offers a wide variety of high-powered courses on art appreciation in all shapes and forms, including one- or two-year full-time programmes, plus short courses (also evening courses and weekly lectures spread over eight weeks). The diploma and certificate courses are validated by the RSA (Royal Society of Arts) examinations board. There is also a year-long diploma course at Glasgow on Decorative Arts, with the emphasis on Arts and Crafts – graduates preferred.

What it's like: A very pleasant space, with library, canteen, lecture rooms, etc., behind Christie's South Ken. auction rooms, and all buzzing with energy. The common-room (used for exhibitions) has notice-boards bristling with information, posters, etc. on the London art scene; exhibitions, openings, music, theatre, job lists and students' own additions of parties, discos and other social events.

Christie's say that the minimum age is 19 'so that students really know what they want, and aren't being pushed into this by their parents'. Students are bright and well-heeled, more females than males, and according to one cynic, 'plenty of people with good collections back home'. One-third of students are from Britain, one-third are North American, one-third from elsewhere (notably the Far East). Necessary qualifications are commitment, enthusiasm, visual alertness, curiosity. Some students are post-degree, some are changing career direction, some are here nourishing interests.

Most popular of all is the London Art Course (non-examination), the one-year course that covers the fine and decorative arts from the Renaissance to the present day. There are tests (slides, questionnaires) and practical exercises, and much time is spent visiting galleries, museums, country houses, collections (often not open to the general public), etc. with tutors and experts. 'My daughter became visually confident,' commented a father. Critics claim that the London Art Course is 'not taken seriously'. Fun and action-packed it certainly is.

The diploma course covering the same era puts emphasis on connoisseurship, investigates questions of identification, attribution and quality, develops visual and analytical skills, and involves writing and research, and students are guided to appropriate careers in the art world. This is an excellent place to get a taste, make contacts, look and learn. Time is also spent behind the scenes in the auction rooms. There are teams of outstanding lecturers, who are specialists in many different fields – and who are by no means limited to Christie's own staff.

For the serious-minded, Christie's Education has a good track record of placing people in jobs in the art world – provided they prove themselves able. Foreign languages, office skills, etc. are highly valued.

Application: Potential students are interviewed in London or New York by two or three members of staff in January and March, when they are given the 'postcard test' – they are shown postcards of works of art for discussion, dating and assessing.

INCHBALD SCHOOL OF DESIGN
32 Eccleston Square, London SW1V 1PB, tel: 0171 630 9011, fax: 0171 730 4937.

See Traditional Alternatives – Indoors chapter, p. 173.

Art appreciation course directors: Mrs Diana Lloyd, an ex-student who has taught here for 20 years 'off and on', and Mr James Bolton, a director since '92.

What it does and what it's like: Inchbald offers career-oriented work programmes. This is high-powered stuff, taken at a brisk pace – and is not for the faint-hearted. 'Tough,' said one young student; 'standards are uncompromising and the work is highly disciplined.'

The 'appreciation' courses most likely to be of interest are: Historical Survey of English Interior Decoration 1500–1935 (10-week certificate course, from September to December), which covers the development of various styles and fashions in English interior domestic buildings, with lectures on contemporary architecture and on the major influences from the Continent. There are detailed analyses: ceilings, mouldings, wall-hangings, wall-papers, carpets, curtain treatments, methods of lighting and picture hanging, etc. are all examined. Students must research, sketch, do water-colours and photograph (cameras essential) for their own records. They learn skills in visual identification and critical analysis as well as how to present ideas. Lots of lectures, lots of field trips. 'It gave me confidence,' said an ex-Wycombe Abbey girl, 'to look at architecture and objects of art in a completely different way.'

The year-long diploma course in Art and Design History concentrates on historic interior-decoration changes (1500–1935) in the first term, examines European furniture and objects during the second term, and in the summer term studies the development of gardens over the same period. There are exams at the end of each term and a huge number of visits and lectures. Skills in research and sketching, photography, etc. are taught as in the short course, but in greater depth. Useful for anyone wanting to find a career as historical advisor in film or television, or even as a background for design journalism.

This is likely to be a daunting establishment for 18-year-olds. Most students are 'mature', often postgraduate, well off; some are mid-life and poised to start a new career, and will probably eventually practise interior design in sophisticated circles in all parts of the world. Staff are largely professionals active in their own fields of art history, and well aware of the importance of keeping course curricula constantly under review. The school has a reputation for being good at monitoring and advising on career opportunities.

JOHN HALL

(Pre-University Interim Course)

12 Gainsborough Road, Ipswich, Suffolk IP4 2UR, tel: 01473 251223, fax: 01473 288009.

Vital statistics: Around 40–50 students (usually equal numbers of boys and girls, mainly from public schools). Age: students are mostly 18 and 19, occasionally older. For information and registration apply to Mrs Clare Augarde. No previous knowledge needed.

Director: Mr John Hall MA (Oxon.), who set up the course in 1965. Keen historian and art historian (and read English at Corpus Christi College). His teaching career included being assistant master at King's School, Canterbury, and later running his own

Art Appreciation

tutorial establishment in London specializing in preparing students for Oxbridge. Very affable, married (more than once), his youngest child is currently at prep school in England. Plans many of Swan Hellenic's art treasure tours in Italy. Lives in Italy, in the Marches, where he enthusiastically cultivates his own vineyards; back in Britain he lectures at public schools drumming up future business.

What it does: Offers a seven-week course (late January to mid-March) on European civilization – art, architecture and music. Specifically designed for students who have just left school. Italian language classes and drawing/painting and photography lessons are also on offer. There is an introductory week in London, then the course moves to Venice. Optional extensions to Florence and Rome are available.

What it's like: Huge fun, and very hard work too. Brilliant lecturers – writers, artists, musicians, university lecturers. 'They're an exceptional battery of wildly enthusiastic experts,' comments John Hall. It's not uncommon for students who have gone on to read History of Art at university to say that no teaching comes up to this standard: the impressive list of teachers currently includes: Peter Lauritzen, Jane Glover, Rodney Milnes, Edward Lucie Smith, Deborah Howard, Charles Hope, *the* Titian expert (Warburg Institute), Peter Phillips, founder of the Tallis Scholars, and other stars from Cambridge, Oxford and the Courtauld Institute. Organization throughout is high-powered, professional and extremely efficient. 'Nothing but the best,' said one parent, forecasting that university life would now seem 'very humdrum'.

In Venice, the centre for lectures is rented from the Dante Alighieri Society (two-thirds of the students opt to do Italian lessons here and all report this to be grindingly hard work); some lectures (there are two each day) are given on site – in a church, in a *palazzo*, in a gallery, etc. There are organized walks, visits, excursions, optional practical classes, and free time for students to explore Venice.

At the end of the course, students take a slide test and choose a project or an essay. They are also faced with a questionnaire which includes the following: What is the maximum time you have spent looking at one painting? Average time? Do you look at a guidebook before looking at art, while looking, or after looking? Which do you think leaves you with a better memory of a painting/building – taking a photo of it or sketching it? And students fill in a form assessing lecturers (with devastating honesty, e.g. 'monotonous voice'; 'very amusing and I didn't look at my watch once'; 'couldn't we have more of him/her?'; 'good but intellectually superior'. They are also asked to comment on the *pensione* (pasta praised but not the meat dishes); hot water – or rather, the lack of – the butt of heavy criticism, 'remains a mystery' according to John Hall, at whose behest the plumbers are often on the premises.

Students stay in (and virtually take over) the simple Pensione Atlantico (where they have breakfast and supper too). John Hall's English/Italian-speaking secretary – 'one of life's universal aunts' according to a parent – mother of university-age children, accompanies students (who adore her) and lives with them in the eye of the storm (a comforting pastoral note for parents). Social life is 'brilliant', comment students: 'You make friends for life.' This is *carnevale* time (expect to hear wild stories).

Above all, this course in this setting 'inspires, teaches you to look, to listen, to assess,' commented one student.

Application: Up to two years ahead (book early, this is sought-after). You fill in the form and pay a deposit – there's no interview.

Cost: £3,150 (not counting the London stay). Extension to Florence: £520; extension to Rome: £385. Expensive, but value for money and worth every penny, parents agree, and most of them admit to envy.

SOTHEBY'S EDUCATIONAL STUDIES

30 Oxford Street, London W1R 1RE, tel: 0171 323 5775, fax: 0171 580 8160.

Vital statistics: 680 students per year, with 350 on full-time courses. Age: 90 per cent of students are over 24 (minimum age: 18). Two-thirds are women. Seventy-five to 80 per cent are non-British (one-third from the US). Impressive team of tutors (ratio 1 tutor to 15 students).

Art Appreciation

Director: Mrs Anne Cersole, a director of Sotheby's Europe. A clever and high-powered Swiss, convinced that more women are needed in the art world (she herself is a specialist in the history of architecture and interiors, French furniture, arts and crafts). She is also convinced that the Sotheby's course is 'good for all art networking aspects', and says of potential students: 'They must have a clear understanding of what they're going to get out of it, and they absolutely must be committed.'

What it does: There are courses of various lengths and levels – a single term to one year, including diploma and postgraduate courses, also evening classes. (Courses are linked with the universities of Manchester and Leeds.) Most suitable for younger students is the Styles in Art course (a.k.a. the 'access course') that runs for 15 weeks (starting September and February). Also offered is the foundation course in the Asian Arts (15 weeks, new from September '95).

What it's like: Courses take place in unlikely premises – four floors at the seedy end of Oxford Street, near Tottenham Court Road, among sex boutiques and fast-food shops. Behind the faceless glass exterior and fortified by entry codes on every door, are the clean, functional seminar rooms, admin offices and a splendid library complete with whizzo computers.

Courses are highly structured, with continuous assessment (marks go towards the final certificate), and with particular emphasis on identifying works of art (regular worksheets are given for this purpose). It is a constant process of learning to assimilate, and gets progressively harder as the course moves forward. There are slide lectures plus visits. The Styles in Art course works through the history of fine and decorative arts, starting in the tenth century BC and ending with post-modernism. The foundation course in the Asian Arts (September till Christmas) gives an overall grounding in the subject, with emphasis on cross-cultural links, trade and patronage. Teaching is partly at SES, partly at the School of Oriental and African Studies (SOAS).

The courses grew out of a series laid on for Sotheby's own experts wanting to expand their knowledge and horizons. All the teaching is object-led, i.e. students start with the close examination of an object (a painting, a piece of jewellery or furniture, for instance). 'They're taught to see what they're looking at and then to make a critical assessment.' They also learn to research for cataloguing at a scholarly level.

Hard work and expensive, the courses at Sotheby's are definitely not a doddle for nice girls or boys whose mothers want them to have dinner-party conversation. Reading, researching, looking, visiting are expected: for those who are really keen, this could be the way to a career in the art world.

Application: Apply two months in advance. Students are carefully interviewed: some historical knowledge is essential. Languages and IT are considered useful assets, also students' potential as business-getters in the art market.

Cost: The 15-week Styles in Art course costs £3,800.

THE STUDY CENTRE FOR THE HISTORY OF THE FINE & DECORATIVE ARTS

6 Beauchamp Place, London SW3 1NQ, tel: 0171 225 3027, fax: 0171 225 3126.

Vital statistics: Approximately 20–30 students on the diploma course; 10 on the Decorative Arts course. Ages: range between 18 and 55. This is an educational charity, with a small scholarship fund for the diploma course. Two A-levels (or the equivalent) are the minimum requirement for entry to the diploma course, although a good proportion of postgraduates are attracted. There are no specific requirements for the Decorative Arts or English Painting course, except for enthusiasm and interest. Any of the courses would be suitable for gap-year students.

Director of studies: Mrs Karen Evans BA (who has worked here since 1979).

What it does: Offers a one-year diploma course (NB affiliated to and validated by the University of Leeds). Two 10-week short courses on Fine and Decorative Arts (autumn and post-Christmas); a six-week summer course on English Painting, Holbein to Hockney (lectures twice daily on Tuesdays, Wednesdays, Thursdays).

Art Appreciation

What it's like: Intense, huge fun, and famous for inspiring and firing students up. Low-key, not smart (no ladies in fur coats).

Overheads are kept down by itinerant use of lecture rooms (at the time of writing, courses are held in borrowed premises in Queen's Gate, and were previously at the Polish Club and the Goethe Institute. A National Gallery private room is also regularly used.) The small admin office is in Beauchamp Place.

This is a pioneer among the private art history courses, with an impressive academic board and advisory committee; it was founded in 1964 by Erica O'Donnell MBE (retired, but keeps an eagle eye), and was originally held at the Victoria & Albert Museum. Extremely well viewed right across the art world, the Study Centre has spawned an impressive and long list of distinguished figures now in the art world (many of whom lecture for the course, also at universities) including, for instance, Giles Waterfield, director of the Dulwich Picture Gallery, Rosalind Savill, Director of the Wallace Collection, numerous luminaries at Christie's, Sotheby's and the National Trust. There is a remarkable quality of teaching, with specific experts called in to talk on their particular subject. Non-commercial attitudes prevail, with never a mention of money values of works of art, this not being connected with any auction house, although the Study Centre has strong links with auction rooms, also dealers, museums and universities through the network of former students.

The short course acts as a general introduction, and is non-examination; though students often take the option of writing essays, and are taught to look, to see, to ask. The diploma course covers the decorative arts plus the study of architecture, painting, sculpture and contemporary issues such as conservation, museology and methodology. There are also tutored visits to Paris and Rome. Essays, discussions and visits are an integral part of study. 'I learnt more in one year here,' said one young graduate, 'than I did in three years of reading History of Art at university.'

Despite (because of?) the lack of common-room, canteen, etc., students and tutors are close-knit, see each other out of hours, and there appears to be a tendency to form lasting bonds and friendships.

Application: Written applications are followed by interviews, students are hand-picked. 'We take those we like', according to course director Mrs Caromy Hoare.

Cost: The one-year diploma course costs approx. £4,700, the 10-week courses on Fine and Decorative Arts approx. £1,500 and the six-week English Painting course, £660.

VICTORIA & ALBERT MUSEUM

South Kensington, London SW7 2RL, tel: 0171 938 8638 (for information), 0171 938 8407 (to book at the box office).

Lecture courses, available to absolutely anyone, on a wide variety of subjects (Late Medieval, Early Renaissance, the Art of Holy Russia) run throughout the year at the V & A. Some are held in the evenings, some are full study days. Booking arrangements are flexible: you can book in for a year, a term, or a day (student day rate is £5). Lecturers are from the V & A's huge pool of experts.

Deservedly popular is the V & A summer course – History of the Fine and Decorative Arts in the West. This runs for the first three weeks in August, with at least two lectures and a gallery talk each day, and romps through Roman art, Greek, early Christian art, Byzantine art, etc. right through to art nouveau and symbolism (at the cost of around £300). The fourth supplementary week covers the twentieth century.

Approximately 100 students attend (all ages, but this has school-leaver appeal; 'It's a taster,' said one). Slide lectures (one in the morning, one in the afternoon) are held in the Museum's lecture theatre, plus a lunch-time talk is given in a gallery.

10

Hands-on Art

The idea of a 'foundation' training in art originated with the Bauhaus movement (the early twentieth-century German architecture school), and it is a considerable strength of the teaching of art in this country. The best art foundation course is at once 'a clearing-house, a stepping-stone and an education in itself', to quote the head of one of the best. It is usually a year between school and a degree or other course, which gives would-be artists and designers a chance to find out what they are best at. A foundation course is meant to be 'diagnostic', i.e. it provides the opportunity to try aspects of art which schools cannot offer owing to lack of time or equipment, and to 'shake out' stereotyped, unoriginal ideas and discover what you *really* want to do.

In practice, only the first term offers real exposure to the huge umbrella of subjects which make up art and design, and in this term most courses follow patterns of, for example, a week or two for fine art, a week for fashion, plus textiles, three-dimensional design, printmaking, graphics, photography, sculpture, etc.; this is followed by a concentration on one area in the second term, at which point (or sooner) students start looking to the degree and other courses they hope to take up the following academic year. The last term is usually spent securing a place (if not already done), and doing some long project (often several weeks of it), which can be shown at exhibition. At the end of the year, if all is well, students are awarded a diploma or BTEC – this last is a useful qualification in its own right.

Which One?

Most art foundation courses are state-run and they are meant to be studied locally with the student living at home, at least as far as the local authorities are concerned. Unfortunately your local course may be mediocre, and it is very much worth while bustling about to get in on a good one. Whether you do depends on (a) your being offered a place, obviously, and (b) if it is outside your local authority area, whether you can pay for (part of) it, or persuade someone else to (see Funding, p. 215).

Also, pause to think about your long-term goals as they are now. If they include a degree course in art, bear in mind that an upheaval to a new place in a year's time is unsettling. If a foundation course is attached to a college of higher education with a good reputation in a field you are currently particularly interested in, it might be a shrewd move to go for this, though foundation course leaders rush to point out that (a) it isn't an advantage, (b) there is no automatic entrance to the degree course on site and (c) you may well change direction.

Sussing out a good foundation course is not that difficult, but you will almost certainly have to do it yourself. Going round art departments when researching for the *Good Schools Guide*, we were amazed at the ignorance and out-of-date-ness of most school art departments in this context. Even boarding schools with students from all over and renowned for their art often have only the vaguest idea of what goes on beyond their gates in the art world at foundation level. Don't rely on them, is our advice, but set your own network going. Visit, and watch out for the following:

1 Teaching – are the staff actually *doing* any?
2 Standard of work – use your own judgement.
3 Efficiency of support staff (in our experience inefficiency and unfriendliness at secretarial level are usually a reflection of inefficiency, etc. elsewhere).

4 How many staff/part-timers/practising artists are there around?

5 Where do students come from? Where do they go on to?

6 How many taught hours a week are there (*key* question, this one), and what do they mean by 'taught'?

7 How much emphasis is there on drawing? 'Drawing underpins everything,' says the principal of a famous college – fashion, commercial, the lot – you must know how to draw, and beware of colleges (mainly in the South) that have in the past tossed out technique in favour of creative let-it-all-hang-out chaos.

8 How big is the course? A small one cannot fund a full range of subjects, but a large state course is tough: fragile flowers may wilt.

9 What is the college's policy on funding? Some Southern colleges (London particularly) have been guilty of packing in *huge* numbers of students in order to qualify for greater government funding, without providing the staff and facilities to support the extra load. Caveat!

10 What are the facilities like – in the best of all possible worlds, can everybody do everything? Is there enough elbow room (will the head get knocked off your creation)? Is there a kiln? Is there really a photographic department? Are the facilities shared with students on other courses? – not necessarily a bad thing, but you may have to queue to use them. Is there a library? If not, which one do they use?

That'll do for a start. All the answers to theses qs should be at the course principal's fingertips. Big courses have open visiting days, often every week in the autumn term, when all qs are answered and you get a chance to look around.

Some colleges are renowned for particular areas, e.g. Wimbledon for theatre design. It can help in getting on to these courses if you are *sure* you know what you want, but unless rock-sure, it is not something to bust a gut over: many students we know have gone up to a course intent on being x and within two weeks have changed their minds to y.

What Are *They* Looking For?

Heads of foundation courses and art colleges we have talked to constantly mention 'commitment' and 'self-motivation', and are on the lookout for students who are going to get the most out of their course; but overwhelmingly what they are looking for is ability, talent: that spark of originality which they hope to detect in your portfolio. However, let it be said that if you can think through and explain your work in an interview, you are more than halfway in (NB interviews are particularly important for borderline cases). You need to be able to demonstrate that you can think for yourself – why did you do this piece of work like this? – not, what did your art master or mother think?

Most courses make noises about the need for GCSEs and/or A-levels, but we have yet to come across one which turned away an outstanding candidate for lack of these. Evidence of ability to use the English language is also stipulated, the idea being that without it you cannot actually get on to the next stage or present work to clients, etc.

A word of warning: colleges differ over whether they are happy to accept candidates who want to treat a foundation course as a way to occupy themselves for a gap year, before going on to read something totally different at university. Some say all are welcome because the whole point of the course is self-discovery; others say you are using up a place which could have gone to a serious student.

Private v. State

The best traditional, diagnostic art foundation courses are state-run. Good state courses have the funds, resources, size, cut and thrust you will find in the competitive outside world. Private courses are useful to know about if either you fail to get into a good state one, or the shock of being ejected from a small private sixth form into the state system is going to be too much for you.

Funding

State

This is complicated. If you get on to your local course it won't normally cost you a penny. (It is paid for mainly by central government, and partially by the local authority concerned.) If you choose to go outside your area, you will probably be asked to cough up around £600 towards the real cost of the course (around £4,000–£5,000). This also applies to EC candidates. Those from elsewhere have to bear the whole cost, though expats who have boarded in the UK for three years or more will qualify, and this is a handy expat wheeze to be aware of. The money provided by your local authority is on a first-come first-served basis, so apply early.

Six hundred pounds is a lot for a student to find, but peanuts compared to private school fees. However, if you live away from home, you still have to pay for accommodation – usually around £30–£70 a week, plus food, plus travel. Here you are v. unlikely to get help and a handily placed granny comes in useful.

NB Increasing pressure on state-funded colleges to 'perform', by which the government means put bums on seats and keep them there, is resulting in an increasingly gung-ho, let-them-all-come attitude, and many colleges are now guilty not only of accepting students in increasing numbers simply in order to pocket more money, but also of awarding certificates at the end of the course regardless of whether the students have come up to scratch.

Private

In most cases if you attend a private course you will have to pay the full fee yourself. The exception to this is if your local authority cannot offer the course you need to follow, in which case it may pay for you to go elsewhere. Local authorities differ hugely in their interpretation of what your needs are versus what they've got to offer.

Scotland

Scotland does not do a foundation year: students go straight from school into four-year degree/diploma courses and there is enormous pressure on places at Scottish institutions. If you are coming from a Southern foundation course, you *should* be good enough to go straight into the second year, but given the Scottish emphasis on technique you may well not be.

Age

State courses require you to be 18 before the course starts, but 'mature' students (by which they mean over 21) are usually very welcome and form a significant percentage of those on the course (and a steadying, broadening influence). Even oldies are welcome – we came across several middle-aged housewives picking up the paintbrush, and even a retired doctor.

Contact

Your initial point of contact is your **local authority** (look in the telephone directory, or ring your local town hall).

Art and Design Admissions Registry: Penn House, 9 Broad Street, Hereford HR4 9AP, tel: 01432 266653, fax 01432 343367. Will supply a list of art foundation courses throughout the UK.

The London Institute: 65 Davies Street, London W1Y 2DA, tel: 0171 514 6000, fax: 0171 514 6175.

The London Institute was set up in 1986 to provide an umbrella for five London art colleges – the College of Printing, the College of Fashion, Chelsea College of Art and Design (see p. 219), Central St Martin's and Camberwell College of Arts (see p. 217). It comprises a fat layer of bureaucracy (it took us three weeks to make an appointment), the real purpose of which is to a create a huge art conglomerate (largest 'single' centre in the UK) which can or could wield much power in the art world, and now awards its own degrees.

Housed in the old British Council building off Oxford Street, the Institute has a good, large gallery showing the work of students who received top marks in the previous year's exams – illuminating – lots of post-post-modern and Andy Warhol-inspired work when we visited; well worth would-be applicants perusing.

Below are just some of the art foundation courses we have visited and, on the whole, found good. The standard varies, but we hope this will give you an idea of the breadth of courses that's available, and will serve as a starting-point.

ART FOUNDATION COURSES

CAMBERWELL COLLEGE OF ARTS
Peckham Road, London SE5 8UF, tel: 0171 703 0987, fax: 0171 703 3689.

Vital statistics: Number of students: approx. 250 (has been increasing). Number of staff: for foundation course, 3 full time, one half time, plus 35 visiting teachers (equivalent of 8 full time). There's a good-value shop in the entrance hall. Students are expected to find their own drawing materials, but the rest is provided (within reason). Thirty-five taught hours a week (but field trips, etc. are included in this figure).

Head of college: Since 1993, Professor Roger Breakwell, previously Executive Director at Liverpool's John Moores University. Has come in big, bouncing, like a dose of the proverbial to stir everything up, with energy and clear aims. It's orderly – a college to watch.

Course director (Foundation Studies): Since 'about 1984', Mr Jim Pearson Dip. A.D. (Sculpture and Drawing) at Camberwell, plus MA in Sculpture from the RCA (Pearson's name, by the way, hardly figures in college literature). A conscientious hard worker who appears slightly bowed down by the huge numbers of students now passing through his hands. He comments: 'If I can put them off, they will not survive'; 'It's about adaptability in a changing world'; and: 'Art is about making mistakes.'

What it does: Students on the foundation course get the chance to try virtually every major discipline. The school is famous for design and craft, particularly ceramics and metalwork. It also offers a wide range of degree courses, evening classes, plus a summer school in conjunction with an American college.

What it's like: An old established art school with an interesting history going back to 1896 and Jon Passmore Edwards, and one which has enjoyed an excellent reputation over the years but has been in the doldrums. The course is part of the famous Camberwell College of Arts, with all the buzz of degree students flying about. Now a member of the London Institute (p. 216) and all that that implies. 'The best year of my life,' reported one student, though this may bring a gasp of surprise from some from sheltered backgrounds. The foundation course is on two sites (stained-glass windows worth a detour on the Peckham Road site). The course is difficult to get to grips with, but there is an energetic policy of informing students every inch of the way – and a v. good booklet on all matters (restaurants, accommodation, local churches, etc.) and a clear statement of what students should expect.

There is a good library. Good, v. cheap, well-patronized canteen. There's also a carnival at the end of the Christmas term. Sixty per cent of the students are school-leavers, 30 per cent 'mature'. In '93, 208 out of 220 completed the course, 188 applied for higher education, of which 20 didn't get places. Thirty-four per cent went on to London Institute establishments. There is a regular foreign contingent on the course – Germans, Japanese, Americans. All students have the opportunity to go to Barcelona to work on the hoof, and there are also trips to New York, Russia, etc. The college has two halls of residence, but there was some doubt about whether foundationers would get into one at time of writing.

Not an ideal site – not on the tube, security is very tight, it's in a poor area, all students have to have ID cards. Lockers and locking drawers are provided for all, however. The main building is large and modern but grotty. Overall impression: it's big, bustling, aiming for a balance between imagination and technique. Not much sign of actual teaching going on when we visited, but there is a dynamic atmosphere none the less. Well worth the trek to visit.

Getting in: You must be 17 by the beginning of the October of the year in which the course begins; five or more GCSEs are required, of which three should be in 'recognized' academic subjects, including one which demonstrates proficiency in English; also a portfolio of between 30 and 50 works, and you *must* visit the college before applying.

CHELSEA COLLEGE OF ART AND DESIGN

Bagley's Lane, Fulham, London SW6 2QB, tel: 0171 371 9494, fax: 0171 371 7330.

Vital statistics: Number of students: huge course, probably the largest in the country, around 300 in '93, growing to 350 in '94. Number of staff: v. approx. 10 full time or equivalent, plus a visiting team of around 50, who 'might average a day a week'. Number of taught hours per week: 'at least 20 "real" '.

Head of college: Since 1993, Mrs Bridget Jackson. Trained at Goldsmith's College of Art (National Diploma in Design), followed by an MA in Philosophy. Mrs Jackson has had an interesting and varied career, and is very lively and enthusiastic.

In charge of Foundation Studies: Since 1988, Mr Andrew Yates, previously head of Foundation Studies at Epsom. Trained at Hornsey College of Art (now Middlesex University). Mr Yates has his office on the Hugon Road site (you might get Reception staff to direct you). Mr Yates himself is thoughtful and outspoken, and comments that all foundation courses are 'simply trying to stand up in a blizzard of change'. He also comments that Chelsea is 'not a typical foundation course'; those who choose it are usually confident, high achievers. Foundation course full-time staff appear to have a good knowledge of degree courses – a big strength.

What it does: Art foundation course, with every possible area of art and design offered and available to all (the foundation course has its own facilities). The college also has a full range of arty degree courses, BTECs (including a two-year introductory course in Design), plus day and evening classes and good summer courses.

What it's like: The foundation course is on two large sites (sketchy canteen on both sites) and students continually shuffle from one to another in the first term, dragging work with them (no lockers for foundation students). The college itself has four sites. This course would suit confident, mature students with zip who know exactly where they're going, already have a thorough grounding in draughtsmanship but need a year's grace to free the imagination and acquire the status of having been at a college with a designer label. A third of Chelsea foundation students are over 22, and range up to 60 years old; a third come from outside the UK – there's a cosmopolitan atmosphere.

Teaching is often confined to large seminars in which the creative content of work is analysed. The bias is very much to modernism and post-modernism, as favoured by the London Institute and by the Tate. Of the two sites, the Bagley's Lane one at the back end of Fulham is 'student-led' (i.e. students get on and do their own thing) with the atmosphere of a giant playground. The other site, Hugon Road, is 'brief-led' (students work to specification). More creative chaos here than any other course we visited. Students seem as happy as sandboys.

In a good year, Mr Yates expects to place 90 per cent into degree and further education courses, in a less good year, it's 80 per cent. A piccie of Dirk Bogarde (former student) holds pride of place in the college prospectus. The college has a lingering reputation for a bias towards the fine arts.

Getting in: Normally you need to be 18 by the end of the December of the year in which the course starts. One A-level is required, plus a minimum of three GCSEs grades A–C, including evidence of proficient use of English, or five GCSEs; there is also an interview and you'll need to show your portfolio.

Accommodation: There are two halls of residence for the college as a whole (in SW11 and SW17), but no specific allocation for foundation students – preferential treatment is given to students coming from outside London.

THE CITY AND GUILDS OF LONDON ART SCHOOL
124 Kennington Park Road, London SE11 4DJ, tel: 0171 735 2306/5201, fax: 0171 582 5361.

Vital statistics: Number of students: 40–50 per year for the foundation course. Size of teaching groups: normally not more than 8 or 10. Number of taught hours a week: 30; a 34-week year.

Foundation course leader: Since 'about 1987', Mr Michael Fell Dip. Fine Art, FSDC. Before that he was a full-time practising artist. Teaches two days a week here. Not exactly garrulous.

What it does: Offers a one-year general foundation course. The college also does degree courses, wonderful Restoration courses, History of Art, and part-time courses in stone-carving, wood-carving (v. good, this), etc. Small summer school and excellent short drawing courses.

What it's like: Not so much a foundation course (lack of room, resources, etc.), more a serious painting/drawing course for smarter folk, and a criticism of it as a foundation course is that students' work tends to be similar. The teaching takes place in Georgian houses just south of the river, with excellent teaching of technique – one of the few places in the South which did not abandon the idea that art must be taught. Much recommended for figurative arts and sculpture. The library is rudimentary by state standards, but staff teach tirelessly and wonderfully. All staff are part time as a policy – they must be practising artists, and everybody is paid the same rate.

The college was established in 1879 in Kennington by the City and Guilds of London Institute as an extension of the Lambeth School of Art, and originally provided training for local art industries. Now it is funded by fee income and donations from, among other illustrious patrons, the Fishmongers' Trust and Paul Hamlyn, not to mention Mrs Roald Dahl, the Mercers' Company, the Laura Ashley Foundation and assorted toffs. Funding is, alas, a constant headache. Ninety-seven per cent of students went on to degree courses last year (two are still struggling to find a place at time of writing). Where they go 'depends on where they want to go'. There were no records on this to hand.

Getting in: Normally five GCSEs at C or higher are needed, or three GCSEs plus one A-level (students may be taken without these, providing they 'top up' during the course) – plus interview and submission of portfolio.

Cost: This is a private college. You may be lucky enough to persuade your local council to give you a discretionary grant (ask the college for advice on this), but more likely you will have to fork out yourself: approximately £4,626 for the course at the time of writing (can be paid in two instalments).

CITY OF BATH COLLEGE
(Foundation Studies)

100 Sydney Place, Bath BA2 6NE, tel: 01225 312191 (main college, for application forms), 01225 464413 (for foundation course inquiries), fax: (main college) 01225 444213.

Vital statistics: Number of students: approx. 74 full time. Number of staff: 4 full time (including admin); 11 part time; average 24 teaching hours a week.

Principal of college: Mr Justin Togher

Head of School of Creative and Performing Arts: Mr Bob Briggs is acting head at time of writing (see v. complicated brochure for bureaucratic chain of command).

Course leader (Foundation Studies): Since 1989, Mr Richard Bell. Trained at Swansea, specializes in ceramics. Mr Bell was given his first teaching job by John Brown at Fettes School. Scottish, wears Auld Alliance rosette and is also assistant head of the School. All staff are practising artists.

What it does: Offers a one-year foundation course; also a part-time foundation course; plus A-level art courses, evening classes, etc.

What it's like: The college is housed in two large Regency dwellings overlooking Sydney Gardens – beautiful to look at but absolutely not well adapted to art-course work – smallish rooms, huge corridors, wonderful mouldings and staircases all over-painted and depressingly run-down. Students beaver cheerfully away in attic rooms on their own (v. cosy). Snacks, cups of coffee, etc. are available. The course is v. oversubscribed, but some of this is undoubtedly due to the attraction of Bath, which is an inspiration in itself.

The course spouts jargon: 'seven sequential modules' lasting for 'four weeks, and in each there are four members of staff offering broad-based projects (half a module)'. One day a week is 'untutored', i.e. you are on your tod. The college has recently lost the use of Bath Further Education College library – there is no library now to speak of. Eighty-five to 90 per cent of students go on to a degree course. Mr Bell comments that he is quite prepared to accept students who are going on to read other subjects at university – the idea at this college is discovery. He expects students to work from 9 a.m. to 9 p.m. 'It's like an 11-day week', but if they don't turn up the college will not chase: 'We try to treat them as adults' (though NB the course is small enough for fellow students to notice if someone is missing for long). Mr Bell is 'sympathetic to part-time jobs', and will try to restructure the timetable to fit in with these. Sixty per cent of students are from the County of Avon, and approx. 15 per cent are over 21.

The School had a top reputation when it was at Corsham, but is now a very different animal. However, Bath is still a Mecca for the young – beautiful and full of temptations. The course is believed to have a bias towards fine arts ('a bit precious,' commented a member of the art department at a local school). Would-be sculptors would be better off elsewhere – no room, no room (and no lockers either). Rudimentary photography and printmaking: the course and buildings are too small to offer a wide range of subjects which might include these.

Getting in: Requirements are normally one A-level and three GCSEs at grade C or above; a command of English language; an interview with portfolio – the hopeful student must demonstrate 'commitment' and 'passion'. Qualification awarded: diploma in Foundation Studies.

Accommodation: Rooms in Bath are around £35–£40 a week (contact the accommodation officer on the main switchboard).

FALMOUTH COLLEGE OF ARTS

Woodlane, Falmouth, Cornwall TR11 4RA, tel: 01326 211077, fax: 01326 211205.

Vital statistics: Number of students: around 100 doing the foundation year. Staff–student ratio 15 to 1. Twenty-four contact teaching hours per week, plus life drawing. There are 1,200 students on other courses at the college. Students are taught in groups of 15.

Principal: Professor Alan Livingstone

Foundation course leader: Mr Philip Booth BA (40s), forceful, energetic, a live wire who has been here since 1980. Manchester-born and trained, he is a sculptor (and like all the staff spends seven weeks per year practising his art, and regularly exhibits in a mixed show at a Cork Street gallery). Keeps up links with Japan where he spent time on a scholarship.

What it does: A foundation course that offers all the usual areas – including computer skills.

Also on offer are postgraduate courses in Broadcast Journalism, Fine Art, History of Modern Art and Design; BA courses in Broadcasting Studies, Fine Art, Graphic Communications, Journalism, Ceramics; plus BTEC Higher National Diploma courses in, among other subjects, Graphic Design, Illustration, Advertising, Copywriting and Art Direction.

What it's like: Thorough on all fronts and exciting with it. Gorgeous setting, with handsome buildings five minutes from the sea, near the centre of Falmouth: the place feels well off, well run and infectiously self-confident. The main building was once a private house with a famous botanical garden, still largely intact. Well-designed glossy new buildings, plus many other studios and workshops spread out into erstwhile schools and sheds. Splendid facilities; space, light (for which this part of Cornwall is of course famous). A place which obviously feels good about itself and looks smart with it – fresh paint on the walls, clean, simple carpets, ditto furniture. There's a notably good canteen (with home-made cakes). 'Not a place to lose weight,' sighed a member of staff. A pleasant old house opposite the main campus acts as halls, chiefly for foreign students: other non-locals find bedsits.

Hands-on Art

A terrifically strong emphasis is placed on drawing throughout the foundation course: there are life-drawing classes three evenings and two afternoons every single week. Also stressed is the aspect of art and design as 'a thinking as well as a doing process', and the development of ideas is highly valued. (All potential students are asked what expectations they have of a foundation course; and all are asked to identify their own strengths and weaknesses.)

Foundation students by and large use the course's own well-resourced facilities (photographic, silk-screen and textile print-up equipment and machines, industrial sewing-machines, wood, metal, clay, plaster in the three-dimensional work area, etc.), but occasionally they make use of the main campus, for photography, for instance (though they have their own mini-darkroom).

Teaching is often done in groups of 30 or even 60, with two or four tutors, 'because we find the energy works better that way'. 'It means we don't get stuck with one tutor,' commented a student. Another said: 'The best thing about Falmouth is the surfing.' (The college's prospectus looks like a brochure for a travel company, with photographs of people surfing and walking on the beach . . .) The proximity of the Tate at St Ives is appreciated. Foundation students are mainly (70–80 per cent) local-ish, but plenty come from far and wide. Sloanes like the place. At the time of writing there are 112 students on the course, including a handful from abroad (Mr Booth was just off to Japan in the hope of attracting Japanese talent). Most staff on the foundation are (coincidentally) from the North.

'Course advisors' (akin to governors) from different disciplines and from widespread higher education art institutions come to give talks and individual advice to students: 'A useful means of fine-tuning our course programmes as well,' comments Mr Booth. Every year he and several colleagues from the college leap into a car immediately the foundation year has finished to go and look at art colleges where they catch the degree shows. (Recently it was a 'swoop up the middle', the year before it was Scotland.) This means there is unusually good advice on hand for students wanting to know which disciplines are best taught at which art colleges. The majority go on to degree courses of one sort or another, and are fairly widespread (sculptors favour Winchester, theatre designers Wimbledon, painters may well stay on at Falmouth, particularly well known for fine art, and entry procedure is on a par with outsiders).

Getting in: Five GCSEs at grade C minimum are required, or three plus one A-level. At least three students apply for each place, all of whom must submit a portfolio and are given an interview.

KINGSTON UNIVERSITY
(Faculty of Design)
Knights Park, Kingston upon Thames, Surrey KT1 2QJ, tel: 0181 547 2000, fax: 0181 547 7011.

Vital statistics: Number of students: 70. Number of staff: 2 full time (plus 'support' admin staff), plus 15 part-time staff for this course; full-time technician for foundation course only (subsidized shop). Number of taught hours: $26\frac{1}{2}$ (broken down into 22 tuition/contact/studio; 1 hour life drawing/visual studies; 1 hour location drawing/photography and $2\frac{1}{2}$ of art history).

Head of Foundation Studies: Mr Paul Stafford BA (Hons.), HDFA. The BA is from Coventry. Mr Stafford also did a postgraduate sculpture course at the Slade and has exhibited internationally (look out for sculpted heads sitting disconsolately on a shelf in his office). He comments that it is important for him and his staff to be taken seriously in the art world, so that students will listen and respect what they are doing: 'We all practise what we preach,' he says. He comments: 'The huge advantage of a foundation course is that it sorts you out.' Does two days a week teaching. Very articulate, young, dynamic, organized and clever. While we were there he was in the throes of organizing an exhibition to take to Bosnia.

What it does: Offers a good old-fashioned wide-ranging foundation course – everything from metalwork to printing, photography to fine art. The university also offers a full range of art and design degree courses.

Hands-on Art

What it's like: Excellent, well-run, properly funded foundation course strong on most fronts, particularly good at technical subjects. This is a serious course – the students all work in what feel like exam conditions, on their own. Absolutely no Sony Walkmans, smoking, etc. – it is very disciplined, perhaps slightly lacking in fun, though students report that they 'love it'. Records of where students go on to (about a quarter continue at Kingston) are freely and proudly offered, which is unusual in our experience.

The course has an excellent success rate of getting students on to 'good' courses: in '94, for example, 65 applied for degree, and 62 at time of writing have been offered places and one is on reserve.

The foundation course is in the middle of the Design Faculty, surrounded by degree students, and sharing to some extent their facilities. This has pros and cons: the pros are access to all facilities and rubbing shoulders with students further along the artistic road, and staff (staff around till 5 p.m., place open till 9/10 p.m.), plus all the backup and support of the university proper (plus wonderful extras – music, drama, gyms, etc). The con is the bewildering size of the place (allow an hour to *find* it if you are arriving by car, and don't expect to be able to park), though students have use of free university bus. Not a cosy course, but Kingston itself has a nice leafy, safe suburban feel, away from the hurly-burly of central London, but near enough to make frequent forays to art galleries, etc. The site (high-rise block) overlooks Hogsmill River – of pre-Raphaelite *Ophelia* fame.

Kingston benefits from the legacy of having been, until the early 1990s, a poly, with a long tradition of art and design and huge resources. The university's current policy is to maintain (more rather than less) the size of the course, making this the only course we have seen which is small enough to give lots of personal attention but well funded enough to offer everything a would-be artist could desire – apart from throwing a pot.

The foundation course happens all in one place – another great strength – and the building houses one of the best (possibly *the* best) art libraries in the country, with bound copies of *Picture Post*, *Punch*, etc. going back to the year dot, with a £43,000 annual budget, 180,000 slides, first editions, and a huge database – ask for a picture of a dancing dog and the computer will give reference points for all dancing dogs in the library. Fabulous, with, not surprisingly, a highly enthusiastic librarian: it's worth applying for the course for the library alone.

Sixty-five per cent of students are from Surrey, the rest from all over – Japan, France, Scotland, etc. There are 10 per cent 'mature' students. Much care and thought are given to students' general welfare – the university has a full-time counsellor on tap, plus a part-time psychotherapist, etc., and an elaborate system to check that no one is left out in the cold – highly efficient, all of this.

Getting in: You need to be aged 18 by 1 October of the year of entry; normally five GCSEs or equivalent are required, or three GCSEs plus one A-level, or two GCSEs and two A-levels; a portfolio including 'personal' (i.e. not school) work; plus evidence of proficiency in English language.

Accommodation: To live in a hall of residence will cost you approx. £600 a term. New halls of residence mean places are now available for all foundation students.

THE LEITH SCHOOL OF ART
25 North Junction Street, Edinburgh EH6 6HW, tel/fax: 0131 554 5761.

Vital statistics: Number of students: 40 on foundation course (has been growing by leaps and bounds), out of which about 18 are mature students. Number of staff: three full time plus six 'dedicated' part-timers (this is the staff quota for all courses offered). Number of taught hours a week: 24 (more in the summer term).

Principal: Since 1991, Mr Philip Archer, who studied at Cardiff and did a postgraduate course at the Royal College of Art where he met up with the Shevertons (see below). Has been a full-time painter, but is now totally committed to the school, although, he says, if he feels it is becoming mediocre he will have no hesitation in recommending to the trustees that it should close. Earnest, hard-working and kind.

Hands-on Art

What it does: One of two places in Scotland which offers a foundation year for would-be art students. It also runs day and evening classes (which help fund the rest) and wonderful things such as painters' tours of north-eastern Turkey.

What it's like: The school was founded in 1988 by Lotte and Mark Sheverton, a charismatic and much loved couple who were tragically killed in a car accident in the same year. Mark had been a disciple of Robin Child at Marlborough College and taught at Edinburgh Academy, where he transformed the art department. Lotte was a star student at Marlborough, went to the Slade and taught at Fettes College. The school reckons to take anyone – signs of genius are not needed. The course is patronized by all – tramps off the street, Edinburgh matrons, teenagers doing the foundation course, etc. Encourages original and innovative work.

The school is housed in a dear old Norwegian church (still consecrated) in Leith, by the sea, with touches of dry rot. Not much in the way of resources, but a new studio has just been opened upstairs of which they are very proud. Besides the staff, there are 'occasional' visitors of different disciplines.

The ethos of the school is that it is more than a nine-to-five place, it is a community. Christian principles are seriously followed, and those daunted by the cut and thrust of large state foundation courses might flourish here: the school fields the occasional refugee from the state system. Some of the charisma may have died with the founders, but still, it is an extraordinary place, and highly regarded in the art world.

The foundation course is too small in numbers and space to be 'diagnostic' in any real sense. Like the City and Guilds course (p. 221), it is much more a grounding in drawing and art history. Art history is not separated from the studio – the two go hand in hand (there's no specialist member of staff). Students work in the church for four days, and on the fifth go out into the highways and byways of East Lothian to do outside projects. Leith would be a very good place to consider (assuming you can afford it) if you are from the South but are hoping to get into a Scottish art college, as the school is much more in tune with Scottish art college needs than the majority of courses in the South. The school much deserves its current success.

Getting in: No formal qualifications are needed – entry is on interview and submission of portfolio.

Cost: The school is privately run and therefore there is little chance of you getting a grant though it is *always* worth trying. It is funded mainly by fee income. The cost of the foundation course at the time of writing is around £1,000 a term. Up to a third of the places are at concessionary rates (i.e. half-price). Fees include a package of materials. A scholarship is given by the owners of the Bruton Gallery in Bath. The school looks for sponsorship with the help of its chairman, Mr Graham Ross, ex-United Biscuit megaman. At time of writing, the Wellcome Foundation hosts the school's summer exhibition in London and pays for students' fares to London. The cost of courses other than the foundation year is high.

LOUGHBOROUGH COLLEGE OF ART AND DESIGN

Radmoor, Loughborough, Leicestershire LE11 3BT, tel: 01509 261515, fax: 01509 265515.

Vital statistics: Number of students: 180 (figure has jumped from 130, and there are 1,200 students at the college as a whole). Number of staff: approximately 26, mostly part time and including 10 'hard-core'. Twenty-one hours of teaching per student per week (recently cut from 24; NB national average is 17 hours). Plus 'access' to 'facilitators' for 40 hours during the week.

College principal: Mr Ieuan Pugh.

Head of Foundation Studies: Since 1992 Mr Alan Bunkum, a sculptor, who studied art at Maidstone, followed by a postgraduate degree at the Slade; he also won a scholarship to the British School in Rome. An articulate, perceptive, and positive man. We were surprised to find he does not miss teaching, and finds management 'enthralling'. Has made considerable changes, especially on the staff front: 'vital – our main resource', and has introduced a substantial number of young part-time staff, all practising artists and designers. Mr Bunkum observes changes in student attitudes, with more wanting to start and finish in the same place; more opting for two-year HND courses (intensive and skills-oriented), rather than three-year degree courses (with the added dimensions of philosophy and ideas). Mr Bunkum is keen on 'reassessing', and looking at better ways of teaching.

What it does: The foundation course covers all areas of art and design. Also offered are a two-year Introductory Studies course, BTEC, Advanced GNVQs and a full range of degree courses (part-time access at all levels). Being introduced (from summer '95) is a fast-track foundation course (13 weeks) for foreign students.

What it's like: The foundation course is housed on four floors of a purpose-built 1930s block – light and bright, with a huge recently acquired neighbouring studio, previously home to Lough-borough's electric generator. Five minutes' walk away is the college's main site, where foundation students take part in timetabled workshops, master-classes, etc., and have access to all facilities such as the library and computer suites. There is a canteen on the main site. The college is very strong on inter-department networking. Links are carefully nurtured with the university (i.e. Loughborough University), with some coming and going between students, departments and staff.

The students are mainly local (Nottinghamshire, Leicester-shire), with a regular trickle from Guernsey, and also South Africa; there are also students from Scotland, Wales and elsewhere, plus a handful of mature students.

This is one of the very few colleges focused entirely on art and design and not attached to, for example, a university or college of higher education (and the only one north of the Thames – the others are Wimbledon, Falmouth, Farnham and the Kent Institute) and it fiercely fights off take-overs. It is funded by the Further Education Funding Council, however, and is proud of being 'in the black'.

The facilities are *not* plush; the buildings are functional, well used, well loved – but the atmosphere is definitely dynamic. Students are excited and keen. Good support from tutors, passivity is strongly discouraged; there's an emphasis on understanding that 'how well you use your abilities is more important than how "talented" you are.' 'A heavy responsibility,' commented a student, 'learning on your own.' That said, teaching is on the rigorous, vigorous side.

The course kicks off with the usual broad introductory programme, which explores a wide range of media, materials and visual thinking. The four main areas are: Fine Art, Textiles and Fashion Design (the college is noted for textiles and all areas of 'making'); Visual Communications, e.g. Graphic Design, Illustration, etc., and Three-dimensional Design and Crafts (including jewellery and interior design). The college traditionally has a strong reputation in drawing, and runs a 'project' with an international competitive element. The emphasis is above all on teaching students 'how to look – so they have options, choices'.

Around 90–95 per cent of students go on to degree courses (with 12–15 per cent opting to stay at Loughborough). Good advice is given on the next step, with appropriate students being offered places at e.g. Goldsmith's, Glasgow, the Slade and Kingston (for graphics), and Central St Martin's and Manchester Metropolitan (for TV and animation).

In order to cover the ground, and give foundation students a head start, the college term starts in mid-August (most others do not begin until mid-September or even October). Not a town where there are many distractions . . .

Getting in: Entry requirements: a minimum of five GCSEs at grades A, B or C. Informal interview (with two members of staff), portfolio submission, and a drawing project set in advance. The college is interested in the whole person, not just the finished A-level work that appears in the portfolio, 'and where they're coming from, how they respond'.

Accommodation: Halls of residence are near by.

NEWCASTLE COLLEGE
Rye Hill Campus, Scotswood Road, Newcastle-upon-Tyne NE4 7SA, tel: 0191 273 8866, fax: 0191 272 4296.

Vital statistics: Number of students: 200 on the art foundation course. There are 2,000–3,000 full-time students at the college in all, and this number swells to 17,000 students counting those on day release, part time, evening courses, short courses, etc. Officially gives 15 hours' contact teaching per week, plus 15 hours' 'directed study'. Staff–student ratio: around 1 to 21. Sixty to 75 per cent of students are from Newcastle, Durham, North Tyneside and South Tyneside. Regular contingents come from Northern Ireland, Eire and Scotland; some from the South; a handful from overseas.

Principal: Since 1979, Mr Michael Rowarth MA (Oxon.) (50s).

Foundation course leader: Since 1990, Mr Phil Bawden MA (late 30s), who has terrific empathy with students, helped by pony-tail and earring, and staff, whom he praises and supports to the hilt. Directs operations from a tiny crammed office (visitors sit on fifties red plush cinema seats). Puts the emphasis throughout the Foundation on 'the why rather than the how'. Phil Bawden trained at the Bath Academy, and headed the foundation graphics department here for nine years before taking over as course leader. Describes the foundation year as 'difficult for students: they must grow up quickly'.

What it does: The course runs for 32 weeks, from early September until mid-May. Full-time Foundation Studies in Art and Design takes place in the Faculty of Visual and Performing Arts (NB this is a new creation: formerly the foundation was under the umbrella of the School of Art and Design at the college, and still is, but this is now under the newly named faculty).

Please note that there are three similar-sounding establishments: Newcastle University (one of the relatively rare, old established universities which does a Fine Arts degree); the University of Northumbria (formerly Newcastle Polytechnic), and this one, i.e. Newcastle College, which is a College of Further Education and offers: GCSEs, A-levels, BTECs, HNDs, GNVQs, City and Guilds, and other diplomas – a *huge* variety of courses and subjects. Coming soon: a modular system working up to a full-blown degree.

What it's like: Comes with a strong reputation and very good facilities – though access to them is by no means always easy.

'It takes a bit of getting to grips with,' commented a student, 'because there are two sites, and so many other students about the place.' In actual fact, foundation students keep themselves to themselves.

Fine Art, Three-dimensional Design (metal, woodwork, plastic), and Graphics are a seven-minute walk from the main campus (two minutes from Newcastle railway station), and occupy a series of studios at Newcastle Art Centre (also home to crafts and workshops), though there is talk of moving to a new site. The main campus consists of a no-expense-spared, bravely high-tech building and splendid facilities. Excellent photography set-up, outstanding computers and design computers, fine fashion department, etc. – but there's a tangible sense of frustration among staff that this is all in use by so many other students so much of the time.

The small team of staff is tight-knit and dedicated. The foundation leader has worked hard at persuading them to work as a team, rather than root for themselves. After the usual diagnostic sessions, students opt for their specialized subject: this is a balancing act managerially, says Phil; certain areas tend to get oversubscribed, though it generally ends up with around 30 doing Fashion, 30 in Three-dimensional Design, 38 in Textiles, 18 each in Photography and Ceramics, and the rest divided between Fine Art and Graphics.

The emphasis throughout is on getting students to 'think for themselves', and staff are very keen on breaking down students' preconceptions, encouraging them to question. Students go on to a wide variety of degree courses, with a steady trickle going to the University of Northumbria, also Kingston (usually for Fashion), and into the second year of Scottish art schools.

Getting in: All potential students (600–800 per year) are interviewed by a group of tutors. 'The baseline is drawing – I know everyone says that, but drawing is the cheapest form of visual thinking.' Mr Bawden explains that he is 'most interested in how a student has arrived at something, and finding out what kind of a learning curve they're on'.

WIMBLEDON SCHOOL OF ART

Palmerston Road, London SW19 1PB, tel: 0181 540 0231, fax: 0181 543 1750.

Vital statistics: Number of students: 180 on the foundation course. Number of staff: five full time, three half-timers and 17 regular part-timers. Taught hours: 30 a week, with a 33-week year.

Principal of college: Dr Colin Painter (YES!)

Head of Foundation Studies: Since 1991, Mrs Yvonne Crossley NDD, ATD. Previously at Epsom School of Art. Trained at Goldsmith's. Runs the course with a permanently open door and – unique in our experience of state affairs – absolutely no time is wasted on bureaucracy. People pop in and out at all hours, problems sorted on the spot. Mrs Crossley is an object-lesson in administrative efficiency: inspiring. Does not now practise art consistently, as she considers running the course a full-time job. Comments: 'The teaching of drawing is fundmental.'

What it does: Offers exposure to a wide range of subjects. Outstanding for Theatre Studies (the college has the best Theatre Design degree course in the country); good Sculpture, Fine Art. Pottery, which might have been the poor relation, now has a new kiln, and a new technician 'inputs'. There's a new five-week pre-foundation course, plus summer school programme, etc.

What it's like: This is a five-star course, firing on all cylinders; it is efficient, well supported by the main college, producing excellent work by any standards (look at the exhibition catalogues for a start). There's room for all students to try everything. The annexe, where the foundation course has its being, has a deeply grotty exterior, but do not be put off. It is a brisk walk from the Northern line tube. The atmosphere is busy and happy, and students are encouraged to get out there and grab what's offered. Staff are all teaching hard, even in the last week of term. Everyone goes to Paris for a week (costs £170 all-in at time of writing), and there's an optional trip to Venice in the second term.

Strong work ethic – students are *ticked in* (i.e. it is not left to them to account for themselves) and non-showers are chased up, making it a good course for students straight from school (though there are around 5–15 students over the age of 30 in any one year). Everyone has lockers and plan drawers.

There is continuous assessment, with one retake allowed at each final stage. Well over 90 per cent of students have been 'successfully placed' in higher education over the past three years. All subjects are taught in the annexe except History of Art, Printmaking and Theatre. The size of the course is growing fast – perhaps too fast?

Getting in: You must be 18 by the December of the year of entry; portfolio submission required; proficiency in English language (usually a GCSE at C or above). Apply early (after the end of January is too late).

Accommodation: There's no hall of residence, but the accommodation officer helps to find digs and vets landladies, and English language classes are arranged for overseas students (Wimbledon was the first state course in the UK to cater for overseas students, in '88).

WINCHESTER SCHOOL OF ART

Park Avenue, Winchester, Hampshire SO23 8DL, tel: 01962 842500, fax: 01962 842496.

Vital statistics: Number of students: about 800 altogether; about 115 on foundation course, plus 25 students in 'year zero' of degree courses (see below). Number of taught hours: 18 a week (three six-hour days) in groups of about 40 with 2–3 tutors; one day a week 'independent working' with a skeleton staff; one day a week History and Theory.

Principal: Mr Michael Sadler-Foster

Head of art foundation course: Mr Roy Naylor BA (Hons.) (Manchester) who went to grammar school and 'hated every minute of it', and as a result still reacts very strongly against pigeon-holing. Came to Winchester in '87 to run the department; has worked at the foundation course in Derby and at the London Guildhall before coming here.

What it does: Offers a 'classic' diagnostic course; also a foundation year (known as 'year zero' in the college) as part of a four-year degree course – similar to the classic course in terms of work undertaken, but it carries a 'mandatory' award (i.e. if you get a place here from anywhere in the UK, the government will pay for it).

What it's like: The course is known if anything for Textiles, and for its Barcelona School – a full-blown art college in a lively city at which you can study at all levels, and may well spend time at during your foundation year.

Winchester is particularly useful to know about for its four-year course. Students are a wide geographical mix by foundation course standards: a handful are from 'overseas' (outside the EC); a handful from Europe; the rest from Hampshire, the Surrey fringes, the Channel Islands, the Isle of Wight: 10–15 per cent are 'mature' (i.e., over 21).

A good place to study if you can rise above middle-class, pastel-clad Winchester: the atmosphere pervades the college. However, a light, leafy environment, safe-ish, tranquil. The course was on two separate sites when we visited, but is scheduled to be brought on to the main college campus, in among the degree students and sharing much of their equipment. Zealous pastoral care – there is clocking in twice a day, etc.

Getting in: Entry is obtained by interview and portfolio submission; 700 apply for the foundation and zero year places. Be sure to go and visit the college before interview.

Accommodation: Study-bedrooms with *en suite* bathrooms, no less, are being built for 387 students, and should include all the foundationers.

PRE-FOUNDATION COURSES: PLUMP UP YOUR PORTFOLIO

Some courses – mostly the private ones – offer 'pre-foundation' courses: short ones which you can join (at a price). These are particularly useful for students wanting to get their portfolios up to scratch. They are well worth considering, and you don't need any qualifications to get in. There are also one or two notably good general courses which you might like to know about, whatever stage you are at.

THE BRITISH INSTITUTE OF FLORENCE

Lungarno Guiccardini 9, 50125 Florence, tel: 00 39 55 28 40 31, fax: 00 39 55 28 95 57.

Offers life classes – taken at the studio of Charles Cecil (see below), who is contracted to work for the Institute one day a week or so. This is serious stuff, however, and not for the dilettante or 'Mummy thought I might like to do art' brigade. See main entry on the British Institute in Languages chapter, p. 109.

Caveat on Florence: in theory it should be perfect for hands-on art. In practice, as David Hockney remarked, it is daunting to be working in the shadow of the all-time greats, and it could be no coincidence that no great painter has come out of Florence for a very long time – talent has been channelled into e.g. fashion, leatherwork.

CHARLES H. CECIL STUDIOS

Borgo San Frediano 68, 50124 Florence, tel: 00 39 55 28 51 02, fax: none (use the British Institute one).

Vital statistics: Number of students: 25–30 at any one time.

Head: Mr Charles Cecil (40s), American, majored in Classics and Art History from Haverford College, who was away when we visited; the fort being held by a favoured young student who did the best he could to field questions. Not an easy man to track down: busy, busy (Cecil spends around two days a week in the studio). Impressive c.v., including grants from the Greenshield Foundation to pursue his studies, and a Julius Hallgarten first prize for oil painting, plus exhibitions at the National Academy of Design in New York. An impressive personality, outstandingly articulate and knowledgeable. 'You think he's going to transform your life when you meet him,' says a student. Full of charm, kind and friendly. Married to a Frenchwoman, they have two small children. Has been teaching in Florence for a decade.

What it does: This is a serious working studio for painters, where they learn to work on their own, grind their own pigment in the old tradition (hugely superior – and cheaper, to boot), meet other painters and present work for exhibitions.

History of Art and museum-visiting are part of the course. The studio also takes drawing courses for the British Institute, which take up some of Mr Cecil's time every week when he is in Florence. Courses are planned on a year basis (September to end of June, with breaks at Christmas and Easter of 'several weeks'), though students may be accepted for one term (or try for less).

What it's like: A nice, casual, professional artisty and inspiring atmosphere. You go up a long flight of narrow dark stairs into what was the Church of San Raffaello Arcangelo, though you wouldn't guess that now to look at it. Two rooms are connected by a narrow corridor with high ceilings and windows high up, designed as a studio by Lorenzo Bartolini, sculptor; and what was good enough for Signor Bartolini should be good enough for you. It is very cramped when the studio is in full swing, but with a great feeling of excitement and hope.

The studio is a three-minute walk towards the old city wall from the British Institute library, on the south bank of the Arno. There are jolly restaurants round about (cheaper than the Uffizi side) and scope for finding digs.

This is emphatically not the place for beginners or those in need of constant tuition. It could be just the place, however, if you have already seriously embarked on a fine art career and are looking for a base from which to work (and it'll sound good on your c.v.). If you stay long enough you may get 'privileges' and be allowed to help. Work as hard as you like here, day and night; there is an old mattress on the floor in an upstairs room which is handy for forty winks.

The serious student is only allowed to start with plaster casts – 'real nineteenth-century traditional stuff,' said a student, who initially found it fantastically frustrating. Then – joyful moment – you graduate to life classes and lots of them. Mr Cecil describes himself as 'in the realist tradition, and one of the few ateliers in Europe to offer a thorough training in the classical techniques of drawing and painting . . . [the] curriculum stems directly from the major realist ateliers of nineteenth-century Paris . . .' Successful former students may aspire to become members of the Royal Society of Portrait Painters (Sargent here I come).

Accommodation: Do your own thing. The studio will dig out (pun) likely apartments/rooms to rent, but don't count on it. Your best bet could be to arrange for b & b for the first week or three, while looking round for something which suits you.

Cost: Around 2 million lire a term.

HEATHERLEY SCHOOL OF FINE ART
Old Ashburnham School, Upcerne Road, London SW10 0SH, tel: 0171 351 4190, fax: 0171 351 6945.

Vital statistics: Number of students: about 10 on the pre-foundation course. Ratio of staff to pupils: 1 to 18. Number of taught hours for both pre- and foundation course: 24 'practical' hours, plus three hours of lectures and three of gallery visits.

Principal: Since 1974 Mr John Walton, who owns the school and runs it as a part-time concern (he is a portrait painter and has a small studio in the school). Trained at the Slade.

What it's like: Very informal. Useful to know about in the context of this book for its pre-foundation course, which consists of two terms of intensive work on different disciplines to assess a student's aptitude. No portfolio or qualifications needed. The school is housed in part of an ex-secondary school at the back end of Chelsea. It's cramped, and unable to offer a wide enough range of subjects for a foundation course proper. A distinguished name in Victorian times.

Cost: This is a private school and each course is different, but a pre-foundation course costs around £2,580 for the two terms.

LORENZO DE' MEDICI
(Language school and Art Institute)
Via Faenza 43, 50123 Florence, tel: 00 39 55 28 31 42,
fax: 00 39 55 239 89 20.

Vital statistics: Number of students: around 400 (including language students) at its busiest. Maximum studio class size: 20 students; Art History: 30 students. Nine staff in administration, 40 full-time teachers in all, 15–25 part-time teachers.

Dean of academic affairs and programme director: Dott. Arch. Gabriella Ganugi, an efficient lady who has been working for the school for 11 years and whose husband works for the university.

What it does: Offers 120 different classes including language courses; photography; Art Restoration; History of Art (in Italian), Art (including four-week summer courses); Ceramics, Watercolours. 'Semesters' are taken in 'blocks', e.g. one Language block, one History of Art, three Studio blocks. Every studio class meets six hours a week: all in all, 90 hours in a semester. There are also monthly summer courses.

What it's like: It's large, all things to all (wo)men, but useful to know about. The centre is on four sites. There is a large building attached to an ex-church (which is used sometimes for lectures); the main art studios are two streets away in the Via Alloro – a good, large, light main studio with the usual students' rather pedestrian life drawings on the walls. Absolutely brilliant photography department in the big cool basement – a real find, open all hours, with a massive amount of equipment; enough for all to have a go, and an enthusiastic head.

Painting restoration courses take place in a dear little house through a door tucked away off the San Lorenzo cloisters – you go up and up rickety stairs and out on to the rooftops. The building was once Donatello's studio, which adds greatly to the excitement of the place.

Very professionally run, but not cosy – the atmosphere is very much Come and get it rather than What can we do for you?, though the Centre boasts a part-time counsellor for 'adjustment' or 'cultural' problems. There is a useful canteen open all day – and all day Saturday – pasta, salad, 'American yoghurt'. Home from home for Americans.

Accommodation: The Institute will help find accommodation (it's a free service) from about 22,000 lire a day for b & b. Most pressure is on single rooms in student apartments (around 400,000–600,000 lire a month at time of writing). Rooms are allocated on a first-come first-served basis, so hurry for this.

VICTORIA & ALBERT MUSEUM
South Kensington, London SW7 2RL, tel: 0171 938 8638 (impossible to get hold of anyone, but there is an answerphone), fax: 0171 938 8635.

Principal of drawing courses: Ms Eileen Graham. Has been working for the V & A for 25 years, and running these particular courses since they started in 1990. Ms Graham is busy, direct. (NB Lord Armstrong, the famous civil servant, is still here, putting his considerable talents to better use.)

What it does: Runs short drawing courses: one day to eight days; the average is three days, plus the possibility of coming once a month (if that is what you can afford). There are around 40 courses a year: everything from Chinese Art, Islamic through to European, all using the museum's collections as the 'source of inspiration'.

What it's like: The V & A has changed radically in the last few years – formerly the courses were esoteric, with teachers doing their own thing in a highbrow way. Now the museum has to make money, and it has changed 'out of all recognition' says a lecturer, producing what the punter wants. A thrilling environment to work in – drawing all the time, working in the gallery from 10.30 in the morning to 5 at night, always using the museum's collections to work with – Chinese life drawing, for example, and japanning.

There is no average student: 'We have everything from 92 down ... it may be a Slade lecturer doing a refresher, or a student working on a portfolio to get into art college, or a USA summer student, or an interior designer, or a dedicated amateur,' says Ms Graham. 'It's a grand mix, and that's how we like it.' There is a useful social side for young artists: mixing with well-established professionals. Minimum class size: 10 students (to break even), maximum 20.

Cost: Not state-funded any more so no free places. Fees cover cost of teachers, materials and hidden extras such as printing.

11

Music

Musical matters tend to be dictated by your prowess as a musician, and would-be pros tend to go straight from school as fast as they can to music college, as a baton beats time at their back. There are, however, a few courses which offer pure joy to the (very) amateur music-lover – we list one or two tried and tested below – as well as specialist schools and courses which offer a standard which a budding professional would be happy to work to. In the fee-paying sector, the outstanding non-specialist secondary schools for music are Winchester, Eton and Uppingham. The specialist schools are Yehudi Menuhin (what a hothouse), Chetham's and Purcell. Wells Cathedral School has a specialist division.

A useful publication is *Music Teacher* magazine, published by Rhinegold Publishing Ltd., 241 Shaftesbury Avenue, London WC2H 8EH, tel: 0171 333 1747. This monthly produces a supplement called *Guide to Leisure Courses* each year around February, and is well worth browsing through (find it at music shops).

MUSIC COURSES

THE BRITISH RECORD INDUSTRY TRUST
PERFORMING ARTS AND TECHNOLOGY SCHOOL
60 The Crescent, Croydon, London CR0 2HN, tel: 0181 665 5242, fax: 0181 665 5197.

Vital statistics: Number of students: around 687 (approx. 450 at 16+). Ages: 14–18. This is a coed day state school.

Principal: Ms Anne Rumney. Previously head of a state comprehensive school, Ms Rumney trained as a dancer.

What it does: The school provides specialist training for students who wish to go into the 'entertainment industry'. GCSEs and A-levels are offered, but the school majors in vocational qualifications.

What it's like: This city technology college, funded jointly by the government and the recording industry (20 per cent from the latter), has been compared to New York's Fame academy. It is alive with students dead keen to be anything from rock stars to TV sound engineers to clapperboard persons. It is too new to have a track record as yet, but is very much worth looking at if you know this is the area you are heading for (though NB it's not the place for the social climber).

The buildings are high-tech in suburbia, all singing and dancing facilities including recording studios, a video-editing room, loads of practice rooms, stage sets, etc.

Getting in: Entry is by interview at 14+ and 16+ – you don't need academic qualifications to get in, but you do need to prove dedication and show spark.

THE DARTINGTON INTERNATIONAL SUMMER SCHOOL OF MUSIC

c/o The Dartington Hall Trust, Totnes, Devon TQ9 6EL, tel: 01803 867068, fax: 01803 868108.

Artistic director: Mr Gavin Henderson, who is principal of the Trinity College of Music in London.

Course manager: Mr Marcus Davey

What it does: A five-week summer music school – all manner of courses are on offer for both professionals and amateurs. There are master-classes, a choir, composition and specialist courses in e.g music for film.

What it's like: This is the business. The management takes over the whole of the Dartington Hall campus for the duration of the school, which draws musicians from all over and gets the biggest names: Stravinsky and Poulenc have been in their time. There is a choir, and chamber music for 'enthusiastic amateurs – we get a lot of those,' says course manager Mr Davey. There is e.g. African drumming and there is opera: in '95 they are doing *Cosi Fan Tutte* and a full-blown production of Purcell's *Diocletian*.

The course is residential, so there are lots of opportunities for professionals and amateurs to get together and discuss the joys of making music. The school is seriously good news both for budding professionals and for closet Pavarottis and Zuckermanns.

DORSET OPERA
Abbot's Acre, Sherborne, Dorset DT9 3JF, tel: 0935 79297, fax: 0935 812030.

Musical director and conductor: Mr Patrick Shelley, who is head of music at Sherborne School.

What it's like: An extremely jolly and serious opera company, a mixture of professionals and amateurs – and heaps of young people. Founded over twenty years ago, it generates terrific enthusiasm and excitement and takes over the town for almost two weeks in the summer (usually late July/early August). People come back year after year (musicians have been known to get stroppy if they aren't invited back), and some local families have been involved at all ages. You'll find language coaches, choreographers, not to mention sewing teams, designers, lighting engineers and construction teams all beavering away. 'We are worked *incredibly* hard,' said an 18-year-old member of the chorus.

Soloist singers, the orchestra, producer, designer, set builder, production manager, etc. – all the key posts, in fact – are paid professionals (often well known), and just about everybody else is amateur, with anything between sixty and eighty people in the chorus. Many of them are young (even lower-sixth-formers).

Getting in: There are no auditions, but 'they need to be pretty good'. Several participants have gone on to music careers and degree courses. This is also a very good springboard for anyone interested in the behind-the-scenes aspect of production – 'a crash course in stage apprenticeship,' said one boy who worked on set-building. Apply by February at the latest: this is hugely popular.

Cost: The course alone costs £70 (and you'll need to find a place to be a paying guest at); the course plus full board is £170. Chorus members must provide their own scores.

ELMHIRST CENTRE

Dartington Hall, Dartington, Totnes, Devon TQ9 6EL, tel: 01803 866688, fax: 01803 863569.

Director: Mrs Helen Challoner

What it does: Offers short courses in all manner of subjects, from music, theatre, visual performance and arts management, language weekends and one-week courses on lacemaking, embroidery, tapestry-weaving and Chinese brush painting.

What it's like: Elmhirst Centre is one of a number of operations run on the Dartington Hall estate which Leonard and Dorothy Elmhirst bought derelict in the twenties, and, on the premise that a 'job is not enough', set about creating 'an environment in which people can work and learn together', a function now carried on by the Dartington Hall Trust.

The estate has 800 acres of working farm (going organic), with miles of trails and wooded walks. However there is no main switchboard; each venture operates entirely separately with no intercommunication.

The Elmhirst Centre uses the Hall, which is set round a Saxon courtyard, and has magical gardens and a superbly re-roofed Great Hall. The bedrooms (with private bathrooms) at the Hall are immaculate, and most of the 'spaces' (Dartington-speak for classrooms) are superb. Food is organic (even the bacon) with a vegetarian option at all meals. Expect to find a sprinkling of hippies in the vicinity. There are also lots of external events attended by locals in the Great Hall.

The Dartington College of Arts in the grounds – a collection of nasty sixties buildings – does three-year music degrees. The estate is also famous for its summer music school – see p. 245.

Cost: As a rule of thumb, it is about £100 per weekend course. Bursaries are available.

HEREFORD SUMMER SCHOOL

c/o 13 Pera Place, Camden, Bath BA1 5NX, tel: 01952 825814.

Musical director: Mr Peter O'Hagan, who lectures at Roehampton, (the 'President' is Vladimir Ashkenazy).

Course organizer: Mrs Clare Orrell

What it does: Offers a feast for the soul of short courses and master-classes including choral singing (you can apply to be the conductor too), solo singing, opera studies (including being the *répétiteur*). The course menu changes from year to year (e.g. this year there's a Young Pianists course for 12- to 16-year-olds).

What it's like: This summer school is held at the Royal National College for the Blind in Hereford (where there are over 150 pianos) and you live in. It is mostly of a reasonably high standard, but low-key and the classes are small. Expect to get to grips with some heavy stuff: past choral singing, for example, has included Ann Boyd, Meyerbeer, Tippett, also lots of Peter Warlock. There are lots of informal concerts, with recitals by the tutors, and of course you get to meet like-minded enthusiasts. You may also take part in the school as an observer, by which they mean a paying audience...

Getting in: Auditions for some of the courses in '95 are by tape (in the spring).

Cost: Around £300 for the week, including accommodation, or £20 a day to be an observer.

MUSICALE HOLIDAYS

The Bourne, 20 Salisbury Avenue, Harpenden, Hertfordshire AL5 2QG, tel: 01582 460978, fax: 01582 767343.

Directors: Mrs Gillian and Mr David Johnston, who have been running the Harpenden Musicale Music School for the past 18 years (1,000 students have passed through the doors after school hours, aged from three upwards).

What it does: Offers short summer non-residential holiday music courses dotted about in schools up and down the country, e.g. at The Hall, Hampstead, and at King's College Choir School, Cambridge. There's also 'Mecca', says Mr Johnston: a residential summer course, taking over St George's School, Harpenden.

Music

There are two 'streams': one for absolute beginners aged 5–10, offering the rudiments of music in the hope that it will inspire them to start learning an instrument; the other for teenagers plus, in an ability range of beginners to grade 6 and higher, geared to a concert at the end of the course, and constructed depending on the ability of those on the course at the time (which varies from year to year, obviously).

Cost: It's around £120 for a summer course, plus about the same again for accommodation on the residential course.

THE MUSICIANS' INSTITUTE
131 Wapping High Street, London E1 9NQ, tel: 0171 265 0284, fax: 0171 488 3658.

Director: The aptly named Mr Tony Muschamp (pronounced Mooschamp).

What it does: Institute courses cover all contemporary music fields, including jazz, blues, pop, etc. Courses include the one-year 'MI Classic' course, part-time courses, a 10-week course and private tuition.

What it's like: This is *the* place if contemporary music is what you are after, but aren't quite sure how to go about it. Lots of rap, rock, bands of all varieties, serious training in harmony, guitar-playing, drums, rhythm, etc., etc. They also teach composition (for advertising jingles for example, or theme music for films), and arranging, not to mention choreography for e.g. video promos – 'another string to your bow'.

There are about a hundred students on the one-year course at the moment – it's expanding – and about five hundred pass through the school in any one year.

The Institute was founded in the early eighties and 'mutated' to become a branch of the Musicians' Institute in '91–'92. (This is a Los Angeles-based music school which now also has a sister school in Japan, as well as this one in London.)

Getting in: Entry is obtained by assessment at the school: 'we don't call it an audition'. No formal qualifications are needed, the assessment puts you at the right level for your ability, and the

Institute can be very flexible. Pony-tails and funky gear abound, there are lots of school-leavers, though the average age is 25–30ish and it is not for the half-hearted.

Cost: It's around £3,250–£3,750 for the year course for UK students (more for foreigners), and rising. Discretionary grants from your local education authority are a possibility.

PETER SYMONDS' COLLEGE

Owens Road, Winchester, Hampshire SO22 6RX, tel: 01962 852830 for further information.

The college runs the Hampshire Specialist Music Course for serious 16–18-year-olds who aim to study music professionally. It works to the London double A-level in Music, plus other A-levels and GCSEs as needed. Lots of opportunities are available for hands-on experience (including regular lunch-time concerts and getting to meet and be taught by e.g. members of the LSO).

Getting in: Entry is by interview and audition: you need to be grade 7–8 on your first instrument. Applications must be in by the middle of January and interviews are held in February for entry in September. See the main entry on the college as a whole on p. 22. This is *the* answer, if you haven't any money.

WEST DEAN COLLEGE

(The Edward James Foundation), West Dean, Chichester, West Sussex PO18 0QZ, tel: 01243 811301, fax: 01243 811343.

Principal: Dr David Lee, who comes to West Dean in September 1995 from the Conservation Unit of the Museums and Galleries Commission and the United Kingdom Institute for Conservation of Historic and Artistic Works.

Music course organizer: Mrs Rosemary Turner

What it does: On the hands-on music front, there are flute master-classes, a wonderful Early Music Performance course and a (classical) guitar festival. The college is also famous for all manner of short and diploma courses (over 140 of them), including antiques restoration, restoration of musical instruments, drawing, not to mention cord- and tassel-making, lacemaking, etc. etc.

Music

What it's like: This is a five-star place on every front. Courses are held in the covered stable yard, which is subdivided into moveable areas; the workshops themselves are in the converted nether regions. For e.g. flute master-classes you need to be grade 5+, but for the guitar festival a 'lower standard' is OK. Teaching is by highly qualified, practising, sometimes brilliant tutors.

The guitar festival takes place over five to six days in August. There is tuition through the day (at different levels) and a concert in the evening and great fun is had by all. The festival is very popular indeed, with students coming from Holland, Germany and even Japan, as well as the UK.

The college is set in 6,000 rolling acres of Sussex farmland (with formal parks all round the house), in the largest flintstone house in England. Apart from roofing over the stable yard and converting the domestic quarters, little has changed externally since it was a private house, and even the internal modifications are unobtrusive and well blended.

It is a joy to visit and work here: West Dean is the most elegant, beautifully furnished and glorious memorial to the famous philanthropist and collector Edward James, who lived in this ravishing place. There's some serious furniture, superb pictures, and, for all that, the trappings of education and learning sit easily here. Accommodation for students is either in the house for short courses, or in the converted dower house for longer courses.

Cost: From around £150 to £500 per course for a single or twin room with bathroom *en suite*. There are reductions for students coming in daily.

12

Money and How to Make It

Whatever you are doing next, you will certainly need to beg, borrow or earn money. It pays to engage brain.

How much money do you need? What for? How much time do you have to get it? What are the time restrictions – can you only earn by night because of a daytime course? Are you only free at weekends?

Draw up a proper budget. Face it realistically. For example, if you are going to Africa for three months in the summer the sort of thing you will have to research is:

* air fare – telephone the bucket-shops for cheap deals – see Travel chapter, p. 271
* airport taxes (in and out)
* the cost to the airport (return)
* inoculations (and medicines if you think you will need to take them with you)
* visas and insurance – see Travel chapter, p. 281 and 277
* kit – what do you *really* need, where can you get it, and how much will it all cost? See Travel chapter, p. 271
* travel in the country of your destination
* daily subsistence rate, and how many days you are actually going to be there. For this, talk to people who've just come back, and contact the tourist office (you'll find it in the telephone directory, or if this fails, ring the embassy concerned).
* last but not least, emergency money

HAND-OUTS

Having worked out your bottom line, now you've got to achieve it. A hand-out is pain-free compared with long sessions on a building site. Start with your parents.

Parent-handling

Choose the *right* moment to ask, i.e. not when they're just dashing out of the house, or are having ten people to dinner. A long car journey is probably the best idea (PS for parents: if *you've* got 'something to discuss' it's worth generating a car journey specifically. It's less threatening all round, there's no escape, and you don't have to look at each other).

Never take parental hand-outs for granted. Once you have left school, you will probably find a shift in attitude. To date, your parents have been funding you as they have seen fit, almost always for educational purposes. Now you are beginning to take control, to have a say. The downside is that they will no longer automatically put their hands in their pockets to fund you. However they are an excellent source of money, usually keen to help if they can. Handle with care – as you would the golden goose.

Parents will react best if you have a plan. They will react even better if it has a slightly worthy sound or educational edge: think of your parents' image, imagine them telling their friends. They will want to know how much you need, and it will help to show them your budget in writing.

Grandparents: the same applies. Or have you thought of your godparents, even rich uncles? All the above is relevant. It might be a good time to get in touch with a long-lost godparent: traditionally godparents relinquish responsibility when you're 21, but now is an equally important moment and it's a good idea to write and tell them exactly what you're trying to do. They will certainly be glad to hear from you anyway.

Golden note: anathema to parents, etc. is serious time-wasting, sleeping in late every day (and going to bed late every night), when you're meant to be getting your act together. *Do something*: appear keen. It is no use moaning about parents' quaint old-fashioned attitudes – parents *are* old-fashioned.

Touching your School

Failing the family – and you may well find they are prepared to pay something (half? a percentage? or match your earnings?) – your next port of call might be your school, especially if it is a rich one. It's well worth approaching the careers staff, to find out if there are any bursaries or scholarships available for school-leavers or for the summer holidays. You will need to know before you put in a bid what these funds are intended for: read the bumf carefully and possibly tailor your project accordingly. For example, a student we know who wanted to travel to Spain was offered a scholarship to travel to France as far as the Spanish–French border.

The late bird will not catch the worm. Again, you need to be very clear in your own mind of what you want, and to give convincing reasons. Saying 'I want to travel' in a vague way will not make the money flow – everyone says that. If you say 'I want to go to Malawi and keep a sketch diary, because I'm planning to produce a book', you are more likely to succeed. Again, think of it from their point of view: they can justify this sort of activity more easily – it sounds more worth while and less like freeloading. You will of course be offering to write for the old school mag., producing photographs and drawings, maybe coming back to talk about your experiences: whatever they want. Show willing.

Grants and Scholarships

There are a surprising number of organizations with money designated to help pay for what *you* want to do. If you *do* know that what you want to do next is save hedgehogs in Timbuktu, this could be your first point of inquiry. See also Gap Expeditions chapter.

You might also find the following useful to know about:

ARTSWORK LTD
TVS, 84 Buckingham Gate, London SW1E 6PD, tel: 0171 976 7199, fax: 0171 799 3536.
Regional Offices:
Artswork North: Tyne Tees Television, City Road, Newcastle-upon-Tyne NE1 2AL, tel: 0191 261 0181 (ext. 2317), fax: 0191 261 2302.
Artswork South: Meridian Broadcasting, Television Centre, Southampton SO9 5HZ, tel: 01703 712246, fax: 01703 236816.

This is a national charity, linked with ITV's regional companies, that creates and promotes lots of opportunities in the arts for 14- to 19-year-olds. Their definition of the arts is satisfyingly broad – anything from circus, fashion and sculpture to every sort of mixed-media performance – and events take place in every imaginable venue. Funding restrictions at the moment mean they are concentrating on getting people involved in projects *they* have initiated, but it is well worth getting in touch with ideas of your own. They will then put you on to your regional coordinator. It is a particularly good opportunity to work with professional artists, musicians and film-makers.

EARTHWATCH
See Gap Expeditions chapter, p. 145.

THE PRINCE'S TRUST
8 Bedford Row, London WC1R 4BA, tel and fax: 0171 405 5799.

255

The Trust covers a number of worthy areas, including 'Partners in Europe', a scheme for people under the age of 25 who are not in full-time education to develop a project or a business idea with partners in other countries, e.g. studying costume design in Italy, setting up a photographic exhibition exchanges between Russia and the UK, making contacts in Switzerland for marketing lightweight wheelchairs. The first stage is an exploratory 'go and see' grant. The second stage – if you've gone and seen and found it good (and so have the Trust) – is a 'go ahead' grant.

The Trust also helps 14- to 25-year-olds to help themselves in some particular venture: for example, it might enable a group of unemployed people to buy musical instruments, or an ice-skater to buy boots and blades to compete in ice-skating championships. It's very encouraging, and easy to apply.

THE WINSTON CHURCHILL MEMORIAL TRUST
15 Queen's Gate Terrace, London SW7 5PR, tel: 0171 584 9315, fax: 0171 581 0410.

One hundred awards are made annually in 10 categories for people to travel and gain knowledge and experience of the lives and work of people overseas, which will benefit their work and community on their return. This is a wonderfully wide net and covers, for example, travelling across America in a bus and keeping a diary of it, and learning to dance in Moscow. Awards are about £3,000–£5,000 at time of writing, open to all UK citizens, and there are no age restrictions. The categories change each year, but 1994 included an open category for projects in Southern Africa, energy conservation, the water industry and the preservation of the water environment. Applications by 29 October.

EARNING MONEY

This section is not about self-fulfilment, but about getting hold of the folding stuff as fast as possible. Don't be proud: you can do anything, even stack supermarket shelves, for a short time – and you'll be surprised who else has. You might suggest to the interviewer that you'd be happy to pack behind the scenes.

Shops

Big department stores and chains take on a lot of extra staff for their summer and New Year sales, and sometimes before Christmas. Some stores have a tradition of employing students or school-leavers on a temporary basis. And, dare we say it, some of the snootier shops frankly have a preference for public school boys and girls (they imagine their friends have more spending power, which may well be rubbish). Put on a medium-posh accent and look smart. You may be working 40 hours a week, more with overtime, and you may have to be there by 8 in the morning: be prepared for a long, possibly boring day. You will probably be asked to wear a suit for the job (dark grey, dark blue or black): visit the second-hand clothes shops, and don't forget Oxfam may have something that is just the ticket. Weekly pay is on average between £120 and £160.

Apply well in advance. Ring up and ask for the Personnel department. Find out when they are recruiting. The day before you go for an interview, go along to case the joint – and ask a friendly-looking assistant if there are any tips about getting work there. Go along to the interview looking tidy and neat. They will want to know your previous work experience (babysitting will do nicely). You probably won't be given a choice on which department you work in, but if you are, be warned: the 'glamorous' departments

257

such as Fashion can be excruciatingly boring whereas the more 'humdrum Haberdashery and Toys can be quite fun,' says an ex-shop-girl, and now a successful journalist, who has tried every department.

Here are well-trodden paths:

HARRODS

Knightsbridge, London SW1X 7XL, tel: 0171 730 1234 (ext. 2211).

Big employers – up to 600 vacancies for temporary work in their New Year and July sales. Call, send in your c.v., or go in person to the Personnel Officer (make sure you know his or her name). Apply mid- to end of August for the next year's sales. Look smart, well groomed, confident – and you should be over 16 and have some retail experience. Standard rates will make you about £160 a week at time of writing, and of course there are hundreds of departments: China is the most hectic, Toys the noisiest. Supervision is strict. Expect lots of talk about A-level results, etc. from school-leavers working with you. Good straightforward money-earner.

HARVEY NICHOLS

Knightsbridge, London SW1X 7RJ, tel: 0171 235 5000.

Summer sales start around 21 June; also sales at New Year – there are about 100 vacancies for each week. Ring up or send your c.v. to the Personnel department. Same requirements as Harrods – the most important things are smart appearance and businesslike manner. It's a 31-hour week.

SELFRIDGES

Oxford Street, London W1A 1AB, tel: 0171 629 1234.

You must be over 18 to work at Selfridges' Christmas and summer sales. Experience is not essential, but good presentation and manners are a must. Apply to the Personnel department by telephone, letter or in person in November for Christmas, and May or June for the summer. It's a 40-hour week; each sale lasts about two weeks. Expect to make about £160 a week.

*

Don't just go for the shops everybody has heard of: try all your local shops. Go in off the street (looking alert and tidy, as usual) and ask politely who you should talk to. Try not to look as if you've been unlucky at all the other shops down the road. Give the impression that you *really* would like to work in this shop. A local bakery may be just as well paid as a big chain.

Some high street names to conjure with: Marks & Spencer, B & Q (for example, they need checkout operators and general assistants); Sainsbury's, your own local supermarket; Next (will take people aged 16+); Benetton (varies – some will employ at 16); John Lewis Partnership (you need to be 18 for this); Laura Ashley (16+). If you telephone (you will probably need to call the big organizations), ask to be put through to the Personnel department and ask if they have a policy on age limits (some will only employ graduates), or a minimum work period. Remember you are asking about temporary work.

Restaurants, Hotels, Waitering, Fast-food Joints

Restaurants are the perfect source of temporary work, since there's always a high turnover and kitchen hands and waiters don't need that much experience. A little bit of bluffing will generally go a long way. But it's not for the thin-skinned or the unfit. Also, beware those flexible hours – some shifts end at 1 a.m., so you need to be 18 to work these, and have a bike or somebody to pick you up because taxis are going to be way past your budget.

An old hand says: 'Kitchens are often a microcosm of society at its worst: pressured, hierarchical and very bad-tempered. The work is hard, fast and if you're washing up, filthy. Waiters often get the worst of both worlds – shouted at by the kitchen and the customers – and there is always at least one moment in the evening when you've got seven things to do simultaneously and you're convinced you're about to spill something very hot or sticky over the next table. The pay isn't spectacular – around £3 an hour, so tips are very important. But the longer you do it, the easier it gets, you get fed and the real life-saver is that most of the other people will be in the same position as you, so you'll have plenty of support and probably make a lot of friends.'

Restaurants advertise in jobcentres and local papers, but the best way to get work is to go in and ask for the manager.

Hotel work is similar – often you have to work shifts at unsociable hours, and again the best way is the personal approach. Hotels start looking for summer staff before Easter. They prefer you to be over 18, because then by law you can work after 10 p.m. and serve alcohol, etc. Chambermaids, night portering, behind the scenes in the kitchens – all the Fawlty Towers jobs (one person reported doing nothing all day but chopping up lettuce leaves to drop into the packet soup so it could be called 'home-made').

Try the Hilton Group (contact your nearest one; you must be aged 16+); Holiday Inns (age 16+), your station hotel (if it still exists), the Sheraton Group (16+), the Forte Group – this is the big one in the UK. A likely bet is your local three-star AA hotel, often desperate for some temporary help in the summer.

Other possibilities are:

SEARCY'S
124 Bolingbroke Grove, London SW11 1DA, tel: 0171 585 0505, fax: 0171 350 1748.

Ask for the Personnel department. You must be over 18 to register with them. Most of the work is in and around London.

TOWN AND COUNTY CATERING/RING AND BRYMER
Manor House, Manor Farm Road, Alperton, Middlesex HA10 1BN, Tel: 0181 998 8880, fax: 0181 991 9636.

These two are the big catering companies, which work at all the main events – Ascot, Henley, the British Open, Wimbledon, Hickstead, the Chelsea Flower Show, as well as seven racecourses all over England. They employ general assistants, waiters, silver service, bar staff. You have to be over 18 for the bar, over 16 for everything else, and each job is roughly for a week. Some are paid by the hour, some daily, between £26 and £40 at time of writing (usually nearer £30). Even if you don't get to see much action, there is generally a good atmosphere, the week will go very fast.

THE YOUTH HOSTEL ASSOCIATION

Trevelyan House, 8 St Stephen's Hill, St Albans, Hertfordshire AL1 2DY, tel: 01727 855215, fax: 01727 844126.

Contact Sharon Cain at the above address if you want to get a job as a temporary warden at one of the 250 youth hostels. You have to be over 18 and you get board and lodging and £300 a month. For Scotland, contact individual youth hostels directly.

Don't forget the ubiquitous McDonalds, Kentucky Fried Chicken, Pizza Hut, Pizzaland, etc. They are a good hunting-ground as there is a high turnover of staff. You need to be over 16 and a half (15 for KFC, 18 for Pizzaland – and some shifts end at 1 a.m., be warned). Contact the branch directly and ask for the manager. Rates of pay vary from about £3 per hour.

You need to be over 18 to serve in pubs.

Employment Agencies

Below we list a handful of tried and tested employment agencies (there are dozens and dozens). Local contacts always come in useful here, but beware the tiny newly-mushroomed agency. Beware the sales talk – don't let them talk you down: it may well be that there are too many people looking for too few jobs but their job is to find you work. If they start saying there is no work, believe them – get up and walk out and on to the next agency. This often flushes out a job.

Be sure to join more than one agency. One student we know joined five and has not been out of work since. 'I will do anything,' she said to the agencies. She presented herself well, talked clearly and politely, and was easy to get hold of during office hours. An answering machine is useful.

Obviously agencies pay their way by charging commission: ask who pays them. Normally it is the employer, but occasionally they take a percentage of your fee. You should be able to join the agency for free, or sometimes for a minimal administration fee, but bear in mind these agencies are often the last port of call for employers because of the expense of using them.

A useful way of finding out the good agencies is to ask the consumer, i.e. the employer for whom you're working, which agencies they use.

If you have done a secretarial course or are a whiz at word processing, so much the better (and better pay): but even if you haven't, give it a whirl if you can find your way round a typewriter. Try major agencies such as Reed, Kelly Girl, Alfred Marks.

Also try general employment agencies such as:

CATCH 22 EMPLOYMENT AGENCY LTD.
199 Victoria Street, London SW1E 5NE, tel: 0171 821 1133, fax: 0171 834 7172.

Employ general staff for temporary jobs such as furniture-moving, driving, warehouse work and message-running. The minimum rate of pay is £3·25 per hour. Very variable hours; they employ on a day-to-day basis. They also employ office staff. Minimum age is 18. Work is available especially in March–April and June–October.

UNIVERSAL AUNTS
19 The Chase, London SW4 0NP, tel: 0171 738 8937.

You have to go in for an interview (but ring up first). Minimum age is 18, and if you are deemed suitable (they are very much interviewing *you*) you can get on to their books. They *prefer* you to be available for a minimum of six months, and there is slightly more scope for females. Jobs might be anything from polishing pews to sitting in the back of a car with a child going to the dentist, to house-sitting.

For nannying work, the following agencies have places for temporary girls (mostly), foreign as well as British. Don't imagine that because they are all in London they only place nannies in London – far from it. All are reliable sources, according to the *Good Nanny Guide*:

Computa Nanny: 80 Elgin Crescent, London W11 2JI, tel: 0171 221 7715.

Connections Nanny Agency: 65 Drakefield Road, London SW17 8RS, tel: 0181 692 1862.

Nanny Connections: Stern House, 85 Gloucester Road, London SW7 4SS, tel: 0171 835 2277.

Occasional and Permanent Nannies: 2 Cromwell Place, London SW7 2JE, tel: 0171 225 1555.

Seasonal Employers

ARDMORE ADVENTURE LTD.
11–15 High Street, Marlow, Buckinghamshire SL7 1AU, tel: 01628 890060, fax: 01628 898141.

Leaders and supervisors (minimum age 19, Easter and summer only) are needed for adventure residential camps for 5- to 14-year-olds, located throughout the UK. Board and lodging is given, plus wages of around £45–£60 a week, depending on hours worked.

BUTLINS LTD.
Head Office: Bognor Regis, West Sussex PO21 1JJ, tel: 01243 860068, fax: 01243 829588.

Butlins has five holiday centres and six hotels. The busiest time is after Easter until the end of October. The minimum age is 18. Pay is 'skill-related' and 'varies from area to area', and your job might be anything from working with a housekeeper to being an assistant behind the bar.

CHESSINGTON WORLD OF ADVENTURES
Leatherhead Road, Chessington, Surrey KT9 2NE, tel: 01372 729560, fax: 01372 725050.

Every year Chessington takes on over 400 temporary staff between Easter and October to work on the rides, in the cafeteria and kiosks, the amusement arcades and in the shops and ticket office. You work about 40 hours a week; pay varies according to age (16+). There is limited accommodation available and a minimum period of work of four weeks. Apply to the Personnel department from February onward – the sooner the better.

FREETIME SUMMER CAMPS
Park House, Moor Lane, Woking, Surrey GU22 9RB, tel: 01483 740242, fax: 01483 750726.

Sports instructors and counsellors are needed at around £100 for a five- to seven-day week, from July to August, for these activity hol. camps for children aged 7–15 at day and residential centres in Surrey, Somerset and Sussex. 'Activities' include archery, arts and crafts, canoeing, rifle shooting, tennis, windsurfing and dinghy sailing.

FUNCOAST WORLD
Skegness, Lincolnshire PE25 1NJ, tel: 01754 762311, fax: 01754 767833.

This holiday centre takes on around 1,000 staff, including that hardy perennial, the Redcoat. You work 39 hours a week, and must be over 18. Apply from mid-January to the Personnel Manager for a season starting in March.

GISELA GRAHAM LIMITED
Main Office: 12 Colworth Grove, London SE17 1LR, tel: 0171 708 4956, fax: 0171 703 9859. Warehouse: Elizabeth Industrial Estate, 2 Juno Way, London SE14, tel: 0181 691 9488.

This Christmas decoration company is just the sort of firm an employment agency will put you on to. They hire a large temporary workforce for the annual despatch season from 2 August to 26 November. Mainly pickers and packers, some fork-lift and van-driving. Work from 8 a.m. to 6 p.m. plus some Saturdays.

Hourly wages vary, but it's above the local average, plus performance bonuses. Mainly a student workforce, and a friendly atmosphere.

WIMBLEDON TENNIS CHAMPIONSHIP
The All England Lawn Tennis and Croquet Club, Church Road, Wimbledon, London SW19 5AE, tel: 0181 944 1066, fax: 0181 947 8752.

Apart from the ballboys and -girls recruited from local schools and tennis clubs, Wimbledon also needs people to work in the press and referees offices, on the scoreboards and in information. You must be over 18, and a connection with tennis is useful. Languages are important for the press and referees office, and a diplomatic nature, since information often means telling people how much longer they'll be standing in a queue. Every day of the two weeks will be a long one, but the atmosphere is great and most people go back year after year: the pay is also better if you've done it before. Write to the Championships department in December or January (the championships are in June).

Fruit Picking

Hundreds of farms around the UK need help with the harvest, which roughly begins in June, with strawberries and gooseberries in the South, and continues until September – hops in Kent and Herefordshire – or October, the end of the apple harvest. Many people follow the harvests round from farm to farm, but you can do it on a short-term basis. It's back-breaking work, so try and pick up the tricks from old hands. Accommodation is often minimal and the pay varies, depending to an extent on the amount of fruit you pick. On a good day, you could earn £25, on a wet one, nothing.

Where else to look

* *The Lady* magazine is a wonderful source for all
kinds of domestic jobs, everything from being a
companion, delivering meals, dog-walking, looking
after children, chambermaids, etc. etc. It is *the* market
leader in 'domestic situations'. It hits the news-stand
officially on Tuesdays, but usually you can buy it on
Monday, and subscribers have already got it on
Saturdays. It's vital to get in there first.
* local press
* the public library
* shop windows, especially newsagents
* your local jobcentre

Horrible Ways to Make Good Money Fast
(You won't have the stamina to do it for long.)

Mortuaries: Ring round hospitals and mortuaries. Ring round
undertakers and funeral parlours via the *Yellow Pages*. Gloomy of
course, and not surprisingly unpopular, but it pays about three
times more than jollier jobs.

Frozen-chicken factories: Pay well. 'My smelliest and coldest
job,' said one teenager (wear gloves). Night shifts pay best – but
think about transport. Try Premier Poultry Ltd., Ram Boulevard,
Foxhill's Industrial Park, Scunthorpe, South Humberside DN15
8QW, tel: 01724 281081, fax: 01724 281082. Bernard Matthews plc:
Great Witchingham Hall, Norwich, Norfolk NR9 5QD, tel: 01603
872611, fax: 01603 872421. He of turkey fame. Not for vegetarians
– but you may become one. Write to the Main Factory Personnel.

Building sites and road works: Builders' labourers' jobs were
two a p in the 80s, but the slump in the property market has clipped

wings here a bit. It's hard, physical work, and very much a man's world. You must have a head for heights, and a sense of humour is crucial. It's an early start – 7 or 8 a.m., finish about 4 p.m. For a 39-hour week, pay ranges from around £70 for a 16-year-old to £140 for an 18-year-old. The only way to get work is to go to a particular site (some have sits vac. noticeboards posted at the entrance) and ask the agent or foreman if there are any vacancies. Sir Robert McAlpine & Sons Ltd., John Laing, and Sunley are names to conjure with, Miller Construction in the North.

Entrepreneurial Note – Doing Your Own Thing

Write out a list of all the things you can do, e.g. filing, shopping, walking the dog, painting the basement railings, babysitting. Get it printed off on your parents'/friend's/school computer, best of all on brightly coloured paper. Post it off, together with several copies, or deliver it to your parents' friends, and all your neighbours; display it in your local post office window, and you should never be out of a job. A covering letter to the friends, asking them kindly to alert *their* friends, broadens the network. A fellow we know (now reading medicine at London University) wrote the following. At the top of the paper he gave his name, address, telephone number plus mobile number. Note his modest charge.

During this Summer I shall be using my endless time and clean driving licence to do the chores listed below, plus any you care to suggest:

1 *Basic household chores, gardening, painting, clearing out attics, garages, sheds, window cleaning, etc.*
2 *Helping with children, babysitting, collecting and delivering from school and parties.*
3 *Shopping – happy to go anywhere.*
4 *Arranging, telephoning, time-consuming tasks like finding specific items, services, tickets perhaps for the theatre or travelling. I can spend time looking for the best and most suitable options for whatever you may need.*

5 *Acting as a chauffeur for when you would like to drink or if you are unable to drive owing to accident or injury.*

6 *Cook basic food such as lasagne, shepherd's pie, chilli con carne and standard meals. (Useful for babysitting.)*

7 *Acting as a butler for dinner parties: this could be done formally or informally.*

8 *Anything involving animals is fine, from gerbils to horses, I am happy; animal-sitting while you are on holiday would be a pleasure.*

9 *Acting as general helper for older people, doing tasks to make life easier, including reading for those with poor sight.*

10 *I will happily drive long-distance if required [he gives a reference].*

11 *Helping with the disabled. [He gives another reference and explains he has experience in this – you may have experience in other fields.]*

I shall be charging £3 per hour, plus 15p per mile for driving expenses. I hope I can be of some use to you, and once again stress that I am open to any suggestions and am available at short notice at any time.

Admin – Pay Slips, Banks

Keep a record of what you earn, pay slips, all the bits of paper that come with it: sooner or later the taxman is going to ask you what you are up to and there is no escaping him. Handle him with care also: he or she can make life hell or be surprisingly helpful, depending to some degree on how you handle them and your affairs. Don't throw letters from the Inland Revenue into the bin: open them and answer them p.d.q., and if you are puzzled, write and tell them so. Sorry to be boring, but open a Tax file (get an A4 wallet from W. H. Smith). You are allowed to earn up to £3,525 per annum at time of writing without paying tax on it (it is called the personal tax allowance). However, you will be taxed automatically on an 'emergency' code if you are working officially, even for a short time. Don't panic: you will get the tax deduction back in due course (via a form to be filled in before 5 April).

SETTING UP YOUR BANK ACCOUNT

This takes time, possibly weeks and weeks. It's useful to use your parents' bank: they act as security, assuming they aren't bankrupt, in which case anywhere else will be better. Don't be seduced by student lures of free tapes, etc. Go into the bank, say you want to open an account. (By the way, you will need another of those wallets for your statements.) A bank in a small market town may well be preferable to the big impersonal bank in the city. Find a human being with whom you can get on, so you can trot in and have a chat. Get them interested in you and your life. They want to know you are a responsible citizen, who is going to make pots of money in due course. A cashcard (with your secret pin number) is a safe bet. You may need a cheque-book, but leave it at home unless you really know you're going to use it.

Set up an 'authorized' overdraft facility, which probably won't cost you. This will save you those huge amounts charged on 'unauthorized' overdrafts (we have heard of a £30 charge on an account going accidentally into the red for a couple of hours). However, don't use your overdraft facility except in a *real* emergency.

Beware of 'student loans' even if the government underpins them – you are going to have to pay the money back, and you don't want to live with a huge debt around your neck (however kindly the interest rate).

Further Information

The Directory of Grant-making Trusts and Charities, published annually by the Charities Aid Foundation. This is the fund-raisers' bible – an enormous tome which you'll find in the local library. It has separate indexes to help you find the relevant charity, and some of them are very specific, you will find.

Directory of Summer Jobs in Britain, published by the Central Bureau for Educational Visits and Exchanges, Seymour Mews House, Seymour Mews, London W1H 9PE, tel: 0171 486 5101.

Teenagers' Vacation Guide to Work, Study and Adventure, Vacation Work Publications, 9 Park End Street, Oxford OX1 1HJ, tel: 01865 241978.

Street-smart corner

* Beware of letting anyone you are working with know that you find this a hellishly boring job: it is not kind, as this may be their life.

* All weekly jobs should pay you on a weekly basis. Don't let the boss get away with not paying you, however nice and full of promises. The recession has made cowboys of most of us. Don't let them trade on your inexperience: the labourer is worthy of his hire. Try and check out the employer if you're in doubt: the local vicar or the Chamber of Commerce will give you some clues.

* Constantly bear in mind that you are up against full-time professionals.

* Your rights – these depend on the health and safety aspects of the job. Someone should tell you when you start work what the score is on coffee, tea breaks, etc.

* That said, you need to be flexible. Don't shout about your rights, a gentle request at some stage will do.

* Keep your financial affairs simple. You must be in control. Regular checks on your bank balance are a good idea – a telephone call to the bank (they won't charge for this); or check with your cashcard (which could be a day or two behind).

* If you don't understand it, don't do it – this applies in general to money matters, everything from 'concessions' and 'special student offers' to Switch cards. It equally applies to those shady-sounding jobs.

The Charities Aid Foundation: 48 Pembury Road, Tonbridge, Kent TN9 2JD, tel: 01732 771333, fax: 01732 350570.

See also Travel chapter, p. 271, and Gap Expeditions chapter, p. 128.

13

A–Z of Travel

Air Travel – *See* Bucket-shops.

Airport – A likely place to pick up useful local information and you're sure to find English-speakers and fellow travellers. Reps are usually a mine of facts. Airports offer good loos and the telephones tend to be working. Remember to keep enough money for airport taxes. Be specially on your guard here, you may be disorientated at this stage, and easy prey for fleecing. Don't allow your baggage to be carried off into the blue by a stranger posing as a porter.

Try to look reasonably human. Long-haired ultra-scruffy backpackers plugged into Sony Walkmans are constant victims of Customs searches.

Banks, etc. – *See* Money Management.

Bargaining – Not an English thing, but prevalent in many countries, where it is expected, and you'll soon get used to it. Very roughly, the seller opens the bidding with one (usually ludicrously high) price; you respond with a low one. In due course you should meet somewhere around the middle. Be prepared to walk away, but never get into a bargaining situation unless you really intend to buy the object. Don't show too much keenness. Pointing out you are a poor student can help: the object in question is surely worth all that money, if *only* you had it . . . Remember it is the seller's livelihood.

Bribes – Bribing is a way of life in some countries, so don't be embarrassed by it. If you are in despair trying to arrange something and there appears to be no other discernible block, then failure to bribe may be the problem. It is a two-edged weapon however: it can open doors, but it also of course entrenches the custom further.

British Consul – *See* Emergencies.

Bucket-shops – These are travel agents specializing in cheap flights. The good-o ones can save you a lot of money. Shop around. You may need to persevere for the deal that suits you. Ask what arrangements the bucket-shop has to protect your money should it go bust. It's worth looking in *Time Out*; the *Sunday Times* is the market leader for travel ads.

These are some of the good agents:

Campus Travel: 52 Grosvenor Gardens, London SW1, European inquiries: 0171 730 3402, worldwide: 0171 730 8111. Arranges special travel rates for students, also for those under 26, with 37 branches in the UK and cooperating agents in 40 countries worldwide.

Symphony Travel: London House, 266 Fulham Road, London SW10 9EN, tel: 0171 351 7661. Good source of deals, particularly for Italy.

Spanish Aviation Services: 72 Lupus Street, London SW1V 3EJ, tel: 0171 821 5801. Specializes in flights to Spain.

Budgeting – Your basic way of working out a budget is to make a plan: How long will you be away? How much money do you need? How much money have you got? What will your daily allowance be? Take advice on how little you can live on, and bear in mind that every now and again you will want to splash out. If you blow your daily allowance on, say, a cup of coffee at Florian's, then you will have to save for several days, or starve till sunset.

Economy tips: Man *can* live on bread alone – for a bit, anyway. Bananas are a cheap and nutritious food in some countries. The end of market-day may flush out some bargains if you turn up looking hungry and hopeful. A request for one serving and two spoons is a time-honoured economy and usually acceptable. A drink at a posh hotel won't be cheap, but may well give you unlimited access to free peanuts, crisps, tapas, olives, etc. One student who recently went round Europe on £2 a day suggests going round to the *back* of restaurants at the end of the evening: you may well be given some leftovers. Overnight trains are the economical way of avoiding hotel bills, and stations are good places to pass the hours without spending money, and without being chivvied. Prices of train tickets often shoot up during business hours, and fast, fancy trains tend to cost fancy prices. 'Parachuting' with parents' friends is another major saver.

Bureaucracy – The other major stumbling-block to arranging things. We don't want to bore you with this, but be prepared for unbelievably lengthy and frustrating delays. Keep your cool. Cultivate a philosophical outlook. *See* Waiting.

Buses – Your extraordinarily cheap way to travel. You will probably travel with a whole variety of people and sometimes, their animals. Bus stations and bus stops are not always marked on the map: start in the market square, ask in the local inn. Most buses in the Third World will stop for you wherever you hail them: be sure you know what they look like. In some countries (e.g. Turkey) the bus services are wonderful; in others (e.g. Tanzania) not even the most intrepid European traveller would choose to use them.

Communication – Try to use their language – you are in their country. Smile, look people in the eye (but not too boldly). Get to grips with the vital words: please, thank you, hello, yes, no, where, when.

Keep an eye and an ear on world events and local events, not just to know if trouble has arisen, but it is also polite to take an interest.

Get your telephone card/*jetons* as soon as you arrive in a new country. Don't wait until panic strikes.

Find telephone directories in airports and hotels.

PS Phone home from time to time to let the old folks know how and where you are. Do you know your parents' fax number?

Contacts – Before you set out, you may feel that the friends and business contacts, etc. of your parents and their friends are deeply boring, not for you, and just what you are trying to escape from. You could be wrong. Such contacts are very often expats or locals. Either way, they are a rich source of good information (not to mention food); when you have been 'on the road' for a bit, you may find home comforts surprisingly welcome; they can be a very present help in trouble. *See also* God Slot.

Diaries – You will of course be keeping a record of your travels, notes of friends you make, sketches, and collecting exotic bus tickets, i.e. a general scrap album. It needs to be fat, but not too unwieldy – it has got to fit in your hand luggage. You need to write it up regularly, even if it's only hurried notes. Serious travel writers write every night.

Directions – In some countries it's loss of face to appear not to know the way, and you may be misdirected. We just thought we would warn you.

Dress – If in doubt, cover up. Keep naked flesh for the beach. Camouflage and adapt. Girls with big breasts should wear shirts that have pockets, advises a female explorer who knows Africa well. Loose clothes and long skirts should be worn in hot countries; skirts (not trousers) for squatting on those long journeys. Have a scarf for your head and shoulders (to get into mosques, etc.). Keep something neat and clean for those invitations you hope you will be getting – you hope this will be a journey of contrasts. Don't underestimate the power of the sun – keep covered and keep in the shade when possible. Get a local haircut (for men, a good way to blend in with the locals); shoes are a whole science in themselves – get a line from people who have trod where you will tread. You'll need more than one pair. You do not want to stick out like a sore thumb.

Drugs – *Don't*, don't and don't accept anything from anyone (you're a sitting target), even, sadly, from that little old lady who says she can't carry her luggage . . . Trains are a classic place for being unwittingly offered drugs: they have even been plied from the official food trolley posing as sweets, for example. Be on your guard. You don't want to wake up two days later wondering what hit you. Headlines in the papers will have alerted you to all this.

E-111 – This is the form entitling you to reciprocal free health care in EC countries. Get one free from any post office. It needs to be stamped, but once you have it, it lasts for ever (or until you use it). Keep it in your passport. NB Countries vary about how health care works; some charge a little, some charge and then reimburse. Don't expect local doctors necessarily to know how their system works for foreigners – it's often news to them and they may argue. Don't be deflected. Wave the E-111 at reception before you start treatment. The drawback to the form is that it feels like hard work if you're really ill.

Emergencies – Ask yourself: is it *really* the end of the world? Often only time and face are lost.

In dire cases, your lifeline is the British Consulate or Embassy. Embassies have a 24-hour duty officer. If you are disappearing into the wilderness, find out the number of the British Embassy before you go. Other possible helplines are the local police (though NB they may be the problem in the first place); the doctor, the priest, and of course, not least, your contacts from home.

Emergency Kit – *See* box on p. 282.

Food and Drink – Go local but don't go mad, particularly when you have just arrived and are not acclimatized. Fruit which you can peel is safest. Be careful when eating salad. Funnily enough, alcohol can be a life-preserver: a generous gin and tonic, for example, is a good germ-killer. Eggs and rice are good for runny tummies.

It is safest to avoid all tap water. Watch out for bottled water – make sure it is sealed when it arrives at the table (an increasingly common practice is to fill old mineral-water bottles with tap water). Pack purifying tablets. Coca-Cola can be your safest bet in a really fly-blown place. In hot climates dehydration sets in faster than you think: keep drinking. A lick of salt can restore the balance like magic.

God Slot – Priests and vicars may well be a sanctuary for young travellers, and the local church may be a good place to meet people, and you are touching base with your own kind. If you're short of contacts in a foreign land, a contact from your local church can be useful. Don't despise it.

Guide Books – The Lonely Planet series published by Lonely Planet Publications are by and large the best, and are particularly useful for cheap hotels, etc. Some of the *Rough Guides*, published by Rough Guide Publications, are also good. Look out for the *Let's Go* series, written by Harvard students.

The Travel Bookshop: 13 Blenheim Crescent, London W11 2EE, tel: 0171 229 5260. Useful for all kinds of books to do with travel, including pocket dictionaries and phrase books and every kind of traveller's tale.

Stanfords: 12–14 Long Acre, Covent Garden, London WC2E 9LP, tel: 0171 836 1321. The largest seller of maps in the world. They also have general travel books – a super-duper place for browsing.

Hospital for Tropical Diseases – Travel Clinic, 4 St Pancras Way, London NW1 0PE, tel: 0171 387 4411. The hospital also has a large department in the City Hospital, 51 Greenbank Drive, Edinburgh EH10 5SB, tel: 0131 536 6000. A useful source of advice, vaccinations, etc., and they can be a lifeline. If necessary, go straight from the airport, and don't forget them if your problem drags on and your GP can't sort you out.

Inoculations – It used to be cheapest to do this via your GP. It is no longer free anywhere. British Airways Health Shops have up-to-the-minute knowledge of what is needed in which country, so do firms such as Trailfinders who are constantly in touch with the world at large. Investigate *well* in advance; some treatments take time, need to be spaced out, and some may need to be ordered specially for you.

Insurance – For good, cheap insurance, go to specialist travel insurance brokers, e.g. Hamilton Barr on 01242 223300 or Endsleigh, tel: 0171 436 4451. Hamilton Barr, for example, are quoting £48 for three months' 'standard' travel in Europe or Australasia, or £63 for everywhere else, covering medical expenses, personal liability, repatriation and personal accident (these are all vital). A more ritzy policy, covering not only the above but also cancellation, luggage, delays, etc. would cost more. Endsleigh do a really cheap 'backpacker's policy'.

Questions you need to ask the insurance broker are: Who is underwriting the policy? Does the word 'worldwide' include America? Please can I have a copy of the policy schedule? DON'T forget to look at the small print before parting with your money.

Iron Rations – It's useful to have tucked away e.g. a small bottle of mineral water, maybe some Kendal mint cake, some biscuits, a packet of nuts.

Loneliness and Homesickness – Quite normal: be prepared, it will pass. Also be prepared for your travelling companion to get totally on your nerves (and vice versa); this is also normal. Tolerance is the watchword.

Loos – Apart from the airport, hotels are usually the best bet (walk boldly in – you don't have to buy anything). Art galleries and museums are also likely spots. Otherwise, it's probably the wide-open spaces.

Manners – Golden rule: never forget you are a *guest* in another country.

Money Management – Don't carry ski-bum bags which, says an experienced traveller, 'are a beacon to thieves', but a body belt worn invisibly under your clothes is an idea. Never let it leave your body. Keep your money in separate places so that if you are robbed you won't lose everything, but make sure you have enough money within easy reach to satisfy a determined thief's immediate needs. Good hidey-holes are: pinned into your bra, sewn invisibly into your trousers, in your socks, as well as in your luggage (in itself, another beacon, of course). Keep a rubber band round your wallet (it's harder for a thief to slide it out of your pocket). Never flash wodges of lolly about in public. A zip-up purse for coins is a good idea.

Take different 'kinds' of money if you're going for a longish time: travellers' cheques (ask the bank's foreign department for advice on the best currency to hold them in); some money in the currency(-ies) you'll be needing (if you can get hold of them, small denominations are very useful); US dollars are still very acceptable in some places (though sterling is catching up fast in others); a credit card (if you can arrange one) is very useful for emergencies. Make sure you have the 24-hour emergency number to contact in case of loss.

Changing money: hotels can be the worst places to change money – and the posher the hotel, the worse the rate. The local bank is usually best. Be aware of the black market. This can land you in big trouble (though a private deal with friends should be fine).

Tip: familiarize yourself with the local currency as a matter of priority: it is only too easy to make serious muddles and it will *always* be to your disadvantage.

Objective – Yours. What is it? Are you travelling for the adventure of it? Or trying to get from A to B? Is cost an overriding factor? Or is time of the essence? Do you want to spread your experiences over a wide canvas, or focus in more detail on a particular area?

Passport – Check your passport expiry date *now*. If by mishap you lose it, report its loss immediately to the nearest British Consul or Embassy.

Poste Restante – Some post offices act as postes restantes to receive letters from home (and money?). Find out via embassies before you leave home. Postes restantes are also a friendly meeting-place for exchanging news and views and plotting out parts of your journey.

Presents – Take advice on this before you go, from someone who knows the country concerned. Something cheap and cheerful such as coloured biros can win a lot of brownie points in some Third World countries. If you know you will be sponging off friends, the best thing is to get in touch before you go and ask what they would like you to bring.

Railcards – Inter-Rail is a cheap pass for under-26-year-olds and operates in seven carefully mapped 'zones' of Europe, plus Morocco. You pick which zones you plan to travel in and the price of (unlimited) rail travel within these countries is worked out to reflect this. At time of writing one 'zone' costs e.g. £179 for 15 days, and two zones £209 for a month (though NB there will be supplements to pay on whizzo trains e.g. the French TGVs). The pass also entitles you to discounts on (some) ferries and on rail travel within the UK. Get your pass (in advance, take your passport) from the International Rail Centre, Victoria Station, London SW1V 1JY, tel: 0171 834 2345 for further information, or from (some) railway stations and some travel agents.

For heaven's sake don't part with your rail passes. Particularly watch out for guards taking the wrong bits. One student traveller we know ended up in jail as a result of this: no one believed her tale, and she was deemed to have been trying to wriggle out of paying.

Safety and Survival – Look purposeful always, as though you know what you're doing. There's usually safety in twos, though one school of thought suggests that going singly is less threatening, and therefore safer. Zipped and/or buckled bags are safer than your loose, open ethnic shoulder number. Don't wander into the blue without knowing what you are doing. Respect and follow the local customs; again, brief yourself on this. Don't stare. Check the Big Three daily: Tickets? Money? Passport?

Sex – Girl-talk: observe the proprieties of the country you are in. Don't appear as a sexy young thing (*see* Dress). Remember that in some countries English girls are considered an easy lay. If asked, say you have a boyfriend (even if it is not true). Don't be carried away by flattery and protestations of undying love. Take a wedding ring as camouflage. Gentle humour is a great defence – be tactful and *never* derisive.

Student Card – Officially the International Student Identity Card, ISIC, distributed by companies such as Campus Travel (*see* Bucket-shops). Costs £5. This little card will produce cut prices and special rates, not just on air and rail travel but also on e.g. exhibitions, theatres, discos – and half a hundred other things you don't want. It is useful at all times for proving you are a student.

The card is valid throughout the academic year. School-leavers taking a year off need to buy their ISIC before they leave school, and may then use it until the end of the calendar year (so, e.g., it could be used to book long-haul tickets before Christmas to leave England the following March). Flexibility is the big advantage: you can change dates and destinations on your ticket at the drop of a hat, at minimal charges, and also get refunds on unused legs of your journey. Check this with your travel agent in advance; it may not apply in every case. The ISIC headquarters is in Denmark, tel: 00 45 33 93 93 03, fax: 00 45 33 93 73 77.

Taxis – Find out from someone at the airport what the going rate is, and also what the official taxi looks like e.g., Mercedes in Cairo (there will be cowboys). Before you put a foot in the taxi, always negotiate a price, even if it is an estimate. Putting luggage in the boot rather than on your lap can cost more. A good wheeze is to sit in the front of the taxi, get out a large map and pretend to be following the route – this curbs the driver's instinct to travel from A to B via Z. Get a receipt if possible; with any luck it will have the taxi's number on it, in case of trouble.

Trailfinders – 42–8 Earls Court Road, London W8 6EJ, tel: 0171 938 3232, fax: 0171 937 9294. Also at 194 High Street, Kensington, London W8 7RG, tel: 0171 938 3444, fax: 0171 938 3305. A one-time bucket-shop, Trailfinders was founded in 1970 by an ex-SAS man, and has grown to be the most useful all-round service for travellers in town. It is thoroughly professional on all fronts. Branches are now open in Bristol, Glasgow, Manchester and Birmingham. All their 'consultants' are very widely travelled and are competent to give advice. They provide cheap flight deals (but no charter flights) and are not keen on changing tickets. They will also organize your visas for you – bliss (it costs a few pounds). There is a library, a travel-goods shop and a very good travel bookshop and insurance – everything you will need under one roof.

Visas – Your travel agent might do it all (for a fee), otherwise it's round to the consulate and queue – check the opening hours, which can be very odd. When form-filling, beware of what you put as your occupation/purpose of visit. Tourism is always a good bet. Be careful: writing 'charity work' or, for example, 'teaching' on a visa application form to a Third World country may well cause difficulties.

Waiting – There is going to be a lot of this, and the cheaper the travel, the more of it. Playing-cards, paperbacks, your diary, a musical instrument will while away the hours.

Work Permit – Canada, America and New Zealand, for example, require you to have one if you are planning to work there. You'll need to find out all about it here (and get it) before you go. Be careful, and be as woolly as you can.

Youth Hostels – Information on the Youth Hostel Association is from: Trevelyan House, St Stephen's Hill, St Alban's, AL1 2DY, tel: 01727 855215. Membership costs £9 per year, and entitles you to stay at youth hostels all over the world. Write for free leaflets listing where to find them, specifying the countries you are travelling to, and, if possible, areas within the country. *Hostelling International* is a publication which gives details of hostels all over the world, and comes in two volumes – Europe and the Mediterranean, and, in the second volume, all other countries. Price: £7 each volume. These books are not available in public libraries, but you will find them in YHA shops.

YHA Adventure Shops plc: there are 18 of these in England, including three in London. The main branch is: 14 Southampton Street, London WC2E 7HY, tel: 0171 836 8541. *The* place to buy your kit – there's everything from water bottles to mosquito nets and proper sleeping-bags.

Emergency kit list

* **Plasters**
* **Swiss army knife (which has scissors on it)**
* **Torch**
* **Savlon**
* **Painkillers**
* **Lomotil for diarrhoea (ask your GP)**
* **Antihistamine cream**
* **Antibiotics (ask your GP – very important for long trips)**
* **Blood transfusion kit where this is advised (GP again; be sure you have the necessary papers to go with it)**
* **Mosquito repellents – the stronger the better**
* **Sun protection cream (including total block)**
* **International adaptor**
* **Universal (bath) plug**
* **Sewing kit, safety pins**
* **Loo paper (emergency supplies)**

Index

Index

Index

Index